FANDOM UNBOUND

FANDOM UNBOUND

Otaku Culture in a Connected World

Edited by

MIZUKO ITO

DAISUKE OKABE

IZUMI TSUJI

Yale UNIVERSITY PRESS

New Haven & London

Yale University Press books may be purchased in quantity for educational, business,
or promotional use. For information, please e-mail sales.press@yale.edu (U.S. office)
or sales@yaleup.co.uk (U.K. office).

Designed by James J. Johnson
Set in Janson Roman, Helvetica Nueve, and Bureau Agency Bold type by Westchester
Book Group, Danbury, CT
Printed in the United States of America

Library of Congress Control Number: 2011937359
ISBN 978-0-300-15864-9 (pbk.: alk. paper)

A catalogue record for this book is available from the British Library.

This paper meets the requirements of ANSI/NISO Z39.48-1992 (Permanence of Paper).

10 9 8 7 6 5 4 3 2 1

Chapter 2, "Database Animals," is excerpted from *Otaku: Japan's Database Animals*
by Hiroki Azuma, translated by Jonathan E. Abel and Shion Kono (Minneapolis:
University of Minnesota Press, 2009), pp. 25–62. Originally published in Japanese as
Dobutsuka suru posutomodan: otaku kara mita nihon shakai (Tokyo: Kodansha Gendai
Shinsho, 2001). Copyright 2001 by Hiroki Azuma. English translation copyright 2009
by the Regents of the University of Minnesota.

Chapter 3, "Japan's Cynical Nationalism," is translated and excerpted from *Wararu
Nihon no "Nationalism"* by Akihiro Kitada (Tokyo: Nihon Housou Shuppan Kyokai,
2005), introduction, pp. 9–23; and chapter 4, pp. 197–216.

Chapter 6, "Otaku and the City: The Rebirth of Akihabara," is translated and
excerpted from *Shuto no Tanjo—Moeru Toshi Akihabara* by Kaichiro Morikawa (Tokyo:
Gentosha, 2003), introduction, pp. 26–36; and chapter 1, pp. 40–78.

Contents

PART II. INFRASTRUCTURE AND PLACE

PART III. COMMUNITY AND IDENTITY

Acknowledgments

The editors would like to thank those who provided invaluable guidance and support in creating this book. We are grateful to Shinji Miyadai for inspiring and helping us conceptualize this volume. Elissa Sato provided not only expert translations but valuable insights on otaku culture. Henry Jenkins and Ellen Seiter gave feedback that critically sharpened the core themes of the book, and Jason Schultz offered expert counsel on matters of intellectual property both practical and theoretical. Mariko Oda helped keep this project on track in so many ways. At Yale University Press, this book was in the capable hands of Alison MacKeen, Christina Tucker, Niamh Cunningham, and Mary Pasti, and at Westchester Book Group, those of Debbie Masi. Very special thanks go to Karen Bleske, who provided editorial support for this project throughout.

Editors' Note on Translation

With the exception of the chapters by Eng and Ito, all of the chapters in this book were written originally in Japanese. The chapter by Azuma was translated by Jonathan E. Abel and Shion Kono. The remaining chapters were translated by Elissa Sato and Mizuko Ito. Although the authors have worked closely with Ito in editing the English versions of the chapters, Ito bears responsibility for any faults in the translation. Karen Bleske also contributed to the editing and readability of all chapters.

Japanese names are written in the Western format, given name first, to avoid confusion in the frequent juxtaposition of Japanese and Western names.

Certain key terms with no direct counterpart in English have been written in romanized Japanese. Japanese nouns have no plural form, thus terms such as "otaku," "anime," and "manga" are treated as both singular and plural.

When figures in Japanese yen are mentioned, we have included a corresponding value in U.S. dollars, at an exchange rate of approximately ¥100 per US$.

Chapter 2, "Database Animals," by Hiroki Azuma, is a reproduction of a previously published work, and as such, some of its style conventions differ from those in the other chapters in this book. Citations and dates appear in the notes, rather than in the text, Japanese names are written last name first, non-English words remain italicized after their first appearance, and some syllables retain their diacritical marks. However, for the sake of clarity, figures have been renumbered and obsolete cross-references removed. To conserve space, the notes have also been renumbered to remove the translator's notes; interested readers should consult the original publication for those.

Introduction

MIZUKO ITO

Otaku culture defies simple definition. Emerging first in Japan in the 1980s as a marginalized and stigmatized geek subculture, it has gradually expanded its sphere of influence to become a major international force, propelled by arguably the most wired fandom on the planet.

Along the way, the term "otaku" has been hotly contested by those inside and outside the subculture. For some, it evokes images of sociopathic shut-ins out of touch with reality. For others, and increasingly, it suggests a distinctive style of geek chic: a postmodern sensibility expressed through arcane knowledge of pop and cyber culture and striking technological fluency. This book seeks to plumb the varied meanings and practices associated with otaku culture, not by pinning it to a single origin story or fixed definition, but by exploring its protean and multifaceted nature in varied social and historical contexts. For the authors in this book, otaku culture references a constellation of "fannish" cultural logics, platforms, and practices that cluster around anime, manga, and Japanese games and are in turn associated with a more generalized set of dispositions toward passionate and participatory engagement with popular culture and technology in a networked world.

This introduction situates otaku culture within these varied historical and social conditions, tracing its diverse manifestations as well as the common set of characteristics that make it recognizable as a unique cultural movement. I begin by describing how otaku culture is situated within the transnational media culture of the Internet age. While otaku culture grows out of familiar processes of cultural exchange between Japan and the rest of the world, its growing visibility is keyed to the unique conditions of our current historical moment, a moment in which networked and digital culture has energized peer-to-peer and participatory forms of media creation and sharing. I then turn to a discussion of the key conceptual frameworks that structure the three sections of this book: the particular cultural logics of otaku culture, the underlying peer-to-peer infrastructures that enable it, and the varied niche subcultures that these logics and infrastructures have encouraged.

OTAKU CULTURE IN A TRANSNATIONAL ARENA

Today's otaku culture is situated at a transnational confluence of social, cultural, and technological trends that are increasingly global in reach. While the origins of otaku culture can be found in the specificities of postwar Japanese experiences and imaginations (see Chapters 1 and 6), the international circulation of these cultural forms grew from a trickle to a torrent in the decades from the 1980s to the present (see Chapter 7). Accelerated by the international expansion of fan activity and emerging forms of digital and networked communications, otaku media and practices have become a media "meganiche" (Shirky 2006) that is decidedly multicultural in fantasy content and human membership. In other words, while otaku culture retains a Japanese cultural identity, it is a notably large tent that is as welcoming to knights as it is to ninja and includes not only the fans who flock to Tokyo's Comic Market but also those who frequent Southern California's Anime Expo and the countless other gatherings that take place regularly around the world.

Historical Antecedents

In many ways, the transnationalization of otaku culture follows a long-standing tradition of cultural cross-pollination between Japan and other parts of the world. In her book *From Impressionism to Anime*, Susan Napier (2007) notes that the European and American impressionists of the nineteenth century and today's anime aficionados are united by common themes: aesthetic pleasure, intercultural fascination, and Japanophilia. Napier suggests that the pleasure that nineteenth- and early twentieth-century Euro-American elites derived from "Oriental" gardens and architecture was punctured by Japan's role as imperialist aggressor in World War II. It was only after the war that the U.S. occupation of Japan in tandem with Japan's postwar recovery created a context to revive the Western cult of Japan. At that point, the countercultural attraction to Japanese spirituality and fascination with Japan's business success became closely intertwined. "Japan Inc." was a source of both fear and fascination, a curious mix of exotic tradition and advanced technocapitalist modernity (Ivy 1995; Miyoshi and Harootunian 1993; Morley and Robbins 1995). Napier sees this long-standing ambivalence as the basis of today's fascination with Japanese popular culture, such as anime, games, and manga.

These cultural fascinations are multidirectional. As Euro-Americans absorbed the tenets of Zen Buddhism, Bushido, and Sony's globalization, the Japanese emulated Euro-American political and economic forms, fashion, and popular culture. Rather than focus on repairing relations with Asian neighbors and building a fully Asian national identity in the period since its economic rise, Japan has developed an identity that is neither completely Western nor Eastern (Iwabuchi 2002, 8–11). Japanese "remaking" of the West (Tobin 1992) has generated both business success and cultural ridicule. The ridicule has focused on stereotypical examples of Japanese cultural mimicry, such as nonsensical "Japlish" or salarymen donning cowboy hats and singing country and western (see, for example, the 1991 documentary *The Japanese Version*). But these stereotypes hardly capture the depth and breadth of Western cultural influences. Osamu Tezuka, generally considered the father of contemporary manga and anime, was a devoted fan of Disney animation (Kelts 2006; Schodt 1983), and many films of today's most celebrated animator, Hayao Miyazaki, are set in the European countryside and cityscapes. While retaining a culturally distinctive style, the content of much of today's anime represents ongoing Western influence as well as a kind of "deodorization" (Iwabuchi 2002) or unmooring from cultural origins.

"Cool Japan"

In 2002, the journalist Douglas McGray published an influential article in *Foreign Policy*, declaring a shift in Japan's international identity from a purveyor of hardware, such as cars and electronics, to one of "software." Describing the influence of Hello Kitty, j-pop, anime, and manga, McGray identified Japan's emerging "soft power" as a form of "gross national cool." McGray's article crystallized what street and fan culture had known for decades—that Japanese popular culture was a wellspring of generative fantasy content that invited the passionate

engagement of media hobbyists around the world. Well before Mc-
Gray's article, influential fans in the United States had been writing
reviews, encyclopedias, and guides to anime and manga culture (Clements and McCarthy 2001; Levi 1996; Patten 2004; Schodt 1983, 1996),
and kids around the world were growing up with Japanese media mixes
such as *Pokémon* and *Yu-Gi-Oh!* as facts of life (Ito 2007; Tobin 2004).
American teenage girl fan-fiction writers were discovering that *doujinshi* (fan-created manga) shared their obsession with homoerotic sub-
texts in popular media (McLelland 2001), while American and European
kids in military and expat banker families based in Japan had been
circulating videotapes of anime to peers in their homelands since the
1980s.

But McGray's article marked the tipping point in a cultural balance of power: high culture and the business sector had lost to youth
and pop culture in their efforts to craft Japan's identity in the international arena. In the 1980s, Japan studies were dominated by college
students with career ambitions in business, and courses were designed
with them in mind. But as Japan's economic fortunes declined, universities saw a shift in the profile of students studying Japanese. In her
survey of students in Japanese classes at the University of California,
Irvine, University of Southern California, and Occidental, Annie Manion (2005) found that the majority cited interest in anime and manga
as one of the primary reasons they were studying the language. As one
Wall Street Journal article put it, "Interest in Japanese is about cool, not
careers" (Parker 2004). Faculty interests also shifted in the 1990s, with
a growing number of course offerings and publications in Japanese
popular culture (Condry 2006; Craig 2000; Gottlieb and McLelland
2003; Kelly 2004; Martinez 1998; Skov and Moeran 1995).

This shift in cultural geopolitics happened in tandem with the mainstreaming of otaku culture domestically and of fan culture more generally in the United States and elsewhere. Henry Jenkins (2007) argues
that in the age of digital and networked culture, fannish engagement
with media, including the creation of fan fiction, videos, and art, have
become much more mainstream and less stigmatized. In Japan, the publication of the otaku love story *Densha-Otoko* (Train Man) in 2004 and
the subsequent TV version in 2005 marked a crucial turning point:
by representing otaku as harmless and endearing, both dramas helped
to remove the subculture's historically more negative and sociopathic

connotations and to recast it in a much more sympathetic light (see Chapter 3). The site where the *Densha-Otoko* story unfolded, 2ch (channel 2), was by then an established feature of Japanese online culture and had achieved the status of the largest online forum in the world. The otaku district of Akihabara became a tourist destination for both local and international visitors (see Chapter 6), and otaku art and "superflat" 2-D aesthetics became enshrined in U.S. modern art museums through the cultural brokering of pop artist Takashi Murakami (2005).

In tandem with the growing domestic and international interest in Japanese popular culture, such as manga, games, and anime, academic attention to otaku culture also grew. In their introduction to the English version of Hiroki Azuma's *Otaku: Japan's Database Animals*, translators Jonathan Abel and Shion Kono (2009, xix–xxi) explain how in the 1980s, before the rise of otaku studies, cultural critics in Japan associated with the "New Academism" popularized highly theoretical and philosophical works by writing about them in books that were accessible to the general public; in the process, these critics became popular icons themselves. Scholars such as Shinji Miyadai (1994), Masachi Osawa (1995), and Tamaki Saito (2000, 2007) came of age within this context and represented the first wave of Japanese scholarship to look specifically at otaku culture. Hiroki Azuma, Kaichiro Morikawa, and Akihiro Kitada, represented in this volume, expanded on this pioneering work, further establishing otaku and popular cultural studies as a legitimate field of scholarly inquiry.

Published in Japan in 2001, Azuma's best-selling book was an important turning point. While the success of the New Academism in promoting accessible genres of writing "paved the way for Azuma's success" (Abel and Kono 2009, xxi), Azuma's book heralded a new era of scholarship devoted to popular and youth culture. In the preface to the English translation, Azuma (2009) describes how the new scholarship on otaku departed from "those critics and theorists of an older sort who ignore such [popular culture] trends and continue to talk about 'the end of literature' and 'the end of criticism.'" He also lamented the fact that the work of popular culture theorists such as Morikawa, Kitada, and Miyadai are largely untranslated and unavailable to English-language readers (Azuma 2009, ix–x).

In English-language scholarship, including Japan studies, the pioneering work of scholars such as Anne Allison (2000, 2006), Sharon

Kinsella (1995, 1998, 2000), Susan Napier (2000, 2007), and Joseph Tobin (2004) has helped establish the study of manga and anime as a legitimate specialty. Today, we see a growing body of scholarly output centered on the study of anime and manga (Bolton, Csicery-Ronay Jr., and Tatsumi 2007; Brown 2006; Lamarre 2009; Lunning 2006). The annual Mechademia series of edited books (Lunning 2006, 2007, 2008, 2009, 2010) is testament to the robust scholarly interest in manga and anime as well as to growing international scholarly cross-pollination. Further, these edited books now often feature translated essays from Japan. Also, while most English-language scholarship on anime and manga has focused on professional creators or media content, we are now beginning to see work that looks at fan activity. The fifth Mechademia volume, *Fanthropologies*, is dedicated to fandom.

In Japan itself, a new generation of fan studies is extending the work of the first pioneers of otaku studies, energized by the growing visibility of otaku culture both domestically and overseas. By focusing on empirically grounded and detailed case studies, this new generation of scholarship highlights the diversity of fan and otaku engagement. This book showcases key texts from both the first wave of otaku scholars (Azuma, Kitada, and Morikawa) and the next generation (Ishida, Kijima, Okabe, Tamagawa, and Tsuji). By translating the work of prominent scholars of otaku culture in Japan, this book contributes to the multidirectionality of cultural flow between Japan and the West and complements earlier work on popular cultural flows within Asia (Iwabuchi 2002, 2004). Our aim is to consolidate some of the key work on the contemporary state of otaku culture and practice by focusing specifically on the U.S.-Japan cultural corridor.

"Cool Japan" of the 2000s belongs to an established tradition of East-West cultural flow, and as an example of Japan's continuous rebranding in the international arena, it also belongs to what Iwabuchi (2010, 90) has described as the broader international trend toward "brand nationalism." It echoes the familiar patterns of exoticism and Japanophilia that have defined the privileged U.S.-Japan cultural and political corridor, and it is in keeping with Japan's ongoing nationalist project insofar as it looks more to the West than to Asian neighbors in order to define Japan's identity in the transnational arena (Iwabuchi 2010, 90–91). In contrast to earlier periods of Japanese culture's overseas influence, however, today's otaku landscape has been built by a mostly lowbrow, youth-driven, and highly distributed networked media ecology. International elites, governmental bureaucrats, and transnational corporations are latecomers to a party already dominated by a scrappier and youth-centered crowd. Roland Kelts describes how this groundswell of overseas interest in anime and manga caught local industries off guard: "The global anime boom of the twenty-first century has taken Japan, whose corporate culture prides itself on knowing the next new thing, almost completely by surprise" (Kelts 2006, 7). Kelts goes on to describe how the Japanese government eventually latched on to McGray's notion of soft power as a way to revitalize Japan's international influence in an era of economic recession (Kelts 2006, 112–113).

Otaku culture is emblematic of the growing force of technological privilege and online networks in dictating the terms of transnational cultural flow. Policy makers are responding to and capitalizing on trends set by the technocultural sector and online networks rather than being in the driver's seat. We can see the power of technological and online leadership in the growing influence of South Korea in transnational cultural flows as well. As Iwabuchi notes (2010, 93–94), Korean media culture, particularly drama, has become hugely popular in Japan. This growing cultural influence cannot be decoupled from South Korea's status as one of the most wired countries on the planet, defining a new techno-pop cultural sensibility within the context of its leadership in online and mobile networks and distribution. In short, today's interests in otaku culture and the branding of cool Japan bring a new twist to the ongoing projects of national identity production and transnational flows as they are intertwined with the growing influence of popular culture and online peer-to-peer networks.

Similarity and Difference

Even as otaku culture is recuperated by elites and the mainstream, and as the terms "anime" and "manga" have become part of a common international lexicon, otaku culture and practice have retained their subcultural credibility. In Japan, much of manga and anime is associated with mainstream consumption; otaku must therefore differentiate themselves from *ippanjin* (regular people) through a proliferating set of niche genres, alternative readings, and derivative works. In the United States, the subcultural cred of anime and manga is buttressed by their status as foreign "cult media." This stance of U.S. fans is not grounded, however, in a simplistic exoticism. Susan Napier suggests that "rather than the traditional Orientalist construction of the West empowering itself by oppressing or patronizing the Eastern Other, these fans gain agency through discovering and then identifying with a society that they clearly recognize as having both universal and culturally specific aspects" (Napier 2007, 189). She describes how U.S. fans most often explain their interests in terms of the works' "thematic complexity and three-dimensional characterization" rather than as an interest in Japan per se (Napier 2007, 177).

Put differently, the international appeal of otaku culture is grounded precisely in its ability to resist totalizing global narratives such as nationalism. The long-running and intricate narrative forms of popular Japanese media represent a platform or, in Hiroki Azuma's terms, a database of referents that are highly amenable to recombination and customization by fans and gamers (see Chapter 2). We can see this in the stunning diversity of doujinshi derived from the same manga series (see Chapters 5 and 9) and in the activities of young *Pokémon* or *Yu-Gi-Oh!* card game players who design their own decks out of the nearly infinite set of possibilities on offer through a growing pantheon of monsters (Buckingham and Sefton-Green 2004; Ito 2007; Sefton-Green 2004; Willett 2004). While certain female fans might look to *Gundam* for source material to tell stories of erotic trysts between the male characters, other fans geek out over building and customizing models of the giant robots.

What unifies otaku culture as a whole is less its certain content and genres and more its malleable narrative platform and mode of participatory niche media engagement (Jenkins 1992, 2006). The media mixes of Japanese popular culture invite fannish engagement through links across multiple media types (games, toys, TV, cinema, manga, novels), intricate and open-ended story lines, and massive databases of characters, monsters, and machines (Ito 2006). Otaku also gravitate toward media forms and communication platforms that enable them to engage in peer-to-peer exchange of knowledge and appropriative DIY creation (see Chapters 10 and 12). While earlier generations of fans relied on conventions and amateur media markets to circulate their work and connect with other fans (see Chapters 5 and 7), the Internet has made these forms of fan communication and sharing widely accessible. Armed with personal digital media and plugged into the end-to-end architecture of the Internet, otaku have truly found their medium.

The Internet has also radically expanded the opportunities for transnational communication and connection. Practices of fan subtitling and translation (Chapter 8) and peer-to-peer Internet distribution have made anime and manga accessible to fans around the world, even in the absence of localization and overseas distribution by the industry. The niches within the meganiche of anime are increasingly uniting fans across national boundaries. For example, the *yaoi* otaku fandom of Japan shares much in common with slash fandoms in the United States. Both are female-centered fandoms that center on "couplings" between male characters in popular series, and cyberpunk science fiction has strong crossovers between Japan and the United States as well. Although we are seeing more instances of U.S. media producers' taking up anime-like styles and themes, or creating their own manga, Japan is likely to retain its role as the central site of production for otaku cultural products. Drawing from an interview with Shinichiro Ishikawa, president of anime studio Gonzo Digimation Holdings, Kelts describes how Japan's media markets are a generative site of experimentation and innovation in manga and anime. Ishikawa emphasizes that in one week, Japan sees the equivalent of a full year's worth of U.S. comic sales (Kelts 2006, 196). The fact that Japan is home to the most diverse and robust market for comics in the world obviously goes a long way toward explaining why it is also the source of the tremendous creative output of both manga and anime. Japan's manga ecology is like a primordial soup supporting narrative mutation, and even in the Internet age, only a fraction of the characters and content circulate outside the domestic market.

Variations in otaku culture between Japan and the United States stem not from irreducible differences in national culture but from specific historical, social, and infrastructural conditions. For example, train otaku culture found fertile ground in Japan because it resonated with the history of Japan's postwar modernization and the train-centered transport systems of the small country (see Chapter 1). But we have seen much less transnational uptake of this variation of otaku culture in the car-centered U.S. context. American fans, most of whom encountered anime and manga in a postdigital era, are also much more likely than their Japanese counterparts to engage with digital variants of fan media and production, such as anime music videos (see Chapter 12) or web comics. In contrast, Japan's otaku culture was well established in the predigital era, and it continues to center on the circulation of physical media such as print doujinshi and physical models and figures. This focus is supported by the compact density of Japan and specialized fan events such as the doujinshi market, Comic Market (see Chapter 5), or Wonderfest, where model makers showcase their work. Fans in the United States need to travel greater distances and therefore attend events with less frequency, and conventions tend to be general-purpose umbrellas for all dimensions of the anime and manga fandom.

While the specificities of particular histories, practices, and places are central to the essays collected in this volume, we do not assume that national culture on its own defines the myriad cultural forms that otaku culture takes. We take a transnational rather than a comparative approach. Our interest is not to identify sources of national difference but rather to trace some of the contours of a transnational subculture. Following the lead of a growing body of work in transnational studies that looks at the flow of culture across national boundaries, we see otaku culture as a lens through which to disrupt the commonsensical isomorphism between culture, people, and places (Appadurai 1996; Gupta and Ferguson 1992, 1997; Iwabuchi 1999, 2002). Even as Japan continues to be the primary source of anime and manga content, it is increasingly non-Japanese fans and makers who are defining what it means to be an otaku and a fan of Japanese popular culture.

UNDERSTANDING OTAKU CULTURE

The essays that follow draw from both Japan- and U.S.-centered scholarship to explore three shared dimensions of otaku culture: its discursive and cultural logics, the infrastructures of communication and media distribution, and the structures of community and community membership. The organization of the volume embodies an argument about commonality and difference, in which otaku culture shares a set of common cultural logics and platforms (sections 1 and 2), which are taken up in diverse ways by niche communities (section 3). These underlying dynamics of connection and distinction making are what unify otaku subcultures regardless of national origin and location. Here I provide an overview of these three themes by way of introduction to the chapters of this book.

The Semiotics of Otaku Culture

The chapters in the first section of the book explore the ways in which otaku culture has evolved as a complex set of resistances and accommodations to modernity, mainstream culture, and other subcultures. According to otaku scholar and spokesperson Toshio Okada (1996), the term originated in the early 1980s as a polite term of address between upper-crust college students who were fans of emergent anime cultures. It was transformed into a social category by columnist Akio Nakamori, who published a column on "Otaku Research" in a manga magazine in 1983. In 1989, a full-blown "moral panic" (Cohen 1972) about otaku arose after the arrest of Tsutomu Miyazaki. Miyazaki had abducted, murdered, and mutilated four girls. Photos and footage of his bedroom, crammed with manga and videotapes, many of the Lolita-complex and pornographic variety, flooded the popular press, and Miyazaki became the poster boy of the otaku subculture. After this, "otaku" came to be used and recognized by the mainstream as a stigmatizing label for somebody who is obsessed with anime, manga, and games and out of touch with everyday social reality. Okada (1996) and others have argued against the stigmatizing use of the term, and a more positive vision of otaku as innovative popular-culture enthusiasts has increasingly taken hold.

In the United States, in tandem with the rise of cyberpunk and geek chic in the 1990s, the term "otaku" started to be used in a largely positive manner to refer to enthusiasts of Japanese media mixes, particularly anime. In Chapter 4, Lawrence Eng describes in detail the trajectory through which this term became established in the U.S. context. Although the term has tended to have relatively positive connotations in the United States, it can still function as a term of stigmatization. Like Okada, however, Eng believes in the positive potential of otaku culture and identifies the key dimensions of "the otaku ethic" as follows: information literacy, subcultural resistance, and affinities with networked sociability and culture.

The other chapters in this section analyze the particular cultural logics behind the rise of otaku culture in Japan. In Chapter 1, Izumi Tsuji looks in depth at early train otaku culture, when the establishment of a high-tech national railway system embodied Japan's dreams of modernization. As Japan entered the postindustrial era, this train hobbyist culture was transformed into a train otaku culture as young men began to turn to fantasy representations of trains and as anime series such as *Galaxy Express 999* began to treat steam locomotives as objects of nostalgia. Tsuji argues that by tracing the historical emergence of train otaku culture, we can understand the changing structure of the imagination as it evolved through different historical periods.

In an excerpt from his longer book on otaku as "database animals," in Chapter 2 Hiroki Azuma argues that today's otaku culture is grounded in the broader postmodern turn that challenged the stability of modern grand narratives. The decline of these grand narratives has led to what Azuma has named "database consumption." Database consumption marks a shift from the late 1990s, when otaku culture was oriented to narrative structures and unique characters, to the early twenty-first century, when it became focused on *moe* elements such as cat ears, glasses, business suits, or particular personality quirks. Moe elements are traits that invite particular forms of otaku affection and that are recognizable across a wide range of anime and manga characters and narratives. Today's moe otaku culture represents a fundamental overturning of the premises of modernist narratives. By positioning the act of appropriation and play of signifiers as the generative foundation of cultural production, it downplays the traditional modernist emphasis on "original" and proprietary narrative constructs.

This implicit challenge to master narratives is also evident in otaku's ironic and reflexive critique of mainstream media and institutions. This attitude is manifest in the snarky commentary on the massive anonymous online forum 2ch (channel 2), which is the subject of Chapter 3. Yet even amid the abrasive social exchanges that characterize the discourse of 2ch, otaku's embrace of social connection is also apparent. In line with Eng's description of the networked culture of U.S. otaku, Kitada argues in Chapter 3 that 2ch represents a "kingdom of social connection" that centers on the traffic in insider knowledge. Characterized by an ironic and snarky one-upmanship, this kind of online communication is also oddly sincere. 2channelers' embrace of the melodramatic *Densha-Otoko* love story, in which an otaku is united with the girl of his dreams, is emblematic of the codependent and highly complex relation between irony and sincerity that Kitada identifies. Although all of the essays in this section describe the ways in which otaku culture emerged through resistance to mainstream narratives and sensibilities, they also trace the ways in which these modes of engagement are becoming much more prevalent and visible in today's networked and digital age.

Peer-to-Peer Platforms and Infrastructures

Undergirding the growing visibility of otaku culture is an increasingly robust social, technical, and place-based infrastructure. Shifting from the previous section's focus on cultural content and process, the chapters in the second section of this book examine these enabling locations and infrastructures. As described earlier, otaku culture has strong affinities with user-configurable digital media and online networks that connect people many-to-many and peer-to-peer, rather than relying on the one-to-many mass broadcast model of communication. Many of the core characteristics of today's networked and digital age were evident even in the early origins of otaku culture. These characteristics include immersion in specialized and fluid niche knowledge networks (Anderson 2006; Hagel, Brown, and Davison 2010), decentralized forms of social organization and production (Benkler 2000, 2006; Shirky 2008), the primacy of participatory amateur and DIY media (Jenkins 1992; Leadbeater 2004; Varnelis 2008), distributed and collective innovation and intelligence (Hippel 2005; Howe 2009; Jenkins 2006; Lakhani and Panetta 2007; Shirky 2010), and an open and nonproprietary approach to intellectual property (Lessig 2004, 2008; Weber 2004).

In Chapter 6, Kaichiro Morikawa describes a physical set of infrastructures for otaku activity that is unique to the dense urban ecologies of Tokyo but that still embodies the properties of peer-based and amateur otaku culture. As otaku culture has flourished in the 1980s and beyond, particular districts of the city have been able to support a high density of otaku-related establishments. Morikawa describes how in the 1990s, in tandem with the *Evangelion* boom, stores dedicated to otaku commercial products and doujinshi began to centralize in the districts of Akihabara and Ikebukuro, dedicated to male and female otaku, respectively. Far from being the result of centralized urban planning, the specialization of these districts represented a kind of coalescing of distributed intelligence as hobbyists and businesspeople with shared interests converged through mutual attraction. Today's Akihabara is a veritable otaku theme park, plastered with posters of cute anime characters and dotted with maid cafés, where young women dress up as fantasy maid characters. It embodies what Morikawa describes as "the architecture of otaku taste."

Although decidedly low-tech in its execution, Comic Market, the biannual event dedicated to the buying and selling of doujinshi, also exemplifies all of the dimensions of a networked, participatory, and peer-to-peer infrastructure. In Chapter 5, Hiroaki Tamagawa describes the early origins of Comic Market in the late 1970s, when a subset of fans broke from the industry-centric convention style dominant at the time. Comic Market was founded as a distribution venue for the amateur arts of doujinshi, and its ethic of nondiscriminatory participation continues to this day. Much like the Internet, the market is a neutral platform that invites fans of all denominations to participate. With the growth of otaku culture, this open-door policy has meant that the event has ballooned in size; while the first markets attracted several hundred participants, today's events mobilize more than 400,000 fans.

This peer-based fan culture is evident in the growth of the U.S. otaku social networks that Eng describes in Chapter 7. The U.S. fandom began in the 1970s and 1980s via a dedicated core of anime lovers who trafficked in insider information and tapes of anime that were extremely difficult to come by at the time. Eventually, fans at universities established clubs that facilitated the sharing and viewing of anime, and other dedicated fans organized conventions that brought together members of the growing fandom. Since very few anime were localized for the U.S. market in these early years, fans took on the task of translating and subtitling the works, as well as distributing them through snail mail, clubs, and conventions. With the advent of the Internet in the 1990s, U.S. fans found an ideal medium to share knowledge and media with other fans around the country. Informational fan sites and fan forums proliferated, and with the advent of peer-to-peer video distribution and digital fansubbing, the online circulation of anime exploded.

In Chapter 8, on fansubbing, I describe how today's digisubbers organize highly disciplined volunteer work teams that translate, subtitle, and distribute anime episodes to millions of fans around the world. Practices such as fansubbing and scanlation (fan translation of manga) are fan localization practices that have been central to the establishment of the overseas fandom for Japanese popular culture. Fansubbing embodies the complicated dynamics of managing intellectual property and the relation between commercial and noncommercial distribution in the digital age. The symbiotic yet fraught relation between fans and commercial anime and manga industries is a persistent feature of otaku practice, and it is nowhere more evident than in the fansub case.

Participatory and DIY Communities

The spirit of volunteerism, contribution, and participation that we see in the organizers of Comic Market and fansubbers is a foundational aspect of how otaku communities are organized. The final section of the book looks at specific cases of niche otaku communities and how they organize membership, status, and identity. Although otaku share common types of cultural referencing and infrastructures, particular genres and forms of expression are highly diverse. Otaku subcultures employ strategies to distinguish themselves from mainstream culture, to distinguish different subsets of otaku culture, and to distinguish internally among members of these different subset niches. Drawing from detailed ethnographic work, the chapters that complete this volume offer a window into the fine-tuned distinctions that characterize the internal workings of specific niche communities within the broader anime and manga fandom.

In Chapter 9, Daisuke Okabe and Kimi Ishida examine the subculture of *fujoshi*, female otaku who specialize in "boys' love" and yaoi narratives that center on homoerotic relationships between characters in mainstream manga for boys and young men. Rewriting mainstream heteronormative manga to center on these boys' love narratives, fujoshi disrupt dominant expectations about their own sexuality and feminine identity. Fujoshi also manage a complex identity formation in which they hide their fujoshi identity from family, boyfriends, and friends at school. Bonding rituals of fujoshi identity display are reserved for moments with other fujoshi friends, when they will self-deprecatingly and ironically describe their irrepressible attraction to the fantasy objects of their affections. While yaoi culture resembles many of the products of female fandoms of U.S. television fans, such as fan art and fan fiction (Bacon-Smith 1991; Jenkins 1992; Penley 1997), the identity management practices of fujoshi are inflected by the particular contexts of Japanese girls' culture.

This complicated set of identity negotiations is also evident in Okabe's study, in Chapter 10, of cosplayers, who dress up as characters from manga, games, and anime. Largely overlapping with the fujoshi fandom, cosplay is a female-dominated niche grounded in a DIY and anticommercial ethic of costume making and performance. Although not characterized by formal forms of evaluation and hierarchy, cosplayers are highly conscious of quality standards for costumes. Only handmade costumes that conform to fujoshi interests and moe pass muster; those cosplayers who dress up outside of otaku-dedicated venues or who display mainstream forms of sexuality to attract the male gaze are ostracized from the community.

With Yoshimasa Kijima's study of hand-to-hand fighting games, in Chapter 11, we are offered a glimpse into a masculine and competitive subculture of game otaku. Kijima describes how fighting game culture evolved through various gaming genres and a network of game arcades. Today these gamers have a highly developed set of competitive practices in which they constantly test their skills in combat with other players, moving from local to regional to national competitions. Like the other otaku communities surveyed in this section, the subculture of fighting game otaku is built on a high degree of camaraderie, but it also has a unique brutally competitive character.

In the final chapter of the book, I describe the U.S.-centered subculture of anime music video (AMV) makers. AMVs involve remixing anime to a soundtrack of the editor's choosing, usually Euro-American popular music. As digital video editing became more accessible, what was once a tiny niche community has expanded into a massive and highly visible online scene. In the process, AMV makers developed various social and technical mechanisms for defining the center and periphery of their community, recognizing high-quality work, and defining an elite crowd of dedicated makers. This dynamic tension between democratic inclusiveness and highly specialized distinction making is central to all of the otaku communities described in this book.

CONCLUSION

The picture of otaku culture that emerges from this volume is one that honors its irreducible diversity and contested nature while also recognizing it as a growing transnational movement with a shared set of infrastructures and cultural practices. As the networked and digital age enters a period of maturity, we might expect that otaku culture will become both a more taken-for-granted feature of the global cultural landscape and one that continues to proliferate unexpected niches, genres, and activities fueled by a growing horde of amateur fan makers. Already, we are beginning to see distinctions and niches becoming ever more fine-tuned within the overall otaku scene as the palette of opportunity and participation expands. Although otaku culture will doubtless always be identified with its Japanese origins, its transnational nature has also become one of its defining characteristics. More than simply a sequel to the well-established narrative of cultural contact between Japan and the West, otaku culture represents a genuinely new symbolic database of transnational flows that has already provided a cast of characters, setting, and back story that invites endless appropriative innovation.

References

Abel, Jonathan, and Shion Kono. 2009. Translators' introduction. In *Otaku: Japan's database animals*, xv–xxix. Minneapolis: University of Minnesota Press.

Allison, Anne. 2000. A challenge to Hollywood? Japanese character goods hit the US. *Japanese Studies* 20 (1): 67–88.

———. 2006. *Millennial monsters: Japanese toys and the global imagination*. Berkeley: University of California Press.

Anderson, Chris. 2006. *The long tail: Why the future of business is selling less of more*. New York: Hyperion.

Appadurai, Arjun. 1996. *Modernity at large: Cultural dimensions of globalization*. Minneapolis: University of Minnesota Press.

Azuma, Hiroki. 2009. *Otaku: Japan's database animals*. Trans. Jonathan Abel and Shion Kono. Minneapolis: University of Minnesota Press.

Bacon-Smith, Camille. 1991. *Enterprising women: Television fandom and the creation of popular myth*. Philadelphia: University of Pennsylvania Press.

Benkler, Yochai. 2000. From consumers to users: Shifting the deeper structures of regulation toward sustainable commons and user access. *Federal Communications Law Journal* 52: 561–579.

———. 2006. *The wealth of networks: How social production transforms markets and freedom.* New Haven, CT: Yale University Press.

Bolton, Christopher, Istvan Csicery-Ronay Jr., and Takayuki Tatsumi, eds. 2007. *Robot ghosts and wired dreams: Japanese science fiction from origins to anime.* Minneapolis: University of Minnesota Press.

Brown, Steven T., ed. 2006. *Cinema anime.* New York: Palgrave Macmillan.

Buckingham, David, and Julian Sefton-Green. 2004. Structure, agency, and pedagogy in children's media culture. In *Pikachu's global adventure: The rise and fall of Pokémon,* ed. Joseph Tobin, 12–33. Durham, NC: Duke University Press.

Clements, Jonathan, and Helen McCarthy. 2001. *The anime encyclopedia: A guide to Japanese animation since 1917.* Berkeley, CA: Stone Bridge Press.

Cohen, Stanley. 1972. *Folk devils and moral panics.* London: MacGibbon and Kee.

Condry, Ian. 2006. *Hip-hop Japan: Rap and the paths of cultural globalization.* Durham, NC: Duke University Press.

Craig, Timothy J., ed. 2000. *Japan pop! Inside the world of Japanese popular culture.* Armonk, NY: M. E. Sharp.

Gottlieb, Nanette, and Mark McLelland, eds. 2003. *Japanese cybercultures.* New York: Routledge.

Gupta, Akhil, and James Ferguson. 1992. Space, identity, and the politics of difference. *Cultural Anthropology* 7 (1): 6–23.

———, eds. 1997. *Culture, power, place: Explorations in critical anthropology.* Durham, NC: Duke University Press.

Hagel, John, John Seely Brown, and Lang Davison. 2010. *The power of pull: How small moves, smartly made, can set big things in motion.* New York: Basic Books.

Hippel, Eric Von. 2005. *Democratizing innovation.* Cambridge, MA: MIT Press.

Howe, Jeff. 2009. *Crowdsourcing: Why the power of the crowd is driving the future of business.* New York: Three Rivers Press.

Ito, Mizuko. 2006. Japanese media mixes and amateur cultural exchange. In *Digital generations: Children, young people, and the new media,* ed. David Buckingham and Rebekah Willet, 49–66. Mahwah, NJ: Lawrence Erlbaum.

———. 2007. Technologies of the childhood imagination: *Yu-Gi-Oh!,* media mixes, and everyday cultural production. In *Structures of participation in digital culture,* ed. Joe Karaganis, 88–110. New York: Social Science Research Council.

Ivy, Marilyn. 1995. *Discourses of the vanishing: Modernity, phantasm, Japan.* Chicago: University of Chicago Press.

Iwabuchi, Koichi. 1999. Return to Asia? Japan in Asian audiovisual markets. In *Consuming ethnicity and nationalism: Asian experiences,* ed. Kosaku Yoshino, 177–199. Honolulu: University of Hawaii Press.

———. 2002. *Recentering globalization: Popular culture and Japanese transnationalism.* Durham, NC: Duke University Press.

———, ed. 2004. *Feeling Asian modernities: Transnational consumption of Japanese TV dramas.* Hong Kong: Hong Kong University Press.

———. 2010. Undoing inter-national fandom in the age of brand nationalism. In *Mechademia 4: Fanthropologies,* ed. Koichi Iwabuchi, 87–98. Minneapolis: University of Minnesota Press.

The Japanese version. 1991. Center for New American Media.

Jenkins, Henry. 1992. *Textual poachers: Television fans and participatory culture.* New York: Routledge.

———. 2006. *Convergence culture: Where old and new media collide.* New York: New York University Press.

———. 2007. The future of fandom. In *Fandom: Identities and communities in a mediated world,* ed. Jonathan Gray, Cornell Sandvoss, and C. Lee Harrington, 357–574. New York: New York University Press.

Kelly, William W., ed. 2004. *Fanning the flames: Fans and consumer culture in contemporary Japan.* Albany: State University of New York.

Kelts, Roland. 2006. *Japanamerica: How Japanese pop culture has invaded the U.S.* New York: Palgrave.

Kinsella, Sharon. 1995. Cuties in Japan. In *Women, media, and consumption in Japan,* ed. Lise Skov and Brian Moeran, 220–254. Honolulu: University of Hawaii Press.

———. 1998. Japanese subculture in the 1980s: Otaku and the amateur manga movement. *Journal of Japanese Studies* 24 (2): 289–316.

———. 2000. *Adult manga: Culture and power in contemporary Japanese society.* Honolulu: University of Hawaii Press.

Lakhani, Karim R., and Jill Panetta. 2007. The principles of distributed innovation. *Innovations: Technology, Governance, Globalization* 2 (3): 97–112.

Lamarre, Thomas. 2009. *The anime machine: A media theory of animation.* Minneapolis: University of Minnesota Press.

Leadbeater, Charles. 2004. *The pro-am revolution: How enthusiasts are changing our economy and society.* London: Demos.

Lessig, Lawrence. 2004. *Free culture: How big media uses technology and the law to lock down culture and control creativity.* New York: Penguin Press.

———. 2008. *Remix: Making art and commerce thrive in the hybrid economy.* New York: Penguin Press.

Levi, Antonia. 1996. *Samurai from outer space: Understanding Japanese animation.* Chicago: Open Court.

Lunning, Frenchy, ed. 2006. *Mechademia 1: Emerging worlds of anime and manga.* Minneapolis: University of Minnesota Press.

———, ed. 2007. *Mechademia 2: Networks of desire.* Minneapolis: University of Minnesota Press.

———, ed. 2008. *Mechademia 3: Limits of the human.* Minneapolis: University of Minnesota Press.

———, ed. 2009. *Mechademia 4: War/time.* Minneapolis: University of Minnesota Press.

———, ed. 2010. *Mechademia 5: Fanthropologies.* Minneapolis: University of Minnesota Press.

Manion, Annie. 2005. *Discovering Japan: Anime and learning Japanese culture.* Master's thesis, East Asian Studies, University of Southern California, Los Angeles.

Martinez, D. P., ed. 1998. *The worlds of Japanese popular culture: Gender, shifting boundaries and global cultures.* Cambridge: Cambridge University Press.

McGray, Douglas. 2002. Japan's gross national cool. *Foreign Policy* (June/July 2002): 44–54.

McLelland, Mark. 2001. Local meanings in global space: A case study of women's "boy love" web sites in Japanese and English. *Mots Pluriels* 19, www.arts.uwa.edu.au/MotsPluriels/MP1901mcl.html (retrieved July 12, 2005).

Miyadai, Shinji. 1994. *Seifuku shojo tachi no sentaku*. Tokyo: Kodansha.

Miyoshi, Masao, and H. D. Harootunian, eds. 1993. *Japan in the world*. Durham, NC: Duke University Press.

Morley, David, and Kevin Robbins. 1995. *Spaces of identity: Global media, electronic landscapes and cultural boundaries*. New York: Routledge.

Murakami, Takashi, ed. 2005. *Little boy: The arts of Japan's exploding subculture*. New Haven, CT: Yale University Press.

Nakamori, Akio. 1983. Otaku no kenkyu 1. *Manga Burikko* (June), www.burikko.net/people/otaku01.html (retrieved January 11, 2011). Alt, Matt, trans. 2008. What kind of otaku are you? *Néojaponisme*, http://neojaponisme.com/2008/04/02/what-kind-of-otaku-are-you (retrieved January 14, 2011).

Napier, Susan J. 2000. *Anime: From Akira to Princess Mononoke*. New York: Palgrave.

———. 2007. *From impressionism to anime: Japan as fantasy and fan cult in the mind of the West*. New York: Palgrave MacMilan.

Okada, Toshio. 1996. *Otakugaku nyuumon*. Tokyo: Ota Shuppan.

Osawa, Masachi. 1995. *Denshi media ron—Shintai no media teki henyou*. Tokyo: Shinyosha.

Parker, Ginny. 2004. Interest in Japanese is about cool, not careers. *Wall Street Journal*, October 11, 2004.

Patten, Fred. 2004. *Watching anime, reading manga: 25 years of essays and reviews*. Berkeley, CA: Stone Bridge Press.

Penley, Constance. 1997. *NASA/TREK: Popular science and sex in America*. London: Verso Books.

Saito, Tamaki. 2000. *Sento bishojo no seishin bunseki*. Tokyo: Ota Shuppan.

———. 2007. Otaku sexuality. Trans. Christopher Bolton. In *Robot ghosts and wired dreams*, ed. Christopher Bolton, Istvan Csicsery-Ronay Jr., and Takyuki Tatsumi, 222–245. Minneapolis: University of Minnesota Press.

Schodt, Frederik. 1983. *Manga! Manga! The world of Japanese comics*. New York: Kodansha America.

———. 1996. *Dreamland Japan: Writings on modern manga*. Berkeley, CA: Stone Bridge Press.

Sefton-Green, Julian. 2004. Initiation rites: A small boy in a Poké-world. In *Pikachu's global adventures: The rise and fall of Pokémon*, ed. Joseph Tobin, 141–164. Durham, NC: Duke University Press.

Shirky, Clay. 2006. Tiny slice, big market. *Wired* 14 (11), www.wired.com/wired/archive/14.11/meganiche.html (retrieved January 11, 2011).

———. 2008. *Here comes everybody: The power of organizing without organizations*. New York: Penguin Press.

———. 2010. *Cognitive surplus: Creativity and generosity in a connected age*. New York: Penguin Press.

Skov, Lise, and Brian Moeran, eds. 1995. *Women, media, and consumption in Japan*. Honolulu: University of Hawaii Press.

Tobin, Joseph J., ed. 1992. *Re-made in Japan: Everyday life and consumer taste in a changing society*. New Haven, CT: Yale University Press.

———. 2004. *Pikachu's global adventure: The rise and fall of Pokémon*. Durham, NC: Duke University Press.

Varnelis, Kazys, ed. 2008. *Networked publics*. Cambridge, MA: MIT Press.

Weber, Steven. 2004. *The success of open source*. Cambridge, MA: Harvard University Press.

Willett, Rebekah. 2004. The multiple identities of Pokémon fans. In *Pikachu's global adventure: The rise and fall of Pokémon*, ed. Joseph Tobin, 226–240. Durham, NC: Duke University Press.

I

CULTURE AND DISCOURSE

1

Why Study Train Otaku?
A Social History of Imagination

....

IZUMI TSUJI

WHAT ARE TRAIN OTAKU?

At the Bottom of the Social Ladder of Boys' School Culture

Although just one among today's varied types of otaku, train otaku are in many ways a seminal category.[1] The purpose of this chapter is to elucidate the development of otaku culture in Japanese society by tracing the history of train otaku. As it is one of the archetypical early types of otaku to emerge in Japan, understanding train otaku's history offers a shortcut to grasping the overall history of otaku culture. As discussed later in this chapter, tracing the path of train otaku culture also makes visible various changes in male otaku culture more broadly. Train otaku culture has a long history with roots reaching as far back as pre–World War II Japan.

Today's otaku culture tends to attract attention because of interest in the fantasy worlds of anime, manga, and games. People typically think of otaku as people who harbor a strong, fanatical sense of attachment to fictive characters such as beautiful girl anime characters (see Chapter 2). In comparison, train otaku may seem staid because their affection is reserved for objects that exist in reality.

This does not necessarily mean that train otaku are firmly committed to "real" society. They tend to be socially awkward, and the vast majority of them have never had relationships with "real" women. Because of these tendencies, train otaku tend to be placed on the bottom rung of the male social ladder.

I have been a train otaku from childhood, and I remember having no choice but to belong to the lowest "caste" throughout my junior high school and high school years in boys' schools. In boys' schools, the most important criterion for belonging to the highest caste is to be popular with "real" girls. Most of these popular boys are jocks. Those attached to fantasy girls, such as anime otaku, belong to a significantly lower caste. Train otaku, who indecisively fail to fully commit to either reality or unreality, are assigned to the lowest caste.

The View from the Bottom Rung

Given such stigmatization, what accounts for the enduring appeal of trains? One factor is the long and decorated history of train otaku. Older, more traditional elite boys' schools that include both middle and high schools, as well as many of the established, prestigious universities, almost always have student railway clubs.[2] Many of these clubs were founded in the post–World War II era, or at least by the time Japan entered its period of rapid economic growth in the 1960s. The Railway Club at Keio University was founded in 1934, making it the oldest railway club still in operation, despite a brief hiatus during World War II.

Another factor contributing to the appeal of trains is that most Japanese men have the experience of becoming enamored by trains at least once in their childhoods. Toy trains are fixtures of boy culture, and one can always find them in a toy store. Although not all boys go on to become train otaku, these early childhood experiences provide an entry point for those who do.

Train otaku have attachments to objects that are not part of the mainstream reality they inhabit every day. This kind of attachment to the "unreal" was a core characteristic of otaku culture during its early history, constituting a kind of archetype and a key reason as to why otaku have been looked down upon by the mainstream. Otaku culture's recent rapid rise in popularity may be due to the growing strength of the fantasy domain and the lack of appeal of more reality-based identities.

If we consider this penchant for the unreal as a kind of culture of the imagination, this trait is ubiquitous in all varieties of otaku culture. Anime otaku, who devote their affections to completely fictional characters, take this attachment to the imagination to one extreme, whereas train otaku are only part of the way down this path to fantasy.

Trains as Media of the Imagination

Practices of cultivating an attachment for the unreal while inhabiting a different everyday reality harken to far earlier times. In fact, this stance has been entrusted to young men for generations. In an earlier era, the scientific imagination, detached from mainstream reality, was a symbol of masculinity.[3] In addition, I describe later how youth were redefined as possessing powers of imagination that exceed the confines of reality. Trains have long served as a bridge between a concrete everyday reality and this expanded role of the imagination.

According to sociologist Munesuke Mita, trains have taken this role because they are a medium of the imagination. In other words, by being "external yet internal, internal yet external" (1984, 11), trains are a multifaceted medium that, while being embedded in the ordinary, is also redolent of the extraordinary. The station of origin is soundly grounded in the everyday here and now, but at the same time, trains evoke desire for the somewhere and sometime of their destination.[4] When did trains become a medium of imagination and become linked to Japanese youth? And how has this imagination changed through time? In particular, when did these youths transform themselves into otaku? This chapter explores these questions by drawing from historical materials and ethnographic research, including interviews conducted with forty-nine rail enthusiasts ranging in age from their teens to their seventies.[5]

THE BIRTH OF THE TRAIN BOYS

Youth in a Society Late to Arrive at Modernity

Youth in an earlier era entrusted their imaginations to various concrete objects. I am not suggesting that postwar youth possessed an innate ability that eludes modern-day otaku but rather that historical circumstances did not give these youths any other options. In the Meiji era (1868–1912), Japan ended its policy of forbidding contact and trade with other countries and began to pursue Westernization and modernization. During that time, Japanese youth were expected to pursue goals divorced from everyday reality; the object of their aspirations vacillated over time between developed Western societies and images of the future. It was in such a climate that they developed their identity. The positioning of trains as a medium of the imagination was a result of historically specific circumstances and a confluence of changing social conditions.

Train boys became visible during the period spanning the end of the Taisho era (1912–1926) and the early Showa era (1926–1989). Although I consider this time period one of origin for train boys, I would first like to consider a series of transformations in the preceding historical period.

Media of Fantasy: Steam Locomotives and Scientific Models

First, let us look back on the birth of the railway itself in Japan. Most peg the origins of the Japanese rail system to the 1872 opening of the Shinbashi-Yokohama route. Railways actually existed in Japan before this, however. In 1853 a Russian visitor, Yevfimy Vasilyevich Putjatin, demonstrated to the Japanese a model steam locomotive aboard his ship. The following year, the American captain Matthew Perry presented a Japanese general with a model of a steam locomotive and its passenger trains. A year after that, inspired by Putjatin's demonstration, some engineers of the Saga clan, among them Kisuke Nakamura, built the first Japanese model steam locomotive (see Figure 1.1).

These trains are in some ways mere models, quite different from the real thing. Given, however, that actual trains did not exist in Japan at the time, they were not really being modeled on reality. In fact, could we not consider these models as marking the beginnings of the railway's becoming a medium of the imagination? They could actually be considered the objects to which imagination was entrusted during that period. It follows, then, that the birth of the railway dates to these models and before the opening of the Shinbashi-Yokohama route. This, in turn, explains why model trains have continued to have a substantial presence and also why they played a prominent role in the emergence of train-centered boys' culture.

More important, the first models were not originally built primarily for the study of steam locomotives. Historian Katsumasa Harada (1986, 4) notes that these models were built as precursors to the construction of steamships. Because of the domestic focus on military buildup and the construction of battleships, Harada posits that the

Figure 1.1. Model locomotive built by Kisuke Nakamura and others of the Saga clan, replica in the Railway Museum's collections. Credit: Photograph by Izumi Tsuji.

Saga clan engineers' main interest was in understanding the steam engine's mechanism.

Starting in the Meiji era, Japan pursued Westernization linked with militarization and growing imperialist ambitions. Post-Meiji Japan's effort at overcoming its current reality was directed at the developed Western world, and the focus of the media of the imagination was not the railway but battleships. Battleships were associated with the expansion of the empire and thus were a medium linked strongly to the imagination of spatial expansion, a kind of medium of fantasy. By the early Showa era, fighter planes also had become a medium of fantasy. Youth magazines at the time indicate that the navy was more popular than the army, which may have been because of the presence of battleships and fighter planes (Hara and Sekikawa 2004) (see Figure 1.2).

It was around the same time that steam locomotives finally began to gain popularity among youth as another medium of fantasy (see Figure 1.3). This marked the beginning of what became known as the first golden age in Japanese rail. The domestic railway network neared completion, express train service began, and railways in Taiwan and Manchuria were constructed to aid the management of these occupied

Figure 1.2. Seaplane model "Flying Battleship." Credit: *Youth Club* magazine (Kodansha).

territories. While in the Meiji era steam locomotives were considered mere supports for steamships, and called *oka-joki* (land steamers), in this later era they earned their own name as *kisha* (trains) (Uda 2007).

Textbooks from this period provide evidence that these media of fantasy were frequent topics in the curriculum (Takano 2006; Uda 2007). More tellingly, in science magazines targeting boys (the most representative being *Kodomo no Kagaku*, or *Science for Children*, founded in 1924), the most popular articles were those describing how these media were built. By focusing on the creation of objects of fantasy, youth invested in these new media of the imagination. Science fiction featuring the adventures of boys traveling with trains to undiscovered lands also became popular around this time (Futagami 1978; Nishi 1997; Ozaki 1997; Satoh 1959; Yamanaka and Yamamoto 1985; Yokota 1986).

The very first issue of *Kodomo no Kagaku* included an article on steam locomotives (Kodomo no Kagaku Henshubu 1978). The first magazine dedicated to trains, *Tetsudou* (Railway), was founded a few years later in 1929 by the winner of the first national model train exhibit, sponsored by *Kodomo no Kagaku* (Aoki 2001). In other words, the birth of the rail boys centered on model trains.

These events illustrate how the rise of the media of fantasy was closely tied to the time in which pro-military boys came of age in an

Figure 1.3. Boy riding model steam locomotive, circa 1941.
Credit: Ishizaka, 2000, cover page.

imperialistic Japan arriving late to modernity. Although train otaku and military otaku eventually parted ways, they were one and the same at their origin. It was significant that during this period, boys were attracted to do-it-yourself (DIY) models, known as "science models." The term used at the time, "model engineering," described an approach to modeling quite different from today's efforts that center on creating high-fidelity replicas of an existing original object. Instead, the intent in this earlier period was to go one step beyond the original and demonstrate ingenuity surpassing the real full-scale version (Yamakita 1930). These models that the boys created with their own hands—battleships, fighter planes, and steam locomotives—became media for their imaginations and were not replicas of objects that they had access to in their everyday lives.

The period leading up to World War II represented the zenith of Japan's imperialist and military ambitions. Pro-military youth born before the war drove the growth of interest in steam locomotives after Japan's defeat in World War II. Many of these early aficionados remain active train fans to this day. They say that their interest in battleships and planes rivaled or surpassed their interest in trains. For example, Saitoh, who resurrected the Keio Railway Club in 1953 after the war ended, writes about the draw of these machines: "Speed, strength, courage—the workings of these machines are an open book, inspiring human longing. The experience of having encountered them never leaves one's mind. Perhaps the massive battleships and agile propeller fighter planes exude a masculine magnetism" (Saitoh 2007, 457).

"Steam locomotives are not merely a means of transportation. Our longing for distant unknown lands and the memories of our joys and sorrows meld with the distinctive smell of coal and the rhythm of the wheels on rail joints, sinking deep into our hearts. And despite being a hulking mass of steel, the locomotive's belabored climb up inclines and dancing rods make it feel like a living thing. It is more than just a machine" (Saitoh 1996, Foreword).

Here, the word "longing" is present in both passages, evidence of the fact that steam locomotives are "not merely a means of transportation" but are a medium of the imagination reaching toward the expansive space of "distant unknown lands." The train culture fantasy of youth who came of age during Japan's pro-military period was centered on this vision of steam locomotives.

Defeat: A Turning Point

Japan's defeat in World War II and subsequent demilitarization was a turning point with a profound influence on the history of train culture. One of the core members of Tokyo University Railway Club (born in 1934), who was present when it was founded in 1955, describes his perceptions at the time: "As someone who had grown up during World War II and received a militaristic education, I loved battleships and planes as much as I did trains. But with Japan's defeat in 1945, both the army and the navy vanished . . . and the train was what remained" (Wakuda 1993, 7).

Such testimonials can be understood in relation to the changes that took place in the science magazines dealing with trains and models. Shown in Figure 1.4 is a table of contents from a postwar issue of *Kagaku to Mokei* (Science and Models), a magazine as popular as *Kodomo no*

Figure 1.4. Table of contents taken from a postwar issue of *Science and Models.*
Credit: *Science and Models,* 1947, February/ March issue (Asahiya).

Kagaku. Battleships and fighter planes have completely disappeared, and the content is practically the same as a rail specialty magazine. Japan's defeat caused battleships and fighter planes to fade from view, leaving trains as the last remaining medium of imagination.

More significant than the simple reduction of numbers in the media of imagination was change on a more qualitative level. The Meiji-era slogan of *Fukoku Kyohei* (Rich Nation, Strong Army) had faded away and only the slogan *Shokusan Kogyo* (Increase Production, Promote Industry) remained from that period. In terms of youth imagination, the loss of occupied territories and the disbanding of the military meant the loss of the expansive space of the imagination, forcing youth to refocus their powers of imagination toward the temporal expanse presented by the society of the future. Trains became the central focus as

a future-oriented medium of the imagination, and the dreams of boys'
train culture increasingly shifted from the steam locomotive to the
more futuristic electric train.

Media of Dreams: Electric Trains and Plastic Models

Electric trains have existed since the Meiji era, long before Japan's
defeat. However, for many years they were limited to intracity transportation, with long-distance transportation being primarily reserved
for steam locomotives. The railway network in Japan had been mostly
completed by the postwar period, so rail development centered on
rapid upgrades and electrification of the rail system rather than spatial
expansion. This period has been dubbed the second golden age of the
Japanese railway.

Although steam locomotives still outnumbered electric trains, the
latter enjoyed greater popularity among boys. The greatest symbol of
this shift was the bullet-train line that opened in 1964 (see Figure 1.5).
Called the Dream Super Express, it was a symbol of a dream future
awaiting a society that had undergone miraculous economic growth in
the postwar years.

The Japanese term for bullet trains, *shinkansen* (new arterial line),
referenced the fact that these trains required rails of a different width
than existing ones, so the lines could not be shared with existing trains.
The bullet trains did not reach new parts of the country but were an
upgrade of existing lines. In other words, bullet trains are a medium of
imagination geared toward temporal rather than spatial expansion,
and high-tech electric trains were a medium of dreams.[6]

This period was also a time when the "real thing" began to gain
dominance over models. Magazines shifted focus from those with a
scientific bent featuring DIY models to rail specialty magazines featuring photographs of existing trains.[7] *Tetsudou Fan* (Railway Fan), now
the most popular rail specialty magazine, was founded during this time,
with its first issue featuring a color photograph of an express train on
the cover (Figure 1.6). It was also around this time that rail photography emerged as a serious hobby.[8]

Even in the model world, attention shifted from the more free-form
models that allowed for imaginative creations to kits and plastic models

Figure 1.5. Bullet train and monorail.
Credit: Drawing by Sadao Kimura in *Norimono Ehon* (*Picture Book of Vehicle*) (supervised by Sekita 2007, 62).

that closely mimicked existing trains. This shift was reflected in the models' scale. During the DIY era, relatively large-scale models such as the O scale (approximately 1:45 scale) were prevalent, allowing modelers to dwell on the details of each locomotive. Now the more accessible HO scale (approximately 1:87 scale) is the norm, with modelers creating interlinked electric cars (Figure 1.7).

Another contributing factor was the popularity of science fiction novels depicting societies in the future, such as those seen in the mystery series from Hayakawa Publishing.[9] In other words, this era of the medium of dreams was one in which boys dreamed of the future and expanded their imaginations by building model kits and taking photographs; the postwar era was one of high economic growth and sci-fi boys. The imagination of the previous era in which steam locomotives stirred longing toward unknown lands was replaced by dreams of the future embodied in electric trains.

Figure 1.6. *Railway Fan* cover (established 1961). Credit: *Koyusha.*

Many of the new rail aficionados were attuned to the future in other ways, eventually becoming highly engaged with new media such as online communications and the Internet. The forum administrator of the largest rail forum community in Japan today (www.railforum.jp) is typical of this orientation (Tetsudou Forum 1998). After graduating from university, he worked for a number of years but eventually quit his job to run the rail forum and serve as its administrator. His interest in trains was piqued by the electric express trains (see Figure 1.6) that were center stage during the second golden age. When he entered elementary school in 1964, it was the year of the Tokyo summer Olympic games as well as the year when the Tokaido bullet-train line opened. Looking back, he described those times as an era "full of dreams," one "when trains were cutting-edge technology."

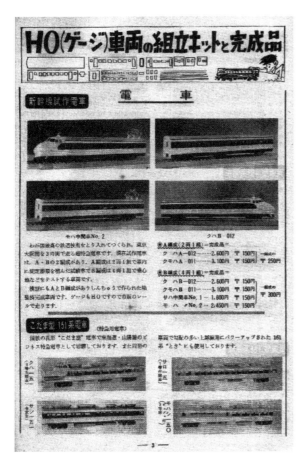

Figure 1.7. HO scale model railway kit and finished product. Credit: *Models and Radio*, 1964, supplemental issue no. 3 (Kagaku Kyozai Sha).

Many youth from this period have remained active in the hobby to this day. Although most have regular day jobs, what differentiates them from their predecessors is that some of the more prominent fans have quit their corporate jobs to pursue careers centered on their hobbies. In a sense, they translated their dreams for their own futures into reality through time. Some scholars have called them "the seminal otaku" (Miyadai 1994) and "first-generation otaku" (Azuma 2001) because of this passionate enthusiasm for their hobbies. It is a subsequent era, however, that heralded the emergence of "authentic" otaku possessing traits typical of otaku today.

THE BIRTH OF TRAIN OTAKU

The Arrival of Postindustrial Society and Consumer Society

The term "otaku" gained notoriety in the 1980s and beyond. The cultural critic Akio Nakamori is credited with having coined the term by writing a series of articles titled "An Investigation of 'Otaku'" in the serial *Manga Burikko* starting in June 1983. In an excerpt from his articles, Nakamori writes:

> Come to think of it, manga freaks and Comiket are only the start of it. There's those guys who camp out before the opening day of anime movies, dudes who nearly get themselves run over trying to capture photos of the "blue train" as it comes down the tracks, guys with every back issue of *SF Magazine* and the Hayakawa science-fiction novels lining their bookshelves, science fair types with coke-bottle glasses who station themselves at the local computer shop, guys who get up early to secure space in line for idol singer and actress autograph sessions, boys who spent their childhoods going to the best cram-schools but turn into timid fish-eyed losers, guys who won't shut up when the topic of audio gear comes around. These people are normally called "maniacs" or "fanatics," or at best *"nekura-zoku"* ("the gloomy tribe"), but none of these terms really hit the mark. For whatever reason, it seems like a single umbrella term that covers these people, or the general phenomenon, hasn't been formally established. So we've decided to designate them as the "otaku," and that's what we'll be calling them from now on. (Nakamori 1983, translation Alt 2008)

In this passage, Nakamori describes train otaku as "dudes who nearly get themselves run over trying to capture photos of the 'blue train.'" Furthermore, phrases such as "guys with every back issue of *SF Magazine* and the Hayakawa science-fiction novels lining their bookshelves" and "science fair types with coke-bottle glasses who station themselves at the local computer shop" also indicate that characteristics and behaviors associated with the eras of fantasy and dreams had already been attached to the definition of otaku. Otaku exhibiting affinity for the unreal also make an appearance in phrases such as "guys who camp out before the opening day of anime movies" and "guys who get up early to secure space in line for idol singer and actress autograph sessions."

They are treated as part of the same category as otaku whose interests lie in real things.

How did train aficionados' behavior come to be considered part of the realm of otaku? Perhaps it was not that they themselves had changed but rather that social changes shaped the outlets they had for their imaginations. What were these specific social changes?

The key transformations took place during the 1970s. Although otaku became a noticeable presence in the 1980s, the underlying changes began earlier with the decline of the Meiji-era slogan of "Increase Production, Promote Industry." Starting in the 1960s, Japan achieved rapid economic growth and industrialization, in what was described at the time as an "economic miracle." The 1973 oil crisis was symbolic of the transition from high to low economic growth, which led to the transition from a production-centric society to a consumption-centric one. In other words, this period signaled the advent of postindustrial society (Bell 1973) and consumer society (Baudrillard 1970).

For rail, this shift marked the beginning of true decline, the passing of the postwar era of rebuilding, inflation, and economic growth. For youth, these changes meant that their imaginations began to lose direction. The term "low growth" indicated a lack of spatial expansion as well as a loss of an expansive imagination of the future. These changes were tied to the rise of contemporary otaku culture and a shift in the culture of imagination as many otaku shifted their imaginations toward unreal objects.

Media of Illusion: SL, Blue Trains, and Anime

The cultural shifts of the 1970s were also salient for train otaku. The train otaku began to relate to their objects of affection as though they were unreal, despite the fact that train technology was real. Such shifts were noticeable in the Blue Train boom mentioned in the quote from Nakamori and in the "SL boom" of the 1970s (see Figure 1.8).[10]

The SL boom was a nationwide phenomenon that was a consequence of the abolition of steam locomotives in the early 1970s, after they had been in circulation for more than a century. By this time, steam locomotives were no longer a medium of fantasy and had become the objects of nostalgia.

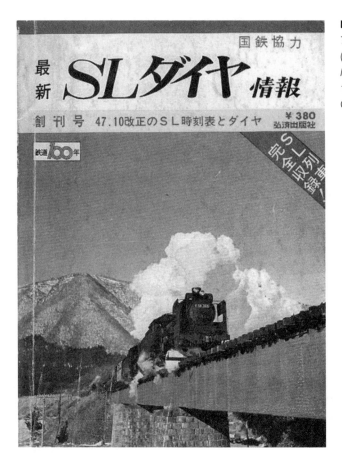

Figure 1.8. *Updated SL Timetable Information* (now titled *Rail Timetable Information*, established 1972).
Credit: *Kotsu Shinbun Sha.*

The subsequent Blue Train boom in the late 1970s shared a similar theme. With the expansion of the bullet-train lines, the large-scale reduction in existing express train service meant that overnight sleeper trains, the Blue Trains, were the only remaining long-distance trains.

SL and Blue Train lines functioned as receptacles of nostalgia toward earlier fantasies, media of the imagination tied to ghosts of the past, or the media of illusions. The animated series *Galaxy Express 999* sparked an SL revival in the late 1970s and 1980s (see Figure 1.9). The setting in outer space is an indicator of how the imagination of the SL in this era could take flight only in such a futuristic fantasy scenario.

The otaku of this period exhibited behavior very similar to that of modern otaku. For instance, during the SL boom, train otaku rushed to regional train lines in great numbers to capture as many images of

Figure 1.9. *Galaxy Express 999,* still being streamed online. Credit: Reiji MATSUMOTO / TOEI ANIMATION.

the trains with their cameras as possible. Collection behavior became highly competitive. Train otaku competed with one another as to who could amass the most information and knowledge, and they engaged in "rail riding," in which they tried to ride as many train lines as possible.

These trends became even more prominent during the Blue Train boom. Anticipating the popularity of national rail, the railways developed a graphic logo for Blue Trains, resulting in huge crowds of train otaku trying to take photographs in major stations such as Tokyo and Ueno (see Figure 1.10). The boom also manifested in the popularity of N-scale model trains. At the relatively small scale of 1:150, the N-scale allowed train otaku to assemble and run Blue Train cars on rails laid down in their own rooms. Trains were no longer being built by hand, the focus having shifted to preassembled models that could be run on a personal miniature landscape. N-scale models that included a set of train cars and a controller became popular as gifts.

As discussed above, Japanese society in the 1970s had entered a transition period as a postindustrial and consumer society. The loss of directional clarity for the imagination was accompanied by a shift away from the future and toward the ghosts of the past, resulting in an

Figure 1.10. Photograph of Tokyo Station in 1978. Credit: Hisashi Morokawa, *Rail Photo Magazine,* 2007, spring issue: 30–31.

era of the imagination of illusion. Given this reversal of interest to the past, we can consider this as a post–electric train era. The sociologist Munesuke Mita (1995) called the same general period "the era of unreality." With their imaginations having undergone a directional shift, some youth came to be called otaku.

These otaku are characterized by an affinity for the unreal and a tendency to have a negative sense of self. I observed these tendencies in one train otaku, born in 1978, whom I interviewed. He belonged to a rail club during his college years, and upon graduation he followed his childhood dream and found employment at a rail company. He now serves as a train operator for express trains. One room in his home is filled with N-scale models and is basically a modeling workshop (Figure 1.11). He still ventures out on train photography trips. Anime-related goods can also be found in one corner of his workshop. He made comments during the interview that indicated a downtrodden attitude: "There is no future in trains. They've fulfilled their purpose. Aside from major cities, especially in rural areas, I think they're about to peter out. I hope I won't be around when it happens." His comments indicate a loss of direction for the imagination and an accompanying pessimism. His attitude is in striking contrast with that of train fans who identified

Figure 1.11. Train otaku (born 1978) and his N-scale collection. Credit: Photograph by Izumi Tsuji.

with the earlier two golden eras and who continue to be active and energetic even today.

The Advent of an Advanced Information-Consumer Society

From the 1990s to the present, Japan has continued its transformation into a consumer society. After the uptake of new media such as the Internet and mobile phones from the mid-1990s onward, the volume of information circulation underwent explosive growth. Modern Japanese society has become an advanced information-consumer society with a stronger emphasis on the collection and transmission of information than in the production of "real" concrete objects.

In a way, this is simply an intensification of the trends that already existed in the preceding era. This could also be considered an indication that Japan has reached its goal of becoming a prosperous society. We are nearing the status of a society in which all the information one could possibly need can be obtained without having to aspire to unrealistic imaginary goals. From a different perspective, it also appears as though the culture of imagination, a longtime province of Japan's male youth, is reaching a certain end point. It is as though imagination is no longer expanding toward an aspirational time and place but is instead fixed in the here and now, capable only of expanding internally and heralding a kind of era of obsessiveness.

The decline of rail continued with the growing presence of personal automobiles and passenger planes. The National Japan Railway was disbanded in 1987 and privatized into seven Japan Rail (JR) companies. Even the JR East Company, the largest rail company in the country, sought to transition to a service-industry conglomerate—a kind of massive information industry—after privatization. For instance, it collaborated with Microsoft to codevelop the Windows XP operating system, and it rapidly built the automatic ticket-gates system that uses an electronic money card called Suica.[11]

Changes such as these indicate a fundamental reversal, where the transportation industry is becoming more of an information industry rather than one concerned primarily with the transportation of physical objects.[12] This turn toward an information society has been debated extensively and is not a new revelation by any means, but what is noteworthy is that the railway companies themselves are working to drive the changes forward. Now that the railway industry is about to become a support system for the networked information industries, we are now in what can be justifiably called the post-rail era.

Media of Obsession: Simulation Games and Figures

Today's train otaku are more purist in their approach to fantasy. Whereas train otaku of the past interacted with real trains to evoke the unreal, today's otaku now interact purely with the unreal. Fantasy has triumphed over reality.

Games are the clearest manifestation of this trend. Taito's 1997 arcade game *Densha de Go!* was an instant hit, spawning a slew of similar types of games, including some in which players could program their own lines and even the scenery. For example, in the 1998 game *Railway Model Simulator* (see Figure 1.12), players create 3-D virtual environments (called layouts) and run trains through them. The game's title is curious, indicating that a model simulator is actually a model of a model. As with the model engineering of an earlier era, perhaps it is possible to imagine and create simulated models that surpass actual concrete

Figure 1.12. *Railway Model Simulator.* Credit: www.imagic.co.jp/hobby/products/V3/v3b157/index.htm.

models. At the moment, however, these simulated models seem to exist solely for entertainment, as a way to have fun in an unreal, virtual world.[13]

More interestingly, model rail manufacturers began to manufacture products other than model trains. One typical example is the Rail Girls series of figures released in 2005 by Tomytec, one of the main manufacturers of N-scale models. Each figure was given a name derived from an existing station or train line and dressed in a corresponding uniform (see Figure 1.13). This product line has enjoyed enormous popularity.

These developments indicate that in the current post-rail era, train otaku are directing their obsessions not toward real objects but toward unreal people or toward relationships with these characters. This obsession directed toward such characters is akin to the now well-known concept of *moe*, where otaku develop attachments, or moe, to particular types of fantasy characters or their attributes. Modern-day train otaku have become one of the *moe-ota* (moe-otaku).[14]

Even if they harbored strong affections toward trains as children, many train-ota turn into moe-ota during adolescence. One of

Figure 1.13. Rail Girls.
Credit: 2005 TOMYTEC /
NATSUKI MIBU.

my informants was a moe-ota who had previously been a member of rail clubs in a boys' private school. He commented that he did not find fulfillment as a train otaku and began going to Comiket (Comic Market) and buying *doujinshi* (fan-created manga; see Chapters 5 and 9) as a ninth-grade student. Compared with the train otaku of previous generations who maintained a strong attachment to trains, these moe-ota converts are unique to today's otaku landscape.

Today marks an era in which the post-1970s cultural shift has reached completion. We live in an advanced information-consumer society and a post-rail era. Sociologist Shinji Miyadai drew on Mita's earlier characterization of the era of unreality (Mita 1995) and described the period after the 1990s as the late era of unreality (Miyadai and Morikawa 2007). We are inhabiting the moe-ota's era of obsession with fantasy information.

THE FUTURE OF JAPANESE SOCIETY AND TRAIN OTAKU

Figure 1.14 represents a summary of this chapter's arguments on the historical development of train otaku culture. The *x*-axis represents increasing spatial expansion to the right; the *y*-axis represents increasing temporal expansion to the bottom.

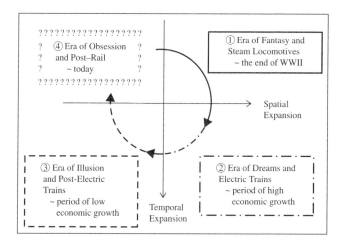

Figure 1.14. Summative diagram of the eras of rail culture.
Credit: Izumi Tsuji.

The upper right quadrant represents the era of fantasy that spanned the period of modernization during the Meiji era to the postwar period. This was the era of the Great Japanese Empire and of pro-military youth. The youth of this era built science models while dreaming of expanding the empire. Battleships and fighter planes took center stage as the media of the imagination, with steam locomotives taking a back seat.

The lower right quadrant represents the era of dreams, high economic growth, postwar Japan, and sci-fi youth. The youth of this era built models that mimicked existing objects while imagining the future of postwar Japan. Trains, especially electric trains, took center stage as the medium of imagination.

Once Japan reached the era of illusion in the lower left quadrant, both Japanese society and the culture of imagination were forced to enter a transition. With the advent of postindustrial consumer society, railways went into decline. This, in turn, signified the advent of an era in which space for fantasies and dreams was limited, and imagination had to turn to fantasy to continue to thrive. It was during this time that otaku culture was born.

Today's train culture has completed one cycle through these four quadrants with the advent of the age of obsessions. Both Japanese society and the culture of imagination have lost direction.

In sum, imagination never halted in its tracks. Rather, depending on changes in social context, imagination could expand with ease during some periods and lost its direction during others. In periods of expansion, young men who let their imaginations take flight were called *shonen* (boys); during periods that lack direction, young men at a loss as to where to direct their imaginations have been labeled otaku.

Contemporary attempts to understand otaku culture tend to be too taken by the peculiarities of otaku behavior and tend to attribute them to their internal peculiarities such as personality and psychology. I have argued, instead, that the imagination is not an unchanging internal reality. Otaku are not a new breed totally divorced from the past but rather should be understood as embedded within a trajectory of historical developments in the culture of imagination.

The history of otaku culture also provides an answer to the more personal question of why I am a train otaku. I was born during the era of illusion and became enamored of Blue Trains. Having written this chapter, however, I would like to avoid limiting the history of otaku to a reminiscence of the past and would like to work toward building a social framework for the future. I am not arguing for the persistence of train otaku culture. Rather, I believe we need to build a new social framework that incorporates a culture of imagination that adapts to social change. This chapter is an effort to contribute to this framework by considering the case of train otaku.

Notes

1. Train otaku fall into several subcategories, the main ones being railroad model otaku, train photography otaku, travel otaku, and train ticket collectors.

2. In the United States, elite universities also have student railway clubs. For instance, in *Hackers: Heroes of the Computer Revolution* (Levy 1984), which traces hacker culture back to its origins, Levy includes a description of the Tech Model Railroad Club at the Massachusetts Institute of Technology during the 1950s.

3. As I will discuss later in this chapter, this appeal of science and technology is tightly linked to the relatively late modernization of Japanese society. With society focused on catching up with and surpassing Western modernity, the rapid development of science and technology was an imperative, thus leading to the appreciation of a masculinity linked to scientific achievements. This thesis is outlined in Tsuji (2009), which investigates the link between the late modernization of Japanese society and the predominance of male rail enthusiasts, and Mosse (1996), who analyzed masculinity in Germany, where modernization was similarly delayed.

4. Though present in other public transportation media, this characteristic is particularly strong with trains. For example, automobiles, especially private ones, do not have predetermined public departure and destination points, rather functioning

more as a method to transport an enclosed space of the everyday sort to various locales.

5. The interviews were conducted between March 2005 and September 2007. Informants were selected based on their high level of interest in train otaku culture and were recruited through rail hobby clubs and research societies. Some were also employees in related fields (for example, rail company employees, rail magazine editors, model-train store employees, and rail-related website administrators). Recruitment was through the snowball sampling method after contact with the relevant organization. Most interviews were conducted one-on-one and lasted an average of two to three hours. A small number of them were group interviews with two or three informants, lasting five to six hours. These semistructured interviews covered common themes with all informants, focusing on self-identity and personal experiences as train aficionados. The list of cooperating organizations and demographics of the final informants are as follows:

Cooperating Organizations
1. Rail Club Mita Chapter (Keio Railway Club Alumni Association)
2. Uwajimia Rail Hobby Club (a rail hobby club in Ehime Prefecture)
3. Teizan Association (a rail travel and mountaineering hobby club in Tokyo)
4. Rail Forums (the largest rail-related website in Japan)
5. Rail Shop Nanpu (a model-train specialty store in Kochi Prefecture)
6. One of the Japan Railways companies
7. Rail clubs in a private unified all-male prep school in Tokyo
Note: Depending on the informant, the informants' names and affiliated organizations were kept anonymous.

Breakdown of Informants by Age Group
Total = 49 informants
10–19 = 20
20–39 = 4
40–59 = 6
over 60 = 19

6. As seen in Figure 1.5, at the same time monorails were also considered the transportation of the future. Since monorails also require their own rails and are spatially limited, they are similar to bullet trains.

7. Although most are not rail models, Tamiya began making its plastic models during this time.

8. The surge in railway photography can also be attributed to the increased quality and lowered cost of cameras.

9. Hayakawa Publishing specialized in science fiction and brought authors such as Phillip K. Dick to Japan.

10. "SL" refers to steam locomotive.

11. *Japanese Railway Technology Today* (Railway Technical Research Institute and East Japan Railway Foundation, eds. 2001) introduces various existing rail technologies. Its final chapter, "When the Train Station Becomes the CyberRail Station," may be symbolizing the future of rail, in which train stations will become hubs in the information network.

12. As the German historian Wolfgang Schivelbusch wrote in *The Railway Journey*, the telegraphic communications industry developed as a support system for railway transportation. To ensure timely operations, telegraph communication systems were built alongside railway tracks (Schivelbusch 1977, 45–48).

13. Aside from the main software, *Railway Model Simulator* offers optional add-ons for more train-car models and more complex parts. The game producer I.Magic posts results of user-generated layout contests on its homepage, providing further evidence that the main purpose of this game is to enjoy it within a virtual realm.

14. Author Toru Honda (2005) has described *moe* as being "romance inside your head." *Moe-ota* train otaku may find it easier to harbor an obsession with pretty girl characters than with trains.

References

Aoki, Eiichi. 2001. Tetsudo shumino ayumi: Tetsudo pictorial no hanseiki to tomoni. *Tetsudo Pictorial, Tetsudo Tosho Kankokai* 703 (51–57): 131–155.

Azuma, Hiroki. 2001. *Dobutsukasuru post modern.* Tokyo: Kodansha.

Baudrillard, Jean. 1970. *La société de consommation: Ses mythes, ses structures.* Paris: Gallimard.

Bell, Daniel. 1973. *The coming of post-industrial society: A venture in social forecasting.* New York: Basic Books.

Futagami, Hirokazu. 1978. *Shonen shosetsu no keifu.* Tokyo: Geneijoh.

Hara, Takeshi, and Natsuo Sekikawa. 2004. Tetsudo wa dokoeyukunoka. *Yuriika tokushu, tetsudo to nihonjin: Senrowa tsuzukuyo* 36 (3): 97–113.

Harada, Katsumasa. 1986. Kaikoku to tetsudo. In *Nihon no tetsudo—Seiritsu to tenkai,* ed. Masaho Noda, Katsumasa Harada, Eiichi Aoki, and Yoshinobu Oikawa, 1–14. Tokyo: Nihon Keizai Hyoronsha.

Honda, Toru. 2005. *Moeru otoko.* Tokyo: Chikuma Shobo.

Ishizaka, Yoshihisa. 2000. *Inubashiri shin.* Tokyo: Mokei Tetsudo Bunkasho.

Kodomo no Kagaku Henshubu, ed. 1987. *Fukkoku daijesutoban kodomo no kagaku 1924–1943.* Tokyo: Seibundo Shinkousha.

Levy, Steven. 1984. *Hackers: Heroes of the computer revolution.* Trans. Yoshie Furuhashi and Nobuko Matsuda. Tokyo: Kogakusha.

Mita, Munesuke. 1984. *Kenji miyazawa: Sonzai no matsuri no nakae.* Tokyo: Iwanami Shoten.

———. 1995. *Gendai nihon no kankaku to shisou.* Tokyo: Kodansha.

Miyadai, Shinji. 1994. *Seifukushoujotachi no sentaku.* Tokyo: Kodansha.

Miyadai, Shinji, and Kaichiro Morikawa. 2007. Ikinobirutameno shisou: Toshi to media no genbakara. *Planets* 3 (9): 174–201.

Mosse, George L. 1996. *Otokono imeji: Danseisei no sohzoh to kindaishakai*. Trans. Minoru Hosoya, Ryoko Kodama, and Keiko Kaizuma. Tokyo: Sakuhinsha.

Nakamori, Akio. 1983. Otaku no kenkyu 1. *Manga Burikko* (June), www.burikko.net/people/otaku01.html (retrieved January 11, 2011). Alt, Matt, trans. 2008. What kind of otaku are you? *Néojaponisme*, http://neojaponisme.com/2008/04/02/what-kind-of-otaku-are-you (retrieved January 14, 2011).

Nishi, Hideo. 1997. *Shonen shosetsu kenkyu. Shonen shosetsu taikei bekkan*, Vol. 5. Tokyo: Sanichi Shobo.

Ozaki, Hotsuki. 1997. *Omoideno shonenkurabu jidai: Natsukashino meisaku hakurankai*. Tokyo: Kodansha.

Railway Technical Research Institute and East Japan Railway Foundation, eds. 2001. *Japanese railway technology today*. Tokyo: Transportation News.

Saitoh, Akira. 1996. *Joki kikansha no kohboh*. Tokyo: NTT Shuppan.

———. 2007. *Joki kikansha 200nenshi*. Tokyo: NTT Shuppan.

Satoh, Tadao. 1993 [1959]. Shonen no risohshugi. In *Taishubunka no genzoh*, 98–114. Tokyo: Iwanami Shoten.

Schivelbusch, Wolfgang. 1977. *Geschichte der Eisenbahnreise—Zur industrialisierung von raum und zeit im 19. Jahrhundert*. Munich: Hanser.

Sekita, Katsutaka. 2007. *Norimonono ehon—Kimura sadao no sekai i*. Tokyo: Froebel Kan.

Takano, Yoshihiro. 2006. *Shoka kyouzaide tadoru kokumin kyoikushi-hananatosedai kara saita sakurasodachi no oboeta uta*. Tokyo: Nihon Tosho Kankokai.

Tetsudou Forum, ed. 1998. *"Tetsudou Forum" koushiki guide book*. Tokyo: Travel Journal.

Tsuji, Izumi. 2009. Naze tetsudo wa otokono roman ni nattanoka-shonenno risohshugi no yukue. In *Otokorashisa no kairaku: Popular bunka karamita sono jittai*, ed. Shinji Miyadai, Izumi Tsuji, and Takayuki Okai, 219–246. Tokyo: Keiso Shobo.

Uda, Tadashi. 2007. *Tetsudo nihon bunkashikoh*. Kyoto: Shibunkaku Shuppan.

Ukai, Masaki. 1999. Tetsudo mania no kohgengaku: Otokorashisa kara ridatsu shita otokotachi no gyakusetsu. In *Kyoudoh kenkyu danseiron*, ed. Yuko Nishikawa and Miho Ogino, 96–121. Kyoto: Jinbun Shoin.

Wakuda, Yasuo. 1993. *Tetsudo wo yomu*. Tokyo: Atene Shobo.

Yamakita, Tohichiro. 1930. *Shonengishi handbook 14 Koukyu denki kikansha no tsukurikata*. Tokyo: Seibundou.

Yamanaka, Hisashi, and Akira Yamamoto, eds. 1985. *Kachinuku bokura shokokumin: Shonen gunnji aikoku shosetsu no sekai*. Kyoto: Sekai Shisosha.

Yokota, Junya, ed. 1986. *Kuusoh kagaku shosetsushu. Shonen shosetsu taikei*, Vol. 8. Tokyo: Sanichi Shobo.

2

Database Animals

· · · · · · · · · · · · · · · · · ·

HIROKI AZUMA

This chapter is excerpted from *Otaku: Japan's Database Animals* by
Hiroki Azuma, translated by Jonathan E. Abel and Shion Kono
(Minneapolis: University of Minnesota Press, 2009) pp. 25–62.[1]

Originally published in Japanese as *Dobutsuka suru posutomodan: otaku kara
mita nihon shakai* (Tokyo: Kodansha Gendai Shinsho, 2001). Copyright 2001
by Hiroki Azuma. English translation copyright 2009 by the Regents of the
University of Minnesota.

PREFACE

The essay excerpted here is from a book published in Japan ten years
ago, in 2001. Please understand that some of what has been written here
on otaku and *moe* is already out of step with the times.

In addition, it is important for English-language readers to understand that this excerpt is from a book on postmodernism, *Doubutsuka
Suru Postmodern*, or "an animal-like postmodernism." This book has
been translated and published in English under the title *Otaku: Japan's
Database Animals*. In the original book, the emergence of otaku is taken
up as one among many examples of how postmodernism has unfolded
in Japan. In fact, when this book was published in Japan, people thought
its key contribution was to position the emergence of otaku culture
within the broader context of postmodernism, rather than analyzing
the internal logic of otaku culture on its own terms. Back in 2001, when
this book was published, the study of otaku culture was not necessarily
a highly valued form of scholarship.

In today's context, in which the significance of otaku culture is
widely acknowledged, this kind of effort may seem both unnecessary

and off the mark. The excerpted text on database consumption may also be difficult to understand in isolation, as it relies heavily on existing theories of postmodernism as well as traditions of literary and social criticism that grew out of the Japanese postwar context. Readers of this current collection may hope that this excerpt will offer a concrete and accessible explanation of the concept of moe. If this is indeed the expectation, I apologize in advance for any confusion and disappointment.

My hope, however, is that for at least some readers, this essay will expand your idea of what it means to contemplate otaku culture.

On the surface, the otaku phenomenon is simply a subcultural genre characterized by sex, violence, and immaturity. In actuality, however, it is a vexing embodiment of many of the key problems that Japan and the world face today. As it becomes commonsensical to consider and discuss otaku culture, we risk forgetting these more vexing issues. If this essay can remind readers of these difficulties, I believe it has served a useful function in this collection.

HIROKI AZUMA 2011

OTAKU AND POSTMODERNITY

The Propagation of Simulacra

My claim that there is a deep relationship between the essence of otaku culture and postmodern social structure is not particularly new. The following two points have already been identified as postmodern characteristics of otaku culture.

One is the existence of *derivative works*. Here I use the phrase "derivative works" as a general term for the largely eroticized rereading and reproduction of original manga, anime, and games sold in the form of fanzines, fan games, fan figures, and the like. They are vigorously bought and sold mainly in the Comic Market (which meets twice a year in Tokyo), but also through countless small-scale exhibits held on the national level, and over the Internet. Founded by a base of amateurs, the market, where numerous copies circulate and a great number of professional authors get their start, formed the nucleus of otaku culture both quantitatively and qualitatively over the past twenty years. If we fail to consider the derivative works of amateurs in favor of only the commercially manufactured projects and products, we will be unable to grasp the trends of otaku culture.

This prominence of derivative works is considered a postmodern characteristic because the high value otaku place on such products is extremely close to the future of the culture industry as envisioned by French sociologist Jean Baudrillard. Baudrillard predicts that in postmodern society the distinction between original products and commodities and their copies weakens, while an interim form called the *simulacrum*, which is neither original nor copy, becomes dominant.[2] The discernment of value by otaku, who consume the original and the parody with equal vigor, certainly seems to move at the level of simulacra where there are no originals and no copies.

Furthermore, that transformation does not end with consumers. There have been many cases recently of best-selling authors who themselves produce and sell fanzines derivative of their own commercial products. For instance, it is well known that the original creator of *Sailor Moon* released products in the Comic Market. And, though they are not strictly derivative works, the company that produces *Evangelion* itself sells much software that parodies the source. Here the distinctions between original and copy have already vanished even for the producer. Moreover, from the beginning the sense of realism in otaku genres has been weak; in many cases, even original works create worlds through citation and imitation of previous works. Without reference to the real world, the original is produced as a simulacrum of preceding works from the start, and in turn the simulacrum of that simulacrum is propagated by fan activities and consumed voraciously. In other words, irrespective of their having been created by an author (in the modern sense), the products of otaku culture are born into a chain of infinite imitations and piracy.

The Decline of the Grand Narrative

The second postmodern characteristic of otaku culture is the *importance placed on fiction* as a mode of action for the otaku. This attitude determines not only their hobby but also how they relate to people. In many cases, the human relations of the otaku, detached from the relations of workplace and family in the so-called social reality, are determined by an alternate principle for which fictional anime and games form the seed. The generation older than the otaku see this behavior only as retrograde, immature acts of the *moratoriamu* period; this is the source of much friction.

The term "otaku" was born in the period from the 1970s to the 1980s when the otaku would refer to each other as *otaku*. Critic Nakajima Azusa in her *Communication Deficiency Syndrome* argues that the essence of otaku is expressed in this alias. She notes: "What the word 'otaku' (meaning 'your home' or 'your family') points to is the assertion that one is identified, not by personal relations but by a relationship to the home unit and one's own territory." This kind of territory is necessary, according to Nakajima, because even after the paternal or national authority has been toppled, otaku must search for a group to which they should belong. The reason the otaku, "no matter where they go, cart around tons of books, magazines, fanzines, and scraps stuffed into huge paper bags like hermit crabs" is that, if they do not ferry around "the shell of their selves"—namely, their fantasies of group affiliation—they cannot be mentally stable.[3] The personal pronoun *otaku* fulfills the function of mutually endorsing the fantasy of group affiliation. Nakajima's point is highly significant. For the otaku, certainly the fictional is taken far more seriously than social reality. And the media often conclude from this kind of observation that the otaku cannot distinguish between reality and games.

However, such a conclusion is imprudent. Since not all otaku are mental patients, it follows that they generally possess the ability to distinguish between fiction and reality. Their preference for fiction, as Nakajima explains, is related to their identity. The otaku choose fiction over social reality not because they cannot distinguish between them but rather as a result of having considered which is the more effective for their human relations, the value standards of social reality or those of fiction. For example, they choose fiction because it is more effective for smoothing out the process of communication between friends, reading the *Asahi Newspaper* and then going to vote, or lining up with anime magazines in hand for an exhibition. And, to that extent, it is they who may be said to be socially engaged and realistic in Japan today, by virtue of not choosing the "social reality." Otaku shut themselves into the hobby community not because they deny sociality but rather because, as social values and standards are already dysfunctional, they feel a pressing need to construct alternative values and standards.

This is a postmodern characteristic because the process by which the coexistence of countless smaller standards replace the loss of the singular and vast social standard corresponds precisely to the "decline of the grand narrative"[4] first identified by the French philosopher Jean-François Lyotard. From the end of the eighteenth century to the mid-twentieth century in modern countries, various systems were consolidated for the purpose of organizing members of society into a unified whole; this movement was a precondition for the management of society. These systems became expressed, for instance, intellectually as the ideas of humanity and reason, politically as the nation-state and revolutionary ideologies, and economically as the primacy of production. *Grand narrative* is a general term for these systems.

Modernity was ruled by the grand narrative. In contrast, in postmodernity the grand narratives break down and the cohesion of the social entirety rapidly weakens. In Japan that weakening was accelerated in the 1970s, when both high-speed economic growth and "the season of politics" ended and when Japan experienced the Oil Shocks and the United Red Army Incident. From this vantage point, we can view the otaku's neurotic construction of "shells of themselves" out of materials from junk subcultures as a behavior pattern that arose to fill the void from the loss of grand narrative.

On this point, sociologist Ōsawa Masachi's theory of otaku might be useful. In his 1995 article "On Otaku" ("Otaku ron"), he claims that, for the otaku, there is a "discord" in distinguishing between the intrinsic other and the transcendental other; and for this reason otaku are strongly attracted to the occult and mysticism.[5] This "distinction between the intrinsic other and the transcendental other," put plainly, means the distinction between the world of the other that surrounds one's own self (the experiential world) and the godly world that transcends it (the transcendental world). The otaku cannot distinguish between these two, with the result that they are easily hooked on pseudoreligions that draw on themes popular in various subcultures. In a modern society, such disorder would have been dismissed as personal immaturity, but in postmodern society it is not so simple, because the very society in which we live is something now characterized by the "disorder" of the grand narrative. The behavioral pattern of the otaku precisely reflects this characteristic of postmodernity. After having failed to grasp the significance of a "god" or "society" supported by tradition, otaku try to fill the void with the subculture at their disposal.

In this way, otaku culture beautifully reflects the social structure of postmodernity on two points—the omnipresence of simulacra and the dysfunctionality of grand narrative. Studies on these two points are accumulating everywhere, so there is no need for me to add to them here. Consequently, I will pose two questions based on these two premises, which act as threads guiding otaku culture. In turn, these questions will help us to develop our consideration of the characteristics of postmodern society wherein they are intensified.

The two questions are:

1. In postmodernity, as the distinction between an original and a copy are extinguished, simulacra increase. If this is valid, then how do they increase? In modernity, the cause for the birth of an original was the concept of "the author." In postmodernity, what is the reason for the birth of the simulacra?

2. In postmodernity, grand narratives are dysfunctional; "god" and "society," too, must be fabricated from junk subculture. If this is correct, how will human beings live in the world? In modernity, god and society secured humanity; the realization of this was borne by religious and educational institutions, but after the loss of the dominance of these institutions, what becomes of the humanity of human beings?

NARRATIVE CONSUMPTION

Theory of Narrative Consumption

Let's begin with the first question. I would like first to draw attention to the *Theory of Narrative Consumption* by Ōtsuka Eiji. More than presuming the omnipresence of simulacra, Ōtsuka goes further in his analysis to consider the kind of logic under which simulacra are produced and consumed. Since I will draw heavily on Ōtsuka, I will cite him at length:

> Comics or toys are not consumed in and of themselves; rather, by virtue of the existence of an order behind these products or of a "grand narrative" of which they comprise a portion, each begins to take on value and

to be consumed. So it becomes possible to sell countless similar products (like the 772 different Bikkuriman stickers), because consumers are led to believe that they themselves approach the overall picture of the "grand narrative." For example, the creators of lines of character "products" such as "Mobile Suit Gundam," "Saint Seiya," "Sylvanian Family," and "Onyanko Club" had prepared a "grand narrative" or an underlying order ahead of time, and this selling of concrete "goods" was directly tied to the consumers' knowledge of it. . . .

Interest in the program itself had been limited to a small group of enthusiasts, but in reality this has clearly become a shared feeling among consumers in certain areas, such as anime, comic, and toys. At this point we can see a new situation confronting today's consumer society. What is being consumed is not the individual "drama" or "goods" but rather the system hidden behind them. However, the system (or the grand narrative) itself cannot be sold, so, in appearance, installments of serialized dramas and "goods" get consumed as single fragments that are cross sections of the system. I want to label this kind of situation "narrative consumption" *(monogatari shōhi)*. . . .

However, products that presuppose this kind of "narrative consumption" have an extremely dangerous side. That is to say, if consumers through their cumulative consumption of "small narratives" get their hands on the entirety of the program that is a "grand narrative," they will freely manufacture "small narratives" with their own hands. For instance, let's consider the following case. Without the permission of the makers who hold the copyright, if someone exactly duplicates one of the Bikkuriman stickers of the 772 beginning with "Super Zeus," it is a crime. A sticker made in this way is a "knockoff." And to date there have been numerous incidents of this sort. On the other hand, what happens when the same person manufactures a 773rd character that is not drawn in the set of 772 stickers and, yet, is consistent with them and in accordance with the "worldview" of Bikkuriman? This is not a copy of any of the 772 originals. And therefore it is not a "knockoff" in that sense. Moreover, because it is consistent with the 772, the 773rd sticker has equal value to the original 772. At this phase of "narrative consumption" cases arise in which there is no distinction between the "real" (genuine, *honmono*) and the "fake" (knockoffs, *nisemono*) in these kinds of individual goods.[6]

From the Tree-Model World to the Database-Model World

Here Ōtsuka uses the phrase "small narrative" to mean a particular narrative within a particular work. By contrast, the "grand narrative" supports that kind of small narrative, but the phrase also refers to the "worldview" or "settings," which cannot be expressed by the surface of a narrative.

So according to Ōtsuka, each work in otaku culture merely functions as an entrance to this grand narrative. What consumers truly value and buy are the settings and the worldview. Yet in reality, it is difficult to sell settings and worldviews themselves as works. Therefore, a dual strategy is effected: although the actual commodities are grand narratives, it happens to be small narratives, which are fragments of grand narratives, that are sold as surrogate products. Ōtsuka labels this situation *narrative consumption*. This is the natural consequence of the inundation of simulacra known as derivative works.

More than an analysis of a subculture, this point is also suggestive of a fundamental theory of postmodernity. To put it simply here, before the arrival of the postmodern, in the era of modernity—when the grand narrative was still functioning—the world could be grasped, roughly, through a kind of *tree model* (or projection model) like the one given in Figure 2.1. On the one hand, there is the surface outer layer of the world that is reflected in our consciousness. On the other hand, there is the deep inner layer, which is equal to the grand narrative that regulates the surface outer layer. In modernity it came to be thought that

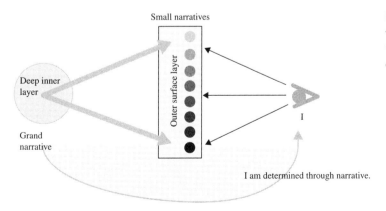

Figure 2.1. The modern world image (the "tree" model). Credit: Hiroki Azuma.

the purpose of scholarship was to clarify the structure of the hidden layer.

However, with the arrival of postmodernity, that tree-model world image collapsed completely. So what kind of structure accrues to the postmodern world? One candidate for explaining the Japan of the 1980s that often seemed borne out in reality was the "rhizome" model, in which signs are linked in diverse patterns over the outer layer alone (the deep inner layer having been extinguished). However, in my mind, it is easier to comprehend the postmodern world through a *database model* (or a reading-up model) such as the one in Figure 2.2.

An easily understandable example of this is the Internet. The Net has no center. That is to say, no hidden grand narrative regulates all Web pages. However, it is not a world established through the combination of outer signs alone, as in the case of the rhizome model. On the Internet, rather, there is distinct *double-layer structure*, wherein, on the one hand, there is an accumulation of encoded information, and, on the other hand, there are individual Web pages made in accordance with the users "reading them up." The major difference between this double-layer structure and the modern tree model is that, with the double-layer structure, the agency that determines the appearance that emerges on the surface outer layer resides on the surface itself rather than in the deep inner layer; i.e., it belongs on the side of the user who is doing the "reading up," rather than with the hidden information itself. In the world of the modern tree model, the surface outer layer is determined by the deep inner layer, but in the world of the postmodern database model,

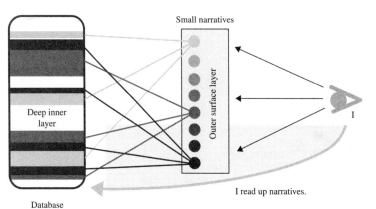

Figure 2.2. The postmodern world image (the "database" model). Credit: Hiroki Azuma.

the surface outer layer is not determined by the deep inner layer; the surface reveals different expressions at those numerous moments of "reading up."

For me, the shift in models is not simply a social shift, such as with the emergence of the Internet, but also was clearly demonstrated in the scholarly world by the ideas of complex systems theory, such as the self-organization of molecules, artificial life, or neural nets, that became widely known in the 1990s. However, I need not go into the details of postmodern theory here. For the purpose of following the argument, it is enough to say that the tree-model world image that is characteristic of modernity stands in opposition to the database model of the postmodern world image; in the deep inner layer of the former there is a grand narrative, but in the deep inner layer of the latter there is not.

Rereading the aforementioned Ōtsuka chapter with the above premise in mind, we can see that the structure of the database model clearly reflects Ōtsuka's structure of narrative consumption. The dual structure of settings and small narratives represents the double-layer structure of information and appearance. In otaku culture ruled by narrative consumption, products have no independent value; they are judged by the quality of the database in the background. So, as these databases display various expressions depending on the differing modes of "reading up" by users, consumers, once they are able to possess the settings, can produce any number of derivative works that differ from the originals. If we think of this situation as occurring only in the surface outer layer, the original product or work can seem swallowed by the chaos of a sea of simulacra. However, in reality, it is better to assume the prior existence of a database (i.e., settings) that enables both an original and the works derived from it, depending on how one "reads up" the database.

That is to say, the otaku consumers, who are extremely sensitive to the double-layer structure of postmodernity, clearly distinguish between *the surface outer layer within which dwell simulacra*, i.e., the works, and *the deep inner layer within which dwells the database*, i.e., settings. Since this double-layer structure will appear many times in what follows, I want to emphasize the point here.

THE GRAND NONNARRATIVE

The Decline of the Grand Narrative and Fiction as Supplement

Even now, Ōtsuka's point has not fundamentally lost its validity. However, here I would like to add one amendment. Ōtsuka calls the settings or worldview a "grand narrative." The reason he uses this word, besides the influence of postmodernism that was then in vogue, is that it was common to discover a worldview or a historical view in the otaku products of the late 1980s. Take *Gundam*, for example: since its first television series was broadcast in 1979, works that continued the series, such as *Mobile Suit Z(eta) Gundam*, *Char's Counterattack*, and *Mobile Suit Double Z Gundam*, were conceived of as belonging to the same fictitious history. Accordingly, the desires of *Gundam* fans necessarily and faithfully embarked on a close examination of this fanciful history; in reality *Gundam*-related books were already shrouded in timelines and mechanical data. Certainly, as Nakajima Azusa has pointed out, at this point a narrative other than reality (i.e., fiction) is constructed.

And the fictional narrative occasionally fulfills the grand role of substituting for the real grand narrative (namely, political ideology). One of the most spectacular examples of this is Aum Shinrikyō, which equipped its doctrines with a subculture imagination and turned ultimately to terrorism. As Ōsawa Masachi explicated in his *The End of the Fictional Age*,[7] the United Red Army of the 1970s and the Aum Shinrikyō of the 1990s differ only in that the former believed in communism, a widely recognized narrative, while the latter believed in a narrative that was still having difficulty winning broad recognition.

In the narrative consumption of the 1980s, too, social circumstances appeared in the background. As a reason for the rise of narrative consumption, Ōtsuka himself points to the extinguishing of "death" or the "mystical underworld" in modern society—that is to say, he points to the extinguishing of the transcendental.[8] Consequently, it is entirely appropriate for him to label the aggregate of worldview and settings supporting a subculture as a "grand narrative," because, in the situation of the 1980s, it must have seemed that the worldview and settings were constructed in order to compensate for the loss of grand narrative.

From Ideology to Fiction

The mechanism that compensates for the decline of grand narrative can be placed in a slightly broader framework. The latter half of the twentieth century (not just in Japan, but globally) was a time of grand change caught between two periods. The world until the 1950s was under the sway of the modern cultural logic, which could be grasped in the form of the tree model. Accordingly, grand narratives were constantly produced, indoctrinated, and desired. An example of this would be the students' immersion into leftist politics.

However, things began greatly to change in the 1960s; from the 1970s, the cultural logic of postmodernism strengthened rapidly. Consequently, grand narratives were already neither produced nor desired. Nevertheless, this kind of change placed a huge burden on the people who came to maturity at this moment. In spite of the global move toward a database model, they were planted with the old tree model (the desire for a grand narrative) in educational institutions and through written works. As a result of this paradox, this particular generation was driven to forge the grand narrative that had been lost. And though I will not elaborate further here, the interest in occult thought and New Age science that grew in America during the 1970s and the global radicalization of the student movements can be seen as results of this drive. The rise of otaku culture in Japan, too, of course shares the same social background. For the first-generation otaku who appeared at that time, knowledge of comics and anime or fan activities played a role extremely similar to the role played by the leftist thought and activism for the All-Campus Joint Struggle generation.

The Appearance of a Generation Disinterested in Grand Narratives

Whether that kind of complex psychology regulates otaku culture even now is a different problem. I think, conversely, that with the evolution from the modern to the postmodern, the necessity for this kind of forgery had to fade. The younger generations that grew up within the postmodern world image imagine the world as a database from the beginning, since they do not need a perspective on the entire world that surveys all—that is to say, *they have no need for forgeries, even as a subculture.*

And if this is the case, in the shift from the generation that needed fiction as a substitute for lost grand narratives to the generation that consumes fictions without such a need—even though they are two parts of the same otaku culture—then a grand transformation is realized in their forms of expression and consumption.

This new tendency became apparent in the 1990s, after the release of Ōtsuka's critique. Compared with the 1980s otaku, those of the 1990s generally adhered to the data and facts of the fictional worlds and were altogether unconcerned with a meaning and message that might have been communicated. Independently and without relation to an original narrative, consumers in the 1990s consumed only such fragmentary illustrations or settings; and this different type of consumption appeared when the individual consumer empathy toward these fragments strengthened. The otaku themselves called this new consumer behavior "*chara-moe*"—the feeling of *moe* toward characters and their alluring characteristics. As previously mentioned, here the otaku coolly consumed only the information that was behind the works without relation to the narrative or message of those works. Consequently, any scheme for analyzing this consumer behavior that proposes that these fragmentary works had already compensated for "the loss of grand narrative" is not really appropriate.

What the *Evangelion* Fans Wanted

Let's consider this through some concrete examples. I've already touched on *Mobile Suit Gundam*. In the 1990s, *Neon Genesis Evangelion* was frequently compared to *Gundam*. Both are science fiction anime with similar protagonists: young boys caught up in battles in the near future. These works were also widely supported by a generation close to that of the respective protagonist, even becoming a topic of conversation for the entire society. However, in reality, both *Neon Genesis Evangelion* and *Gundam* can be thought of as works that were consumed and supported by fans with entirely different attitudes about narratives.

As described above, numerous fans of *Gundam* desired the completion and close examination of a singular *Gundam* world. That is to say, in their case they preserved the current passion for a fictitious grand narrative. However, even during the peak of the craze, the fans of *Evan-*

gelion who appeared in the mid-1990s—especially those of the younger generation (the third generation of otaku)—did not really have a concern for the entire world of *Evangelion*. Instead they focused exclusively on the settings and character designs as objects for excessive interpretation or "reading up" (exemplified in derivative works), and for *chara-moe*.

For them, a grand narrative or fiction with a *Gundam*-style world was no longer desirable, even as a fantasy. *Gundam* fans' extraordinary adherence to the consistency of the timeline of the "space century" or to mechanical reality is well known. By contrast, many *Evangelion* fans required settings to empathize with the story's protagonist, to draw erotic illustrations of the heroine, and to build enormous robot figures, and showed obsessive interest in data to that extent, but beyond that they seldom immersed themselves into the world of the works.

This shift clearly appears again not only on the side of the consumers or the creators of derivative works but also from the point of view of the original creators. The first television broadcast of *Gundam* in 1979 was followed by several well-known sequels. Most of those were developed along the lines of a single fictitious history under the supervision of the general director, Tomino Yoshiyuki. In the case of *Evangelion*, however, there were no sequels and no plans to make sequels. Instead, the original creator's production company, Gainax, developed the derivative works sold in the Comic Market and at the same time created plans for related concepts; for instance, there are mahjong games, erotic telephone card designs using the *Evangelion* characters, and even simulation games in which players nurture the heroine Ayanami Rei. These are all far removed from the originals.

The important point here is that this change exercised a strong influence on the structure of the original itself, as well as on the recycling of the originals and the related projects. In contrast to the *Gundam* director Tomino, Anno Hideaki (the director of *Evangelion*) anticipated the appearance of derivative works in the Comic Market from the beginning, setting up various gimmicks within the originals to promote those products. For instance, a scene from a parallel *Evangelion* world is inserted in the final episode of the television series. In that parallel world with a completely different history, an Ayanami Rei dwells with a completely different personality. But in fact the scene depicted there was already a parody of an image that had been widely circulated as a derivative work at the time of the original broadcast. That is to say, an extremely warped relationship is interwoven into this work, where the original simulates in advance the simulacra.

Although two versions of this work were released for the cinema, both were framed as more than direct continuations of the television series, reworking the story with different versions of that fictional world. This characteristic is apparent in the 1997 *Evangelion Death*, which was made as an omnibus edition. This omnibus edition transforms video images from the TV series into the raw materials for remixing, presenting them as fragments without a unified narrative.

All of these characteristics indicate that, from the outset, the anime *Evangelion* was launched not as a privileged original but as a simulacrum at the same level as derivative works. In other words, this thing that Gainax was offering was certainly more than a single grand narrative, with the TV series as an entrance. Rather, it was an aggregate of information without a narrative, into which all viewers could empathize of their own accord and each could read up convenient narratives.

I call this realm that exists behind small narratives but lacks any form of narrativity *a grand nonnarrative*, in contrast to Ōtsuka's "grand narrative." Many consumers of *Evangelion* neither appreciate a complete anime as a work (in the traditional mode of consumption) nor consume a worldview in the background as in *Gundam* (in narrative consumption): from the beginning they need only nonnarratives or information.

MOE-ELEMENTS

Narratives and Coffee Mugs as the Same Class of Merchandise

One might argue that the original TV series of *Evangelion* continued to function as *an entry into the database*, if not into a grand narrative. However, otaku culture of the few years since *Evangelion* is rapidly abandoning the need for even this kind of an entry point. The rise of multimedia plays an important role here. In today's market for otaku culture, the previously accepted order is no longer dominant; no more do original comics versions debut, followed by anime releases, and finally the related products and fanzines. For example, a proposal for an anime series may make its way into a PC game, and even before the

anime production is complete it garners fan support through radio dra-
matizations and fan events, and even spawns related products that
hit the market. Or, conversely, the commercial success of a PC game
or trading cards could lead to the publication of fan anthologies (a
collection of derivative works made with the permission of the original
author) or novelizations, with the anime and comic versions only
following later. There are multiple layers of these kinds of intricate
circuits. In such a situation, it is quite ambiguous what the original is
or who the original author is, and the consumers rarely become aware of
the author or the original. For them, the distinction between the original and the spin-off products (as copies) does not exist; the only valid
distinction for them is between the settings created anonymously (a
database at a deep inner layer) and the individual works that each artist
has concretized from the information (a simulacrum on the surface
outer layer). Here, even the idea that the original functions as an entry
point into the settings or the worldview is becoming inappropriate.

The most important example in understanding this trend is the
character called Di Gi Charat or Digiko, created in 1998 (Figure 2.3).
This character was originally created as a mascot for a dealer of anime
and gaming-related products. Therefore, no narratives existed behind
it. However, the character gradually gained popularity in the latter half
of 1998, broke out as a TV commercial in 1999, followed by anime and
novels in 2000, and has established a solid world of its own.

What is noteworthy in this process is that the stories and settings
that form its world were created collectively and anonymously as a response to the market, after the character design of Digiko alone gained
support. For example, Usada Hikaru (or Rabi~en~Rose) and Petit Charat
are characters associated with Digiko, but they were released only in
1999, and even the name of the former was decided by a fan poll (Figure 2.4). Furthermore, although Digiko is now known to be "cocky and
carefree," these settings did not exist from the start but were added in
the anime version as a sort of self-parody.

Moreover, unlike *Evangelion*, this development was not managed
by a particular author or production company, because it was just part
of a corporate ad campaign. In such a situation, it does not make sense
to ask what the original of Di Gi Charat is, who the author is, or what
kind of message is implied. The entire project was driven by the
power of fragments; projects such as the anime or the novel, formerly

Figure 2.3. *Di Gi Charat.*

discussed independently as a "work," are merely related products, just like character mugs and loose-leaf binders. The narrative is only a surplus item, added to the settings and illustrations (the nonnarrative).

Combinations of *Moe*-Elements

Another interesting point is that Di Gi Charat uses excessively advanced skill to trigger *chara-moe*, as if to compensate for the absence of story and message. I wrote earlier that the design of Digiko alone found support at first. However, one cannot quite say that the design was particularly original or attractive. In fact, the design of Digiko is a result of sampling and combining popular elements from recent otaku culture, as if to downplay the authorship of the designer. I have identified some of the major elements in Figure 2.5.

I will not describe the characteristics of each element here, but note that each element, with its own origins and background, constitutes a category that has been developed in order to stimulate the inter-

Figure 2.4. Usada Hikaru (Rabi~en~Rose) and Petit Charat.
Credit: *Di Gi Charat.*
Produced by Broccoli.

est of the consumers. It is not a simple fetish object, but a sign that emerged through market principles. For example, it is well known that the "maid costume" originated in the X-rated anime series *Cream Lemon: Black Cat Mansion* in the 1980s and gained popularity in the "visual novels" of the 1990s.[9] Also, in my observation, "hair springing up like an antennae" was popularized in the visual novel *The Scar (Kizuato)* (Figure 2.6), and it has become a standard element seen in anime and games. From this point on, let us call these elements, developed to effectively stimulate the *moe* of the consumers, "*moe*-elements" (*moe yōso*). Most of the *moe*-elements are visual, but there are other kinds of *moe*-elements, such as a particular way of speaking, settings, stereotypical narrative development, and the specific curves of a figurine.

As one can immediately see in specialty stores in the Akihabara or Shinjuku parts of Tokyo, the *moe*-elements are proliferating within otaku culture. The "characters" circulating in these stores are not unique

hair sticking up like antennae   cat ears

Figure 2.5. *Moe-elements that constitute Di Gi Charat.*

bells

green hair

maid uniform

tail

big, loose socks

designs created by the individual talent of the author but an output generated from preregistered elements and combined according to the marketing program of each work.

The otaku themselves are aware of this situation. The otaku search engine TINAMI launched in 1996 signifies this awareness with an actual device (Figure 2.7).[10] To enable the user to find illustrations from tens of thousands of registered sites, this searchable database classifies and quantifies various characteristics of otaku illustrations in detail. The site is equipped with selectable parameters so that the user can search for *moe*-elements. That is to say, the user can search for the desired characteristics of things like "cat ears" and "maid costumes," or can set "the percentage of characters appearing" at more than 75 percent, "the age of character" at between 10 and 15, and "the degree of déformé" at 5 in order to find desired characters categorized in the database. Figure 2.8 shows the actual search window of TINAMI. Some of the "categories" lined up at the bottom half of the figure are

Figure 2.6. An "antenna hair" as a *moe*-element seen in *The Scar (Kizuato)*. Credit: *The Scar (Kizuato)*. Produced by Leaf.

moe-elements, such as "cat ears," "animal," "angels," "maid costumes," and "glasses."

As the Internet spread and the site of otaku activities moved to the Web during the late 1990s, search engines such as TINAMI began to play a prominent role. In such an environment, the producers, like it or not, must have been conscious of their position relative to the whole of otaku culture. As soon as the characters are created, they are broken up into elements, categorized, and registered to a database. If there is no appropriate classification, a new element or category simply will be added. In this sense, the originality of an "original" character can only exist as a simulacrum.

There used to be a narrative behind a work. But as the importance of narrative has declined, the characters have become more important in otaku culture. Subsequently, a database for *moe*-elements that generates the characters has been established. Otaku culture of the 1990s has followed this general trend, but *Di Gi Charat*, which emerged at the end of the 1990s, marks the terminal point of this trend.

In fact, the characters in this work were created with intentionally excessive *moe*-elements. The novelization describes Digiko as having "the maid costume with lots of frills, a cap with white cat ears, cat gloves, cat boots, and a cat tail. Perfect and fully equipped with double-*moe*-options," while Puchiko is described as wearing "a tiger-striped hat

Figure 2.7. TINAMI homepage.
Credit: Screen capture by Hiroki Azuma.

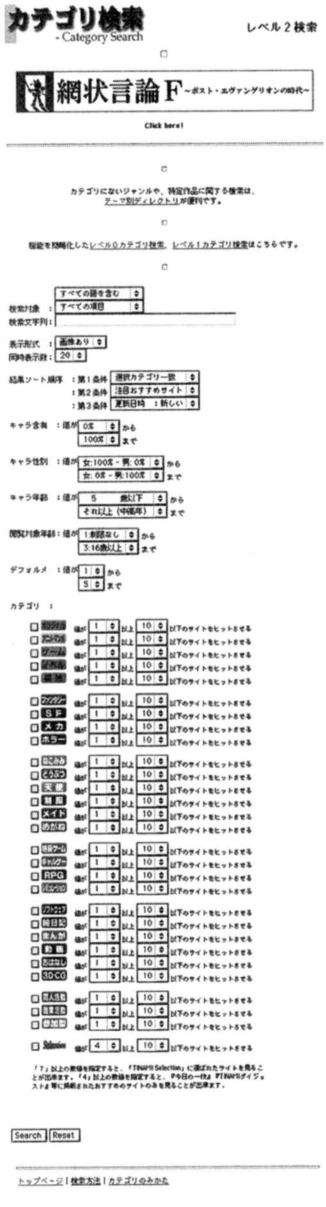

Figure 2.8. TINAMI search screen. Credit: Screen capture by Hiroki Azuma.

with cat ears, a girls' school uniform ('sailor suits') and bloomers, a tiger cat tail. A double-*moe* costume, quite evil and foul for fans."[11] These self-parodying descriptions clearly indicate the fragile position of this work. Digiko has cat ears and speaks with "-*nyo*" (the Japanese sound for "meow") at the end of her sentences. This is not because cat ears or the "-*nyo*" endings are exactly attractive themselves, but because both cat ears and peculiar sentence endings are *moe*-elements and, to be exact, because the otaku of the 1990s accepted them as *moe*-elements as they became aware of the whole structure of this process. In this sense, *Di Gi Charat* is not so much a project that naively relies on the desire of *chara-moe* but a complex project that, by pushing that desire to the limit, has become a satire for the present market dominated by *moe*-related designs.

DATABASE CONSUMPTION

Attractive Characters, Rather than Quality of Individual Works

The organization of the *moe*-elements has rapidly advanced in the 1990s. The term *moe* is said to have emerged in the late 1980s, originally referring to the fictional desire for characters of comics, anime, and games or for pop idols. Since those who feel *moe* toward a particular character tend to buy its related goods excessively, the success of a project for the producers of such goods is directly determined not by the quality of the work itself but by its ability to evoke the *moe* desire through character design and illustrations. This tendency goes back to the 1970s, but its significance decisively increased in the context of the 1990s multimedia trend.

With the new multimedia, various kinds of projects can progress simultaneously while leaving the status of the original quite ambiguous. Therefore, the common ground for all of these projects is neither the authorship of the original creator nor a message but a common world of the work and characters, or, in extreme cases, characters alone. For example, the only reason (other than copyright) for categorizing the TV and film series *Evangelion*, directed by Anno Hideaki, with the "nurturing" simulation game *Ayanami Nurturing Project* as "*Evangelion*-connected" works, or categorizing novel games such as *Droplet* ("Shizuku") and *The Scar* ("Kizuato") created by Leaf and its parodied trading card game *Leaf Fight* as "Leaf-connected" works, is that they feature the same characters. Since the continuity in terms of content between these works is extremely weak, the fans of *Evangelion* and *Droplet* could very well have shown little interest in *Ayanami Nurturing Project* or *Leaf Fight*. Such consumer behavior could have been dominant; it even would have been easier to understand outside of the otaku market.

But the otaku market of the 1990s systematically raised consumers who accepted both versions within a single spectrum and, in fact, the market expanded its size on the basis of the inundation of such "related goods." As a result, instead of narratives creating characters, it has become a general strategy to create character settings first, followed by works and projects, *including the stories*. Given this situation, the attractiveness of characters is more important than the degree of perfection of individual works, and the know-how for enhancing the attractiveness (through the art of the *moe*-element) has rapidly accumulated. Under such circumstances, the development of *moe*-element databases has become a necessity.

Connections between Characters across Individual Works

As a result, many of the otaku characters created in recent years are connected to many characters across individual works, rather than emerging from a single author or a work. For example, Figures 2.9 through 2.12 show four characters: Hoshino Ruri from *Martian Successor Nadesico*, Ayanami Rei from *Evangelion*, Tsukishima Ruriko from *Droplet*, and Ōtorii Tsubame from *Cyber Team in Akihabara (Akihabara Dennōgumi)*. These characters have many things in common in terms of settings and designs.

Such connections, frequently seen in otaku works, have been called "quotations," "influences," and "parodies." However, notions such as "quotations" and "influences" unconsciously presuppose a unit such as an author or a work. For example, there is a notion that an author is influenced by another author's work, and he or she quotes it or sometimes parodies it. Even now we can say that the activities of otaku works lie within such a model. For example, it is not incorrect to trace the genealogy of our four characters as follows: Ruriko was created under the influence of Rei, and Ruri was created as quotations from both, and Tsubame is a parody of Ruri.

Figure 2.9. Hoshino Ruri.
Credit: Designed by
Goto-Keiji. *Martian
Successor Nadesico.*
Produced by XEBEC.

Figure 2.10. Ayanami
Rei.
Credit: Designed by
Sadamoto Yoshiyuki.
Neon Genesis Evangelion.
Produced by Gainax.

Figure 2.11. Tsukishima
Ruriko.
Credit: Designed by
Minazuki Tōru. *Droplet*.
Produced by Leaf.

However, the validity of this model is limited. Let us say that Ruri
is a quotation of Rei or Ruriko. But who did the quoting? In comparison with *Evangelion*, where the roles of Anno as a director and Sadamoto
Yoshiyuki as a character designer were relatively clear, it is difficult to
determine the involvement of Sato Tatsuo and Mamiya Kia in the complex production process of *Nadesico*. Moreover, the example in Figures
2.9 through 2.12 is just a tip of the iceberg.

In fact, in the late 1990s, characters bearing a close resemblance to
Ayanami Rei have been produced and consumed on a massive scale—in
comics, anime, and novelizations, both in the commercial market and
the fanzine market. It does not seem wise to attribute this expanse to
the "influence" of *Evangelion*.

I believe that it is more appropriate to use the image of the database
to grasp this current situation. The emergence of Ayanami Rei did not

Figure 2.12. Ōtorii
Tsubame.
Credit: Designed by
Kotobuki Tsukasa. *Cyber
Team in Akihabara*.
Produced by Ashi
Production.

influence many authors so much as change the rules of the *moe*-elements
sustaining otaku culture. As a result, even those authors who were not
deliberately thinking of *Evangelion* unconsciously began to produce
characters closely resembling Rei, using newly registered *moe*-elements
(quiet personality, blue hair, white skin, mysterious power). Such a model
is close to the reality of the late 1990s. Beyond Rei, characters emerging in otaku works were not unique to individual works but were
immediately broken into *moe*-elements and recorded by consumers,
and then the elements reemerged later as material for creating new
characters. Therefore, each time a popular character appeared, the
moe-element database changed accordingly, and as a result, in the next
season there were heated battles among the new generation of characters featuring new *moe*-elements.

The Double-Layer Structure of Consumption
as Seen in *Chara-Moe*

As these observations make clear, the *chara-moe*, which represents
otaku culture of the 1990s, is not the simple act of empathy (as the
otaku themselves wish to believe). It is a quite postmodern consumer
behavior, sustained by the movements back and forth between the
characters (the simulacra) and the *moe*-elements (the database). Within
the consumer behavior of feeling *moe* for a specific character, along
with the blind obsession, there is hidden a peculiarly cool, detached
dimension—one that takes apart the object into *moe*-elements and ob-
jectifies them within a database. I will discuss this double-layer structure in detail below, with visual novels as an example, but suffice it to
say that *chara-moe* cannot be explained away merely as a fanatical consumer behavior.

The otaku's *moe* sensibility is doubled between the level of individual characters and the level of *moe*-elements, and that is exactly why the
otaku are able to swap the objects of the *moe* so quickly. If the otaku were
selecting the characters simply according to their own tastes without
the level of *moe*-elements, then the fans of each character would be
unrelated to those of another character. If this had been the case, then
the "character business" that bloomed in the 1990s would not have been
possible.

From "Narrative Consumption" to "Database Consumption"

To summarize the discussion up to this point, there is no longer a
narrative in the deep inner layer, beneath the works and products such
as comics, anime, games, novels, illustrations, trading cards, figurines,
and so on. In the multimedia environment of the 1990s, it is only characters that unite various works and products. The consumer, knowing
this, moves easily back and forth between projects with a narrative
(comics, anime, novels) and projects without one (illustrations and figurines). Here, the individual projects are the simulacra and behind them
is the database of characters and settings.

At yet another level, however, each character is merely a simulacrum, derived from the database of *moe*-elements. In other words, the
double-layer structure of the simulacra and the database is again doubled,

forming a complex system. The otaku first consume individual works, and sometimes are moved by them. But they are also aware that, in fact, the works are merely simulacra, consisting only of the characters. Then they consume characters, and sometimes feel *moe* in them. But they are also aware that, in fact, the characters are just simulacra, consisting only of combinations of *moe*-elements. In my observation, *Di Gi Charat* is a project created with a high degree of self-awareness of the doubled (and perhaps even tripled) consciousness of the otaku.

Therefore, to consume *Di Gi Charat* is not simply to consume a work (a small narrative) or a worldview behind it (a grand narrative), nor to consume characters and settings (a grand nonnarrative). Rather, it is linked to consuming the database of otaku culture as a whole. I call this consumer behavior *database consumption*, in contrast with Ōtsuka's "narrative consumption."

In the shift from modernity to postmodernity, our world image is experiencing a sea change, from one sustained by a narrative-like, cinematic perspective on the entire world to one read-up by search engines, characterized by databases and interfaces. Amid this change, the Japanese otaku lost the grand narrative in the 1970s, learned to fabricate the lost grand narrative in the 1980s (narrative consumption), and in the 1990s, abandoned the necessity for even such fabrication and learned simply to desire the database (database consumption). Roughly speaking, such a trend may be surmised from Ōtsuka's critical essay and my own observation. Figures 2.13 and 2.14 show the difference between narrative consumption and database consumption. Figures 2.13 and 2.14 correspond to the aforementioned Figures 2.1 and 2.2, respectively.

The Novels of "Anime/Manga-Like Realism"

It is unavoidable that many examples of otaku culture are visually oriented, but let me cite a different example of how the rise of the *chara-moe* and database consumption is beginning to exert tremendous influence on print culture. In the mass media, the "novel" is still categorized as either "literature" or "entertainment." In reality, however, for ten years the otaku market has been producing and consuming numerous novels that cannot be classified as either. Sometimes labeled with existing categories such as "mystery," "science fiction," and "fantasy" and sometimes labeled with reference to their readership or producers such

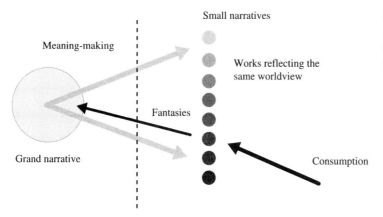

Small narratives

Meaning-making

Works reflecting the
same worldview

Fantasies

Grand narrative

Consumption

Figure 2.13. The
structure of narrative
consumption.
Credit: Hiroki Azuma.

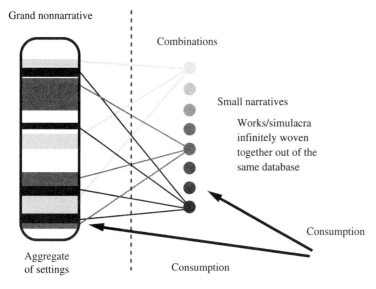

Grand nonnarrative

Combinations

Small narratives

Works/simulacra
infinitely woven
together out of the
same database

Consumption

Aggregate
of settings

Consumption

Figure 2.14. The
structure of database
consumption.
Credit: Hiroki Azuma.

as "junior novels," "game novels," and "young adult (juvenile)," these works have a fictional world with a unique logic that differs from the traditional classification as either literary or entertaining. For this reason, their general reputation is poor. But their logic can be naturally understood in the context of otaku culture, as discussed above.

Perhaps the most appropriate example of this new and different breed of novels may be found in the works of Seiryōin Ryūsui. Seiryōin was born in 1974, falling between the second and third generations of otaku. His debut novel, *Cosmic* (1996), is a mystery novel in which a dozen or so detectives try to solve several dozen locked-room murder cases. That setting is already original, but in addition each detective is given an impressive name and characteristics: Yaiba Somahito ("The Blade Wizard"), who reasons with a dialectic method called "Jin-suiri" ("Syn-llogism"); Tsukumo Jūku ("Ninety-nine Nineteen"), who uses intuition called "Jintsū Riki" ("Divine wisdom and cosmology"); and Amagiri Fuyuka ("Rain-mist Winter-aroma"), who speculates in her sleep, a talent referred to as "Gori Muchū" (Enlightenment and reason in the dream). The resolutions of the mysteries are also extremely absurd. In addition, these superhuman characters appear in a subsequent series of novels, including *Joker, Jukebox,* and *Carnival.* Since his debut, Seiryōin has been declaring that these novels together form a "Great Story of the Water Stream" ("Ryūsui Taisetsu"). In short, his novels may not emphasize the quality of an individual work, but they contribute to the attractiveness of individual characters and consequently the quality of "the Seiryōin world" that they constitute as a series. This author consistently has garnered strong support among teenagers, but some veteran mystery writers have reacted negatively.

Referring to Ōtsuka again, he points out that, behind the rise of this sort of novel, realism itself has begun to transform itself.[12] The modern Japanese novel is said to reflect reality vividly (*shasei*); the otaku novel reflects fiction vividly. The characters and stories that Seiryōin depicts are never realistic, but they are possible in the world of comics and anime already published, and therefore the reader accepts them as real. Ōtsuka called such an attitude "anime/manga-like Realism" and identified its origin in the science fiction writer Arai Motoko's statement at the end of the 1970s that she "wanted to write the print version of the comics *Lupin the Third.*" Ōtsuka argues that, although the naturalistic realism (of the modern Japanese novel) and the "anime/manga-like Realism" give very different impressions on the surface, the progression from the former to the latter was a matter of necessity, because in Japan the former was fictional to begin with.

Elements of Mystery Fiction as *Moe*-Elements

Once again, I agree with Ōtsuka's observation in general, but I must emphasize that the very fiction supposed to be "reflected vividly" has already been broken up into individual elements and collected in the database. It is well known that Seiryōin's novels are influenced by Kurumada Masami's popular manga *Saint Seiya*. At the same time, Seiryōin constructs his world by extracting and freely combining various elements from all of the numerous neo-orthodox mystery novels of the mid-1980s to mid-1990s. Here, the reader shares the same database. That the author can quickly write dozens of discernibly different locked-room murder mysteries with a dozen or so different detectives—and that the readers accept it as a matter of course—is only possible because images of detectives, tricks, and ways of solving mysteries have already become *moe*-elements.

Such self-referential awareness of the conditions of the genre is probably inherited from the writers of a previous generation, such as Ayatsuji Yukito and Norizuki Rintarō. But one great distinction is that, where the previous generation directed their consciousness to the rules (codes) of mystery, Seiryōin's consciousness is directed toward the database of *moe*-elements. It is commonly accepted that the market for mystery greatly expanded in the 1990s, but as far as the young readership is concerned, such growth was sustained by readers differing from the "orthodox" fans who enjoyed clever tricks; the new readers felt *moe* toward characters created by Kyōgoku Natsuhiko and Mori Hiroshi, drew illustrations of them, and embarked on derivative works from them.

This situation spreads beyond the mystery genre. Otaku print culture as a whole is beginning to obey a different kind of logic, one oriented toward characters rather than individual works. Seiryōin's novels, in fact, not only presuppose this as a condition but even satirize it. For example, in Japan Detective Club, 350 detectives are "divided into Groups 1 through 7" and "during the Group Switch every two months the overachievers of a lower group are promoted while the underachievers of a higher group are demoted without mercy."[13] This setting of the Japan Detective Club can be read as a parody of the whole situation, if one keeps in mind the character-oriented state of the market.

Neither literature nor entertainment, the otaku novels are already being sold and consumed according to a logic similar to that of video games and illustrations. Commercially speaking, the change from naturalist realism to "anime/manga-like realism" is sustained by this change in the market. As far as I know, Seiryōin is the author who reacted to this change most responsively and changed how he writes novels most fundamentally. Here, it is neither reality (naturalism) or an earlier fiction (narrative consumption) but the database of *moe*-elements that is felt as most real.

THE SIMULACRA AND THE DATABASE

Drawbacks of the Simulacra Theory

In the above discussion, otaku culture gives us an answer to the first of the two questions I asked at the beginning of this chapter: in postmodernity, how do simulacra increase? The surface outer layer of otaku culture is covered with simulacra, or derivative works. But in the deep inner layer lies the database of settings and characters, and further down, the database of *moe*-elements. The consumer behavior of the otaku, which might seem like a chaotic inundation of simulacra, becomes more ordered and understandable once we turn our eyes to the level of the database.

These observations, beyond an analysis of subculture, provide insights that would change the existing notion of the simulacra. In earlier theories on postmodernity, the increase in simulacra has been considered a chaotic phenomenon emerging after the demise of the distinction between the original and the copy. Such an argument cites, first and foremost, "The Work of Art in the Age of Mechanical Reproduction," a short essay written by Walter Benjamin more than sixty years ago. In it Benjamin famously argues that the sense of originality (called "aura") residing within a particular work of art is based upon the "singularity" of the "ritual" that gave birth to the work, but that the technology of mechanical reproduction voids such a sense.[14] This argument later became a core of simulacra theory.

Benjamin's grasp of "aura" here clearly reflects the aforementioned tree model. In front of an original, the viewer feels a connection with the "ritual" beyond the work at hand. There is no such connection with a copy. In other words, an original and a copy are distinguished by the presence of the connection with the ritual (i.e., the presence of the aura). This aesthetic indeed reflects a modern worldview. Figure 2.15 indicates this idea, based on Figure 2.1. The omnipresence of simula-

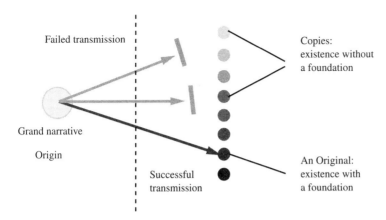

Failed transmission

Copies:
existence without
a foundation

Figure 2.15. The original
and the copy.
Credit: Hiroki Azuma.

Grand narrative

Origin

Successful
transmission

An Original:
existence with
a foundation

cra represents a situation in which, having lost the very criteria for this connection, an original and a copy have come to have the same value and all signs have begun to float without their foundation.

Therefore, in the context of the earlier theories of postmodernity, the two phenomena I mentioned at the beginning of this chapter—"the omnipresence of simulacra" and "the decline of the grand narrative"— can in fact be grasped as two aspects of a single change: the collapse of the tree model. Of course, there is a fundamental difference between these two phenomena, in that the former is a change caused mainly by technological advances while the latter is a social, ideological change. Still, there is undeniably a common change in the worldview underlying these two phenomena. In fact, Benjamin's essay discusses the age of mechanical reproduction and the decline of ideologies as related phenomena, and Baudrillard grasps these two trends in relation to each other, arguing, "no more ideology, only simulacra."[15]

However, previous theories on postmodernity failed to understand that the tree model did not simply collapse but *was replaced by* the database model. Of course, some discussions have suggested such a point. For example, Baudrillard argues that, in contemporary society, permeated by marketing and semiotic consumption, "we live less as users than as readers and selectors, reading cells."[16] His argument that differentiated goods and signs are stocked and circulated in quantity (the totality of which Baudrillard calls "hyperreality") and that consumers can express their personality or originality only as a combination of them grasps a reality that very closely resembles what I have been calling the database model. However, even in this discussion, the level of the simulacra and the level of the database have never been clearly distinguished, nor has the whole been grasped as a double-layer structure. Baudrillardian "hyperreality" covers both the world of the simulacra and the world of the database. In the example of otaku culture, the inundation of derivative works, narrative consumption, *chara-moe*, and even the so-called deformed designs such as Di Gi Charat would all be explained by the concept of "hyperreality."

From "Original versus Copy" to "Database versus Simulacra"

In contrast, in the present study I wish to show that the simulacra that are filling up this society have never propagated in a chaotic fashion but that their effective functioning is warranted first and foremost by the level of the database.

Otaku culture is filled with derivative works; originals and derivative works are produced and consumed as if they were of "equal value." However, not all of such derivative works actually have the same value; otherwise the market would not grow. In fact, underneath the simulacra exists a database, a device that sorts good simulacra from bad ones regulating the flow of derivative works. The 773rd Bikkuriman sticker must adequately share a common database with the previous 772 stickers, or it would not be regarded as a derivative work to begin with. *Ayanami Nurturing Project* must adequately share a worldview with *Evangelion*, and the design of Di Gi Charat must adequately sample *moe*-elements from the late 1990s. Simulacra created without recognition of these processes will be weeded out by the market and disappear.

In other words, in postmodernity, a new opposition is emerging between the simulacra and the database, in place of the previous opposition between the original and the copy. In the past, the original work was "an original" and the derivative work "a copy." Only herein exists the criterion for judging the quality of a work. For example, in the case of *Evangelion*, the TV series created by Anno Hideaki is a "work" connected with the authorship and his original message, while derivative works by amateurs and related commercial projects are mere copies. People are supposed to strictly distinguish between these two in consuming them.

However, in reality, over the past twenty years a consumer behavior that does not discriminate between these two categories has been gaining more and more power. Instead, as I mentioned above, the database of characters, settings, and *moe*-elements is on the rise and with it a different variety of standards applied to the database. On the rise instead are the database of character settings and *moe*-elements, as I have argued above, and emerging with it are a different kind of criteria based on one's relation to this database. A copy is judged not by its distance from an original but by its distance from the database. Figure 2.16 indicates this new relationship.

In contemporary thought, the magical attraction of the original as an original is sometimes called "the myth of authorship." As we survey the history of otaku culture from the 1980s to the 1990s to the 2000s, we find that even this myth has been rapidly declining. Most readers and experts in the field would agree that it is easy to name authors of major comics and anime that represent the 1980s, but it is more difficult to do the same for the 1990s. This observation might be seen as a symptom of the genre's decline, but in actuality, the very fact that it is

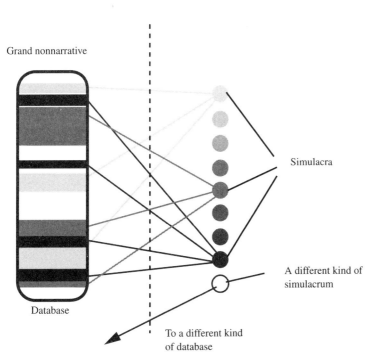

Figure 2.16. The database and the simulacra. Credit: Hiroki Azuma.

Grand nonnarrative

Simulacra

Database

A different kind of simulacrum

To a different kind of database

difficult to name an author points to the essence of otaku culture in the 1990s. Now the author is no longer a god and therefore cannot be named. Instead, *moe*-elements have become gods. A moderately knowledgeable consumer should be able to name several major *moe*-elements representing the 1990s.

Notes

1. As this is a reproduction of a previously published work, some of its style conventions differ from those in the other chapters in this book. Please see translation notes in the frontmatter of this book for a more complete explanation of what has been altered from the original text.

2. For more on the Baudrillardian notion of "simulacra," see, for example, Jean Baudrillard, *Symbolic Exchange and Death* (London: Sage Publications, 1993), and Jean Baudrillard, *Simulacra and Simulation, The Body, in Theory* (Ann Arbor: University of Michigan Press, 1994).

3. Nakajima Azuza, *Kommyunikēshon fuzen shōkōgun* [Communication deficiency syndrome] (Tokyo: Chikuma Bunko, 1995), 44, 49.

4. The most fundamental work on the "decline of the grand narrative" is Jean-François Lyotard, *Postmodern Condition* (Minneapolis: University of Minnesota Press, 1984). The analysis of this book mainly concerns changes in the academic world, but the interpretation of this term coined by Lyotard has been stretched, and it has been circulating as a useful concept for grasping the characteristics of the world since the 1970s. Hence, the term "the decline of the grand narrative" in this book is used as an extended concept, including various such extended interpretations, rather than the original concept of Lyotard.

5. Ōsawa Masachi, "Otaku ron" [On otaku], in *Denshi media ron* [Theory of electronic media], 242–293 (Tokyo: Shin'yosha, 1995), 259ff.

6. Ōtsuka, *Monogatari shōhiron*, 13–14, 17–18, 18–19.

7. Ōsawa Masachi, *Kyokō no jidai no hate* [The end of the fictional age] (Tokyo: Chikuma Shinsho, 1996), 52ff.

8. Ōtsuka, *Monogatari shōhiron*, 26ff.

9. See Shiota Nobuyuki and CB's Project, eds., *Fukakutei sekai no tantei shinshi: Wārudo gaidansu* [The detective gentleman of the uncertain world: A guidance to the world] (Tokyo: Softbank Publishing, 2000), 129ff.

10. www.tinami.com.

11. Nanohana Koneko, *Di Gi Charat*, vol. 2 (Tokyo: Kadokawa Dengeki Bunko, 2000), 12, 19–20.

12. Ōtsuka Eiji, *Monogatari no taisō* [Workouts of fiction] (Tokyo: Asahi Shinbunsha, 2000), 198ff.

13. Seiryōin Ryūsui, *Kozumikku* [Cosmic] (Tokyo: Kōdansha Novels, 1996), 275.

14. Walter Benjamin, "The Work of Art in the Age of Mechanical Reproduction," in *Illuminations*, ed. Hannah Arendt, trans. Harry Zohn, 217–252 (New York: Schocken Books, 1969).

15. Baudrillard, *Symbolic Exchange and Death*, 2.

16. Ibid., 64.

3

Japan's Cynical Nationalism

· ·

AKIHIRO KITADA

IRONIC COMMUNICATION SPACE

Let me start with the story of *Densha-Otoko* (Train Man).

According to the book jacket, *Train Man* is the "greatest pure love story of the century." Born on the Internet megaforum 2channel (2ch), *Train Man* became an instant best seller after being released as a book in October 2004, with more than 300,000 copies sold within three weeks.[1] One might expect that a book coming out of a web forum means it was a novel written by collective input. In fact, however, the book consists of forum posts with nominal editing.[2] This means that tens of thousands of people have paid 1,365 yen (approximately US$13) to read posts from a 2ch subforum for single men.

The plot is, to put it bluntly, mediocre. The story goes as follows: a lackluster *Akiba-kei* (Akihabara type; see Chapter 6) male otaku happens to become acquainted with an older, beautiful, and sophisticated woman because of a certain incident on a train and then overcomes various obstacles to eventually win her heart. As insipid as that may sound, it is, surprisingly enough, quite the tearjerker. I sat glued to the computer for two hours reading the online version of *Train Man*, cried, and then went on to view related flash animations and cried some more. For the record, I thought *Fuyuno Sonata* (Winter Sonata) was ridiculous, and I was enraged by *Sekai no Chuushin de Ai wo Sakebu* (Crying out Love in the Center of the World).[3]

Given my experience, I would hesitate to put *Train Man* into the same category as the sentimental dramas *Winter Sonata* and *Crying out Love*. I believe many of the anonymous contributors to *Train Man* are cynics who dislike such works.

What is notable here is that these 2channelers (2ch users), who are generally considered cynics, managed to create a moving piece of work that puts *Crying out Love* to shame. Let me provide some background in case you are unfamiliar with 2ch. Established in 1999, 2ch is an anonymous web forum. 2channelers have developed a distinctive writing style, posting ironic critiques of the media and social phenomena. The site is often thought to represent the dark side of the Internet because participants frequently reveal the private information of others, or they circulate damaging gossip on the site. In fact, when the news covers criminal activity on "Internet forums," nine times out of ten it is referring to 2ch. 2ch consists of thematic subforums on current affairs, with ongoing specialized discussions framed in a distinctive communication style (Figure 3.1). For example, the "Breaking News+" forum covers the most recent news on TV and in newspapers; the "Media" forum addresses general journalistic practices and reported

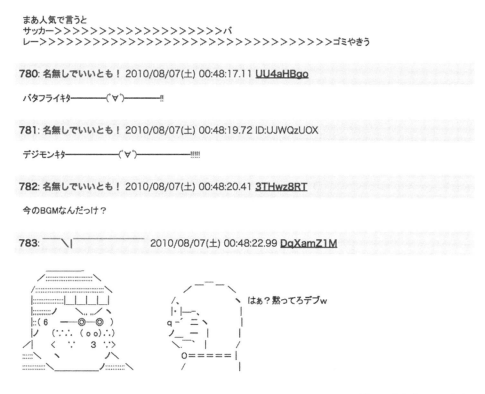

Figure 3.1. Screen shot from 2ch.
Credit: Screen capture by Daisuke Okabe.

content; and the "Live Coverage" forum follows TV programs as they air. In these forums, users engage in discussions replete with 2chanisms and ASCII art, similar to insider jokes among classmates but with a more dry, snarky edge that makes the communication a play in irony.

The media are not the sole target of 2channelers' scorn. Novels, manga, information technology, pop music, blogs, websites, teachers, friends, and their own everyday lives are all considered fair game. In the 2ch universe, anything and everything serves as source material for specialized discussions among forum users. Of course, some 2ch subforums do not demand a cynical attitude, but the most typical communication style on 2ch is trading snarky commentary on specific kinds of source material. The communication is intimate but harsh; the harshness is itself a kind of intimacy. 2ch is a social space in which this curious mode of communication is systematized into a kind of grammar.

The Empathy and Irony Collective

Train Man comes from a subsection of 2ch, the "Single Men" subforum. As such, it is not a narrative in the strict sense of the word. It is instead a record of ongoing real-time communication among individuals, mediated by a computer screen. This means *Train Man* has a realism that a novel could never achieve (Figure 3.2).

2ch's distinct sarcasm is also important. Even though *Train Man* involves empathetic interaction, scorn and ridicule are also directed at the self and others. Sarcasm accentuates the boundary between those who "get it" and those who do not. Readers who understand 2ch's distinct language and atmosphere gain a greater sense of being an insider in *Train Man*'s world. As readers progress through the story, the posts in the online forum become the medium through which they become part of the cynical collective. The reader does not identify with Train Man himself but experiences pleasure and emotion by occupying the role of a 2channeler.

The popularity of *Train Man* may be an indication of how the triggers for our emotional responses are becoming more and more 2ch-like. It is not the story itself that readers find moving but rather the fact that they could be part of Train Man's trials and tribulations

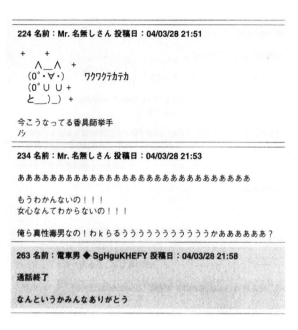

Figure 3.2. Excerpt from the *Train Man* book, 84. Credit: *Train Man.*

as 2channelers, creating a self-referential, moving narrative with other anonymous comrades. Fully aware that emotions can be manufactured in this way, participants take a cynical view while also letting themselves be moved. Perhaps *Train Man* is a haven for those cynics who sneer at melodrama yet are still in search of something that will move them.

My Topic

This chapter examines the development of this antinomy of irony and empathy in modern youth culture, as it is seen in *Train Man*.

This antinomy came to the forefront in the 1990s, underscored by a structural shift in Japan's ironic sensibilities. Irony, in the original sense of the word, is a way of maintaining a distance between the self and the world. Most would consider it paradoxical for this distancing process to coexist with empathy, which is essentially viewing the world as being one with the self. However, it is important to remember that irony is a social behavior embedded in specific times and social codes. What defines irony, the key elements of irony, and the value of irony are all influenced by historical and social circumstances.

Some scholars argue that today's youth are not capable of irony, but I disagree. Compared to the irony of the 1980s, the post-1980s period may appear rather clichéd. However, as 2ch indicates, the spirit of irony continues to live on in spite of, or perhaps even because of, today's cultural context. I would argue that irony has not vanished, but rather its social and discursive value has changed in that it can now be linked to a more clichéd and sincere cultural sensibility. It is meaningless to debate whether we are living in an ironic or sincere era. Instead, we should examine the historic origins of the discursive structure enabling this coexistence of irony and sincerity.

RELATING THROUGH AFFILIATION: CYNICISM AND ROMANTICISM IN 2CH

The Birth of a Massive Inner Circle

2ch is the world's largest web forum. Established in 1999, 2ch by some accounts is being accessed by more than 10 percent of Japan's "netizens." In one section of the forum, "Warriors of Patriotism," nationalistic users who have vowed to fight left-wingers have been unleashing vicious attacks on the media and on populists. These attacks, which are mainly directed toward *Mainichi News,* have generated a miasma of brutal nationalism in that subsection of 2ch. These activities are not sophisticated enough to be considered a form of political conservatism but display a strange passion that is far beyond that of a conventional conservative pundit. Where does this passion come from?

Here I aim to examine 2ch's antimedia, nationalistic elements without idealizing them as expressions of an authentic popular voice nor dismissing them as mere bathroom-stall graffiti generated by faceless rabble.

To understand 2ch's cynical antimedia principles, we must first understand the distance 2channelers place between themselves and the media. Although many have discussed the opposition between 2ch and mainstream media, I would like to draw attention to how 2channelers' behavior also exhibits an excessive *love* of the media. 2channelers' scorn for the media does not arise from some festering resentment. Rather, the media nurtured an ironic sensibility in this population, and they are now directing that very sensibility to the media that they adore.

Because of the anonymous nature of 2ch, it is extremely difficult to study the demographics of 2ch's core users in depth. Based on a review of 2ch posts related to media experiences and net ratings surveys (Figure 3.3), it appears that the first 2channelers were the generation whose members experienced the early Internet, were born during the mid-1960s to the mid-1970s, had access to a color TV set in their living rooms since early childhood, and were in junior high and high school during the late 1970s through the 1980s in the heyday of *All Night Nippon* and the Fuji TV network.[4] Unlike the prior generation that grew up in an era dominated by genres of public television, 2channelers experienced childhood and adolescence in a period dominated by private TV networks centered on a more self-reflective popular and consumer culture. I call the genres of comedic variety, talk, and game shows established during this period "pure TV." People who belong to this later TV generation experienced ironic media that could not be understood unless they themselves adopted a cynical attitude. Consequently, they have a shared "insider literacy" that allows them to read between the lines.

In the 1980s, a new genre of variety show became popular; it centered on informal, snarky conversations between hosts and featured insider knowledge about the show and popular culture more broadly.[5] These kinds of shows began to squeeze out the earlier generation of

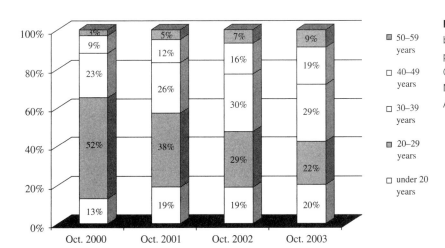

Figure 3.3. Age breakdown of 2ch participants. Credit: Nielsen / NetRatings, NetView AMS.

shows, which featured more staged and scripted performances and skits.[6] In these new shows, the clichés developed by television in the 1960s and 1970s were repurposed and transformed into material to be parodied. The humor of these shows targeted viewers who were able to supply the subtext behind these parodies, such as the personal lives of guests on the shows and insider knowledge of the industry (for example, the assistant director's nickname and personality). To derive humor from the topic at hand, viewers needed to possess "insider literacy"— the ability to access information external to the media at hand. This was an unwritten rule for the pure TV programs in the 1980s, a period commonly referred to as the era of Fuji TV.

This advanced literacy in media gimmicks led these viewers to scoff at clichés. For the purposes of this chapter, I will call this attitude pure TV–style irony. The popularization of this literacy and its attitude has two sociologically significant outcomes.

First, an odd social space, a kind of massive inner circle, was established. This led in turn to the cultivation of insider knowledge needed to enjoy comedy, ads, and parodies that would appear absurd otherwise. Before the 1980s, only a few cynical cultural elites possessed this kind of ironic consumer knowledge. During the 1980s, this selective sensibility was transformed into consumerist cynicism, a mundane device that allowed more viewers to derive entertainment from the mass medium of TV. To enjoy TV's offerings to the fullest extent, viewers had to remain well versed in pertinent information such as the personal data of participants and production staff. Thus, McLuhan's (1964) TV-mediated global village became realized in Japan during the 1980s through comedy and parody.

Cynical Intimacy with TV

This megacommunity did not limit itself to forging a complicit relationship between the content creators, who were reveling in their wit as they churned out industry-insider jokes, and the content viewers, who in turn shared a strong affinity for the industry. The ironic distance between viewers and clichés cultivated in the TV culture of the 1980s simultaneously gave rise to a general cynicism toward TV and the media at large. This paradox is the second outcome with important social implications.

"Irony" refers to an attitude that discerns the boundary between communicated content and its genre by reserving judgment on the content itself while honing the aesthetic judgment of the genre, or form. This formalist aestheticism allows the viewer to escape the confines of a normative and sincere evaluation standard and to acquire a metaposition that allows the viewer to adopt a cynical and ironic attitude. Clichéd and formulaic laughter lacks the reflexive, critical stance toward form and genre conventions, thus becoming the object of derision by the ironic viewer.

Upon further analysis, however, I would argue that the mass media as a whole, including news and op-ed content, are more responsible than humor for the dissociation between content and form. In particular, the dissociation between the principles and realities of journalism became all too evident after the 1980s as news programs increasingly incorporated tabloid elements and began airing a constant stream of sensational content. The connoisseurs of irony would never have failed to notice this dissociation—or, in Niklas Luhmann's (1985) words, the discrepancies between mass media systems and journalism. Consequently, the irony mobilized in appreciation of the Tunnels' humor was transformed into a cynical approach toward mass media as a whole. In this way, the TV culture of the 1980s gave rise to a population that approached the TV industry not only with an ironic literacy and an intimate relationship but also with cynicism.

In summary, pure TV of the 1980s cultivated the following: (1) love for the media in the form of commitment to an insider megacommunity that was welded together via communications media, and (2) cynicism toward the media. These two developments paved the way toward establishing an ambivalent viewership that possessed cynicism born from intimacy. This in turn became the foundation for the 2channeler mind-set.

The Happy Marriage of Irony and an Insider Culture

The ironic attitude toward the media that characterized the 1980s and the antimedia mentality that gained purchase from the year 2000 onward are not identical. The antimedia culture in 2ch materialized in many forms. One example is the formulaic and ongoing criticism of the Asahi newspaper and TV network, because they represent the dominant news media. Another more specific example is the Shonan Trash Pickup Off[line] plan organized on 2ch. Participants subverted a beach cleanup organized by Fuji TV's *27-Hour TV Show* in the Shonan area by arriving earlier and picking up all the trash before the TV crew and official participants arrived. 2channelers were protesting Fuji TV's exclusive coverage of the World Cup, during which it devoted airtime to the fourth-place Korean team, which was a sponsoring country, but did not give any coverage to Turkey, which had come in third place. Another example of this antimedia attitude is the feverish accusations leveraged at NHK (Japan's public television network) about a special program featuring a mentally impaired child. 2channelers picked apart details of the program and insisted that the child's performance was faked. 2ch's antimedia sentiment seems too zealous to be summed up as mere cynicism. Where does this emotional excess come from?

To understand where this excess comes from, we must first recognize some key differences between the audiences of the 1980s and today. In the 1980s, the insider megacommunity was sustained by the mass media industry, and the two were in a complicit relationship. In contrast, the interactive space of 2ch subtly devalues the role of mass media.

In the 1980s, the identity of "the industry" was clear; insider knowledge existed precisely because the media industry defined and purveyed backstage information. Though this may seem obvious, insider knowledge such as the comedian Sanma Akaishi's womanizing or the spacey personality of the Tunnels' manager was not actually hidden from the audience. The viewers' desire for comedy drove the constant stockpiling of insider information accessed through radio shows, TV programs, and magazines. The privilege of defining the boundaries of the insider community—what was on the surface (the sincere) and what lay beneath (the ironic)—belonged to the media. The insider community was underwritten by the third party of the mass media industry and followed its lead.

In contrast, 2channelers place primary value on communication that maintains the insider community culture and relationships. Rather than occupying the role of an outside party that underwrites the community's existence, the mass media industry becomes a fellow interlocutor providing source material for engagement and conversation. For example, in a forum thread about live evening-news programs, comments disparage the cheap sense of justice displayed by reporters and commentators. For example, users mobilized 2ch's unique lexicon to ridicule a reporter stationed at a railroad crossing who yelled at pedestrians trying to slip by the closing gates, "What makes you think you have the right to do that?!" 2channelers are primarily concerned with perpetuating their ironic 2chisms and ASCII art–filled communication. To them, TV and newspapers are merely source materials for their own communication.

The inner circle no longer exists for the media; the media exist for the inner circle. From a sociological point of view, 2ch marks a departure from an instrumental rationality that supports the existing social order. Instead, it is a social space that produces an extreme form of *connective* rationality that supports ongoing communicative actions and reactions that maintain the community.

In this space centering on the maintenance of social connections, mass media are one of many sources of discussion topics, part of the mix with other sources such as personal journal sites and webcam footage. Despite losing their privileged position as a source of information, mass media continue to posture as watchdogs and the voice of the people. Confident in their ability to see through this pretense, the cynics attack the disparity between ideology and reality, scornfully bursting the inflated ego of the mass media. This dynamic has produced a happy union between the insider community's desire for social connection and its cynical scrutiny of the mass media. In the 1980s, viewers related to the mass media but not to one another as cynical viewers, so these two propensities were kept separate. The uniting of these viewer propensities through the medium of 2ch resulted in an effervescence of fervent critique of the mass media.

The subtle codependence between 2ch and the mass media means that the discourse about 2ch tends to be polarized between those who celebrate 2ch as a form of alternative media and those who dismiss 2ch as "bathroom graffiti." The former laud 2channelers' cynicism toward mass media as proof of their advanced media literacy, and the latter point to 2channelers' self-serving avoidance of serious discourse as proof that they lack literacy. As Otsuka (2004) has also stated, neither view takes 2ch's complexity sufficiently into account, failing to see the deep link between 2ch's irony and focus on social connection. 2channelers are not trying to resist the media as much as 2ch's proponents would like to believe. Conversely, while 2channelers may be simply having fun, they are not as oblivious to their own crudeness as the critics would like to believe, either.[7] This obstinate refusal to cater to either side is what separates 2ch from the cynicism of the 1980s, which danced to the tune of corporations and the media industry.

The Structural Transformation of Communication

Why did 2ch's peculiar mode of communication emerge in the late 1990s?

The primary factor was the popularization of the Internet, beginning with the spread of consumer software and the web in the mid-1990s. Before that period, users primarily participated in highly organized public debates in online forums purveyed by commercial media industries. As the 1990s drew to a close, the Internet suddenly became a mass communications medium (Shibauchi 2003). What inevitably followed from this period of online growth was the birth of online forums with an "underground" feel, such as *Ayashii World* (Sketchy World) and *Amezou*, and its official successor, 2ch.

Some saw the birth of 2ch as an indicator of the decline of online communication, but in many ways 2ch embodies the potential of the Internet. Its unique characteristics, such as the uncensored synchronous exchange of opinion, anonymity, and the self-satisfying goal of community maintenance, drove interaction on the site.[8] 2ch's threaded-forum format and lack of user IP logging merely accelerated the realization of the inherent potential of the Internet. The popularization of the Internet in the late 1990s was the technical backdrop for the happy union.

More significantly, the late 1990s also saw a structural change in communication between youth—the increasing importance of social connection relative to that of social order.

For example, in the consumerist culture of the 1980s, youth were expected to display symbols of social status by digesting and mobilizing the value system presented to them by the mass media. Although cynicism did exist to an extent, youth constrained their status displays to the symbolic order prescribed by the mass media. In this sense, a performative relationship existed between youth and mass media. The external entity of the mass media continuously defined value systems, which were performed by the audience consumers from their own vantage points.

Starting in the mid-1990s, however, youth commitment to value systems provided by what Lacan (1968) would term "the Other" began to weaken. Instead, youth began to give priority to their connections with peers and friends. Notably, these connections were not reinforced by shared hobbies and other external topics but rather by the fact that maintaining these connections was a goal in and of itself. For example, young people took up mobile phones for self-contained communication intended to maintain social connection rather than to convey information. In a community that lacks grounding in shared values and ideologies, it becomes more important to avoid actions that may disrupt the inner circle than to remain within the Other's prescribed order. The demise of the mass media's domination over youth culture thus paved the path toward the furtive yet determined rise of a kingdom of social connection embodied by 2ch.[9]

This shift in youth culture during the 1990s has been the subject of ongoing scrutiny. For example, sociologist Tomohiko Asano (1999) conducted studies in 1992 and 1993 and characterized youth as exhibiting: (1) high mobility in and out of communities, with multiple affiliations; (2) pursuit of intimacy within their communities of choice; (3) a "consummatory" inclination to enjoy social connection as an end in itself. Asano has described the "selective commitment" observed in communication among youth: "The first two conditions would be met by consumer and market-centered transactions that support relationships with limited contexts, and with no interpersonal interaction. However, such relations are a means to a specific end, such as maximizing profit or improving productivity. By contrast, selective commitment means that people are interacting because of the pleasure in the social communication itself. For example, in instant messaging and forum postings, many users enjoy the act itself rather than what is being communicated" (51).

In other words, it is not that youth interpersonal relations have become diluted; their relationships are undergoing a transformation in which they seek affiliation in numerous, discrete communities. Other sociologists have also analyzed the changes in youth sociability that Asano observed and put forth their own theories. For example, Shinji Miyadai's (1995) youth-culture theory centers on the shift from "meaning" to "intensity" as the driver of social relationships. Ken Ohira (1995) has developed a theory of the emerging ethic of "kindness," and Hiroki

Azuma (2001; republished as Chapter 2 in this volume) argues that the otaku subculture has entered an "animalistic" era that lacks narrative depth.

This kingdom of social connections is not the sole domain of a small number of 2ch troublemakers. Many youth abhor 2ch, but they may actually inhabit a similar social space, using their cell phones to send "live" commentary to their friends about the creepy middle-aged man they encountered on the train or the lame pun their teacher just made in class. Looking to their everyday world for source material for reinforcing social connections, such youth are no different from 2ch users who draw on TV programs and use computers. 2ch is both symbol and symptom of an interactive reality produced from a desire for social connection, where media content is a servant to the maintenance of this particular form of communication.

Romanticism at the Far Reaches of Irony

In this space of self-generating social connections, mass media's discrepancy between ideology and reality is repurposed as source material to maintain connectedness. I do not think this is a reality that we should condemn, as it is not lamentable. Hidemi Suga (2003) has argued that 2ch-esque irony provides opportunities to criticize the mass media and the intellectual community, both of which had become self-aggrandizing cartels through the years. However, 2ch's pursuit of social connection has eroded its cynicism in recent years, resulting in a twisted political romanticism centered on the pursuit of emotional thrills and empathy.

I have stated above that irony is a cultural form that notes and foregrounds discrepancies between information (content) and its delivery method (form). This attitude is indispensible in criticism employing parody, satire, and other rhetorical devices. Because of the lack of focus on content and concept, however, irony can too easily become an end in itself.

What began as principled attacks on discrepancies between mass media's ideology and reality have changed into an activity seeking to perpetuate ironic communication, leading to a paranoid attitude that aggressively seeks discrepancies between form and content. *Uyo-chu* users who now infest 2ch exhibit this tendency. The term is derived from *uyoku* (right-wingers) and *chuubou* (middle-school kids) and refers to those who indulge themselves in immature, extremely reactionary postings. The actual intentions and content delivered by media companies such as Asahi are unimportant to uyo-chu, who fixate on the format and institution itself. Even if Asahi were to produce content they approved of, they would put a conspiratorial spin on it with comments such as "This is part of Asahi's plan" and "Asahi's desperate to redeem itself." No matter how substantive a news piece may be, it is automatically categorized as source material for cynicism if it is published by Asahi.

Eiji Oguma and Yoko Ueno (2003) have written about the anti-Asahi stance of a local chapter of the Japanese Society for History Textbook Reform.[10] "It seemed as though you'd have something to talk about with people sitting next to you who weren't the same age as you and came from totally different backgrounds as long as you criticized Asahi" (138). Critique has lost its function as critical irony and has become merely a mechanism to maintain social connection with an insider community.

This reification of irony is simultaneously giving rise to twisted romanticism. I have often come across analyses arguing that 2ch's anti-media principles are an outburst of sincere outrage toward the hypocrisy of the media industry, but I believe this is jumping to an unjustified conclusion.

To describe the opposition between 2ch and commercial media as a fight between truthfulness and hypocrisy is a simple restatement of 2channelers' charges about the discrepancy between the mass media's ideology and reality. For example, the anti-Korean and anti-leftist rhetoric of uyo-chu 2ch participants should not be understood as candor as much as a symbolic display of what participants pass off as candor for their inner circle. The flexible nature of these displays makes pinning down "truthfulness" or "candor" even more challenging. Deliberately taking up unpopular positions, 2channelers are in many ways idealists who construct a romantic self-image as whistle-blowers of hidden realities, and not as realists who make brutally honest statements. They seem to believe in journalistic integrity even more than do journalists themselves. 2channelers sometimes exhibit extraordinary acts of heroic justice and shed tears over old-fashioned narratives such as *Train Man* that are far from being ironic.

After an arsonist set fire to the origami cranes in Hiroshima's Peace Memorial Park in 2003, 2ch initiated the 140,000 Origami Cranes project. The project's slogans were "No Political Ideology" and "Stop Bitching and Just Fold." As Peter Sloterdijk (1988) noted in explicating the link between Nazism and cynicism, when irony becomes purified to the extreme, it erodes irony itself and causes a recurrence of its naive, utter opposite, romanticism. 2channelers like to believe that their commitments are not in anti-leftist sentiments but in romanticism that transcends leftist and rightist ideologies.

How we find romanticism at the far reaches of irony, and sincerity emerging from social communication and critique of mass media, follows that same path as pure TV's transformation of cynicism into empathy and the emergence of the social discursive spaces in the 1990s from the mass media of the 1980s.

We now have a cynicism in which critique has been eroded by the fact that irony itself has become its purpose, and by a romanticism that is all too simplistic. Put differently, it is cynicism for the purpose of cynicism combined with an empathetic ethic that resides at the logical conclusion of cynicism. The two sustain 2ch's social space by forging an ambiguous, complicit relationship with each other. It is not a relationship of action and reaction or of a series of backlashes, nor is it characterized by realism in the form of honest outbursts or revolts against the mainstream citizen. We can discern neither these formalists' political romanticism nor their existential stake in formalism if we focus on the leftist and rightist content of their posts. As Sloterdijk (1988) stated, "Instinct is the vanity of the cynic; cynical people perform the self as a kind of style and a kind of demonstration. At the core of this is a kind of existentialism" (118).

2ch continues to waver between the spirit of irony cultivated in the 1980s and the instinctive communication method of the 1990s that foregrounded social connection. An adequate description of 2ch's ambivalence is the starting point for a true critique of Japan's cynical nationalism or cynical romanticism.

Notes

1. 2channel, 2ch.net, or "channel 2," is pronounced "nichanneru," or "nichan" for short. The term is derived from the fact that the two public television channels are Channels 1 and 3 in Japan, and there is no Channel 2.

2. Some posit that this edited version is the definitive version of the narrative. For instance, Genichiro Takahashi (*Asahi Shimbun*, November 28, 2004) has stated the following: "Strictly speaking, *Train Man*'s narrative occurred between March 14th and May 17th. However, the book omitted the last day's worth of posts without comment. The reason for this was that the online *Train Man* continued to post after the 'happy ending' and wrote about events leading almost right up to when he and 'Hermes' finally had sex. . . . The book succeeds in presenting itself as a pure romance by omitting the posts of May 17th, keeping the final events shrouded in mystery." I actually agree that this tactic worked for the book. Deriding the book's innocent portrayal of events was a common occurrence in 2ch from early on, however. Comments ran the gamut from "So it was all staged after all" to "We know that, but we're enjoying it anyway." I would therefore like to emphasize that readers were cognizant of this fact. *Train Man* was born in a social space in which the desire to expose the gimmicks of media production mingled with the inclination toward ironic empathy. In that sense, I believe that analysis sites such as *Train Man's Timetable* are the twin brothers of the book version of the narrative.

3. *Winter Sonata* is a Korean television romantic drama series that was released in 2003 in Japan by satellite television and then broadcast TV in 2004 by the Japanese public television network NHK. The series became extremely popular in Japan, as in particular did the lead actor, Bae Yong Joon. *Crying out Love*, published in 2001, is the best-selling novel of all time in Japan. In 2004, it was released as a movie and then adapted for television. The story focuses on a bittersweet teenage love story.

4. *All Night Nippon* is a popular late-night radio program that began in 1967 and continues today. The program mixes music with DJ commentary and guest appearances, and it is considered a key source of popular culture referents and information. The Fuji TV network is one of the five major private television networks. During the 1970s and 1980s, the network pioneered shows that developed a uniquely wacky child-and-youth cultural style and attitude that were in opposition to the more established, serious, and "adult" culture that dominated the other networks, the public NHK network in particular.

5. Some of the key shows in this genre included Takeshi Kitano's *Genki ga Deru Terebi* (TV That Gives You Energy) and *Oretachi Hyokin-Zoku* (We Are the Goofy Gang), and shows featuring the comedy pair the Tunnels as hosts, such as *Minasan no Okagedesu* (Thanks to You All).

6. The most popular show in this genre is *Hachijidayo—Zennin Shuugou!* (It's Eight O'Clock—Everyone Get Together!).

7. Zenhitei (2002) has said the following regarding 2ch festivals: "[2channelers] deliberately get worked up by *matsuri* (festivals/celebrations). To be more precise, they have decided that it is more fun for them to be ruled by this group excitement. From their perspective, they are not actual idiots, but are instead having fun acting the role of the duped idiot" (74).

8. Initially, the posts did not display any form of user ID, and IP addresses were not logged.

9. Within this kingdom of social connection, anonymity paradoxically causes users to desire self-affirmation from others and from themselves. Eiji Otsuka (2004) commented, "I am getting the sense that self-esteem and pride, which have become specters of the modern ego 'I,' have become even more inflated—or perhaps just more conspicuous—in online environments. Currently, useful freeware and individuals who translate subtitles, even if the act is illegal, are respected in online communities. Even if the individuals are only identified by handle names, validating their actions by gaining respect for 'I' is indicative of their desire for self-affirmation based on a modern yet old-fashioned sense of self-esteem" (155).

10. The Japanese Society for History Textbook Reform is a group that developed to advocate for a version of a history textbook with a nationalist stance.

References

Asada, Akira. 1987. Parody no shuen, moden he no kaiki. *Nikkei Image Kisho Kansoku*, October.

Asano, Tomohiko. 1999. Shinmitsusei no atarashii katachi e. In *Minna bocchi no sekai*, ed. Hidenori Tomita and Masayuki Fujimura, 41–57. Tokyo: Kouseisha Kouseikaku.

Azuma, Hiroki. 2001. *Dobutsu ka suru postmodern: Otaku kara mita nihon shakai*. Tokyo: Kodansha.

Lacan, Jacques. 1968. *The language of the self: The function of language in psychoanalysis*. Baltimore: Johns Hopkins University Press.

Luhmann, Niklas. 1985. *A sociological theory of law*. Trans. Klaus A. Ziegert. Oxford: Oxford University Press.

McLuhan, Marshall. 1964. *Understanding media: The extensions of man*. New York: McGraw-Hill.

Miyadai, Shinji. 1995. *Owari naki nichijo wo ikiro*. Tokyo: Chikuma Shobo.

Nakano, Hitori. 2004. *Densha otoko*. Tokyo: Shinkosha.

Oguma, Eiji, and Yoko Ueno. 2003. *"Iyashi" no nationalism*. Tokyo: Keio University Press.

Ohira, Ken. 1995. *Yasashisa no seishin byori*. Tokyo: Iwanami Shoten.

Otsuka, Eiji. 2004. *Monogatari shoumetsu-ron: Character ka suru "watashi," ideology ka suru "monogatari."* Tokyo: Kadokawa Shoten.

Shibauchi, Yasufumi. 2003. Shiron to yoron no henkan souchi: Net yoron no yukue. In *Sengo yoron no media shakaigaku*, ed. Takumi Sato, 243–265. Tokyo: Kashiwa Shobo.

Sloterdijk, Peter. 1988. *Critique of cynical reason*. Trans. Michael Eldred, foreword Andreas Huyssen. Minneapolis: University of Minnesota Press.

Suga, Hidemi. 2003. *JUNK no gyakushuu*. Tokyo: Sakuhinsha.

Zenhitei. 2002. Tako tsuboteki sekai deno ikari, soshite 2 channel. In *Hacker Japan: 2ch chudoku*, ed. Hacker Japan, 74–76. Tokyo: Byakuya Shobo.

4

Strategies of Engagement: Discovering, Defining, and Describing Otaku Culture in the United States

....

LAWRENCE ENG

More than two decades after the word "otaku" entered the vocabulary of young anime and science fiction enthusiasts in Osaka, Japan, the term remains highly contested and fraught with controversy. From its origins to the present day, its use by various parties and across multiple continents has fragmented its meaning. Of course, individual observers will have developed local, fixed meanings of "otaku," but in observing the landscape of how otaku are perceived locally, transnationally, and through time, one sees that the contours are more fluid than ever. The variation and ambiguity surrounding the meaning of "otaku" reminds us that otaku are a distinct subculture composed of individuals who refuse to be pinned down and easily categorized. This complexity and detail surrounding the topic of "otakudom" makes otaku culture an ideal topic of otaku self-/meta-reflection. It is no surprise, therefore, that otaku themselves are often the ones who argue most heatedly about the implications of their subcultural identity. Unpacking arguments such as those are an important foundation of my own otaku studies.

In this chapter, I describe the ways in which the concept of "otaku" was imported to the United States and how it evolved through the period of the 1990s to the present. Looking at specific historical circumstances and the overall shape of that evolution, I propose an "otaku ethic" to define otaku subculture as an object of inquiry that is of value to both researchers and otaku themselves. After first introducing my own otaku identity, this chapter describes the history of how the term was imported and adapted in the United States, and how it is tied to what I have identified as a unique otaku ethic of U.S.-based otaku cultures.

A CARD-CARRYING ACA/OTAKU

If Henry Jenkins (2006) describes himself as an "aca/fan," focusing his academic attentions on the implications of fan-related activities, then perhaps I am an aca/otaku. Whereas Jenkins decided to study fans to justify his own fan identity, I became interested in otaku when I recognized something in otaku culture that resonated with my worldview as a young adult learning to navigate mass media, popular culture, and the larger world of information being opened to me as a fledgling Internet user and brand-new university student.

Another important difference between Jenkins and me is that my otaku identity preceded my academic identity. I went to college and grad school, initially, to become a laboratory scientist, and being an anime otaku was a secondary diversion. As my intellectual trajectory moved toward Science and Technology Studies (STS), however, the importance and significance of otaku (beyond, and possibly even irrespective of, anime and Japan) stayed with me, and the goal of understanding otaku would come to dominate every aspect of my graduate studies. I completed my doctoral dissertation in 2006, focusing on anime otaku culture in the United States, which is the primary topic of this chapter.

In my doctoral work, I drew heavily on my experiences as an anime fan, but I also learned to take a step back from fandom (when appropriate) to create proper distance as an observer. It also gave me a chance to reenter anime otaku culture anew, with the fresh enthusiasm of a new fan, but also with an anthropological eye for detail, looking into corners of fandom that I normally would have ignored. I was an otaku turned academic who became an otaku once more, making me wonder which part of the label ("aca" versus "otaku") takes precedence.

I have been an anime fan since 1980 or so, grew up as part of the generation watching shows such as *Robotech* and other adapted anime on American television, and became a bona fide member of anime fandom when I joined the Cornell Japanese Animation Society as a college freshman in 1994. Through the years, I have been a member of several university anime clubs, participated heavily in anime-related online communities, attended numerous anime conventions, spoken on panels at several of those conventions, produced websites and a blog about anime, and collected thousands of dollars worth of anime-related merchandise. That does not include the additional events I attended or at which I spoke, interviews I conducted, and other informational resources that I collected as part of my formal research on American otaku. I continue to write about otaku online and in print, and I try to attend several conventions each year to talk to my fellow fans about otaku culture.

OTAKU IN THE UNITED STATES

Today's U.S. anime fandom has evolved from a small group of enthusiasts in the 1970s to what is now a massive and diverse subculture. In Chapter 7 I describe this history of how anime was introduced in the United States in tandem with the growth of otaku subcultures. While the fandom has grown and diversified through these decades, the influence of some of the early defining cultural frames and social practices remains resilient even today. In particular, the period from the mid-1980s to late 1990s, when otaku culture emerged as a distinct subculture, was a pivotal time in solidifying the contours of anime fandom. As a member of the generation of U.S. anime fans that thrived in the mid-1990s, I have a particularly strong connection to what we did during that period, how it grew out of the activities and worldview of the previous generation, and how our activities continue to shape the face of fandom today. At the center of what we did and who we were is the term "otaku," which we used to describe ourselves and our culture without fully understanding what it all meant from a larger point of view. For many years, I have tried to unpack the otaku concept as my fellow fans and I understood it and to link it to the evolution of anime and anime fandom in the United States. For us, being otaku meant that we were instrumental in bringing anime to the United States on our own terms, independently and sometimes irrespective of commercial interests. It had to do with our sense of individualism, a do-it-yourself attitude, a philosophy and ethic that delineated right and wrong within our community, as well as best practices and high standards. It was a time when the media we dealt with were rare but common enough that we could form a community around them, and each of us could seek a meaningful role within that community.

In the years following the birth and rise of the Otaku Generation, the word "otaku" became widespread and attracted mainstream media attention in Japan. "Otaku" has been widely used to label and describe (in various, often contradictory, ways) a subculture consisting of fans of mass media and popular culture. The competing meanings and interpretations of otaku culture, especially among English-speaking fans in the United States, is discussed in the section to follow. In this section, I consider how the term was imported into the English-speaking world, eventually entering into the consciousness of many Americans, fans and nonfans alike.

The first widespread exposure that U.S. fans had to the term was in 1988. A fledgling anime studio in Japan, Gainax, produced an OAV known as *Aim for the Top! Gunbuster*.[1] Gainax consisted of young animators who grew up as die-hard fans of anime, got together as amateurs to create their own works, and eventually became professionals. Representing the spirit of the Otaku Generation like no other anime studio before or since, Gainax became legendary and much beloved by otaku. *Gunbuster* deserves special mention here because it is one of the earliest (if not the earliest) anime in which "otaku" is used to refer to fans. In particular, the main protagonist, Noriko Takaya, is called an otaku by her friend Kazumi, who teases her playfully about her knowledge of anime and science fiction. *Gunbuster* also has the distinction of being one of the very first anime videos released in the United States that retained its original Japanese-language audio track and was subtitled in English. Hence, American fans were exposed to "otaku" equals "fan" as early as March 1990, when *Gunbuster* was released in the United States.

It took much more than this single anime series, however, to push the term into widespread recognition in the United States. The term was popularized through a combination of forces: communication at the fan layer, uptake by U.S. media and commentators, and references in actual anime.

Some of the earliest mentions of the term among U.S. fans can be found on Usenet, a communication forum that was central to the early fandom.[2] Usenet archives, therefore, are a useful tool for looking back in time to uncover the history of "otaku" in the United States as a whole.

Below, I present a few representative examples of early writing about otaku in the English language, with quite a few of them appearing on Usenet; those examples highlight the strong emotional reactions and controversy surrounding the word, even when it was initially introduced to American anime fandom.

The very first mention of otaku (in English) on Usenet was on October 10, 1990, in the rec.games.video newsgroup. The post, titled "Which portable is best for you? (LONG)," is a quiz (translated from *Famicon Tsushin*, a Japanese gaming magazine) that readers could take to determine which handheld gaming system he or she should buy (Leo 1990). One of the yes/no questions was:

> 6. "Otaku" sounds kind of perverted. I hate that word.
> [Note: "Otaku" is a word for someone who stays indoors all the time, for example playing video games.]

Since "otaku" is a Japanese word, it is unsurprising that references to "otaku" in English will refer, directly or indirectly, to Japanese sources of information. It is notable that the question itself starts with a negative framing of otaku as sounding "perverted" and generating feelings of "hate." This may be related to the negative fallout and moral panic surrounding the Tsutomu Miyazaki child kidnappings and murders that took place in 1988 through 1989 before Miyazaki's eventual arrest (Kinsella 2000).

On December 7, 1990, a mention of otaku in the soc.culture.japan newsgroup specifically brought up the Miyazaki child kidnappings and murders in Japan: "Also there are some attempts to attribute his crime to a manifestation of a Japanese youth sub-culture, so-called 'OTAKU-ZOKU.' This sub-culture seems to have Japanese origin and nothing related to foreign influence" (Kitagawa 1990). This was a very minor mention in the context of a much longer discussion thread ("Ignorance of Foreign Cultures") about Japanese perceptions of American culture. The author of the quoted post appears to be Japanese, working for NTT Research Labs in Japan.

A seminal article in otaku studies was written by Volker Grassmuck (1990), whose " 'I'm alone, but not lonely': Japanese *Otaku*-Kids Colonize the Realm of Information and Media: A Tale of Sex and Crime from a Faraway Place" was written in December of that year. It is difficult to know, however, when and where it first appeared online, though it was certainly on the web by the mid- to late 1990s, when I first encountered it. Grassmuck's insightful analysis of otaku in Japan did not appear to make a large impact on English-speaking fandom, and his essay was discussed only a handful of times on Usenet between 1993 and 2000. That said, Grassmuck's analysis of otaku remains relevant, and it had a significant impact on journalists and scholars who would later write on the subject.

On May 17, 1991, in the sci.lang.japan newsgroup, Maiko Covington posted "WOTD—May 17, 1991 (the second one)," in which she discussed various Japanese words and their usage. One of the words was "otaku": "-otaku—this is someone who is really really absorbed in a hobby. So you can say 'keiba otaku' 'anime otaku' like that. See, they are so involved in the hobby that they don't have any friends, and so always talk politely (like you do to strangers) to other people, calling them not 'kimi' but 'otaku' instead. All of these people together are referred to as 'otaku zoku' (zoku in kanji)" (Covington 1991). This post reinforces the stereotype that otaku are socially isolated because of their heavy absorption in their hobbies, a theme we will see repeated again and again in fan discussions and debates about otaku.

For anime fans in the United States, the most important exposure to the term came from *Otaku no Video* (1991), a two-part anime OAV created by Gainax. *Otaku no Video* is a fictionalized retelling of Gainax's origins as otaku turned anime professionals, and it also included live-action "documentary" segments that humorously and self-mockingly expounded upon the different types of otaku in Japan. Founding Gainax member Yasuhiro Takeda, in his *The Notenki Memoirs* (2002), writes of *Otaku no Video*: "In the US, this OVA is widely regarded as the otaku bible" (175).

The first public showing of *Otaku no Video*, interestingly enough, was held in the United States on September 1, 1991, at a video room at AnimeCon '91, of which Gainax was a major sponsor.[3] *Otaku no Video* was shown on 16-mm film to an audience of nine people, according to a rec.arts.anime posting by Noel Gamboa (whose Operation X group would later fansub both parts of *Otaku no Video* before its official U.S. release) (Gamboa 1991).

On October 4, 1991, also on rec.arts.anime, David Mou reported that he picked up *Otaku no Video* (part 1 of 2) from Mikado (presumably Mikado Laser in San Francisco's Japantown) (Mou 1991). In the discussion thread that followed, Hitoshi Doi (a longtime anime fan and well-known figure in the online anime community at the time) expressed his displeasure at *Otaku no Video*'s portrayal of otaku, whereas Enrique Conty (another well-known fan on rec.arts.anime) countered by encouraging anime fans to express pride in being part of fandom (Conty and Doi 1991). *Otaku no Video*, officially released in the United States by Animeigo in 1993, became an instant classic among anime fans and remains an important introduction and reference work for anyone interested in otaku culture.

In April 1994, Annalee Newitz wrote a controversial article about otaku in the journal *Bad Subjects* (Newitz 1994). The article, "Anime Otaku: Japanese Animation Fans outside Japan," was widely criticized by fans online who did not appreciate her psychoanalytic and postcolonial interpretation of fandom and anime, which they thought was self-indulgent and overreaching in its conclusions. This article is notable in that it was written by an outsider to fandom who provoked a strong negative reaction among fans.

In September 1994, *Fortune* magazine mentioned otaku in an article about Japan's Internet use: "Many of IIJ's subscribers are corporate users, who account for 60% of the country's E-mail traffic, conducted mostly in their native tongue. Others are otaku, Japan's version of cyberpunks, who were once turned on by high-tech computer animation and cutting-edge comic books. Now they're logging on to and learning about the Internet" (Terry 1994). The *Fortune* article is one of many that would appear describing otaku as a subculture on the cutting edge of technology, especially the Internet. Science fiction author William Gibson also became enamored of otaku, including otaku characters in some of his later novels, including *Idoru* (1997) and *Pattern Recognition* (2003). He describes otaku as "the passionate obsessive, the information age's embodiment of the connoisseur, more concerned with the accumulation of data than of objects" (Gibson 2001).

This overview of early English-language uptake indicates how the term was contested from the start, embodying both negative stereotypes that came from mainstream Japanese perception as well as more fan-centric positive connotations. When "otaku" was imported to the United States, it was not completely stripped of the various connotations it had acquired in Japan, and those connotations would be referenced and revisited often by scholars and fans alike as they sought to delineate the meaning of the term. Some of those connotations were quite negative, echoing the moral panic induced by the Miyazaki murders. Even though some Japanese scholars and academics also saw positive social potential in otaku culture, it was the otaku turned professionals, via *Otaku no Video*, who had the biggest influence on American otaku culture's self-image. Despite some good-natured self-mockery, *Otaku no Video* presented otaku as champions and idealists, facing misunderstanding and difficult odds but triumphing beyond all expectations. *Otaku no Video* resonated with American anime fans who saw like minds and kindred spirits in that anime's characters. While observers of the subculture use the word from time to time, "otaku" is still primarily used among fans as a shared form of self-identification that nonetheless remains problematic among members of that community.

EVOLUTION OF THE OTAKU CONCEPT IN THE UNITED STATES

Even within fandom, the meaning of "otaku" has been a difficult concept to pin down. Its flexibility as a concept has allowed various groups and individuals to use it in widely divergent ways. While "otaku" is often used in America to mean anime/manga fan, without strong positive or negative connotations, some fans use it in a stronger sense, either using "otaku" as a label of sorts for the media, art, genres, and characters they like or as a pejorative, in the same way it has been used by some parties in Japan. When "otaku" is used pejoratively in the United States, we see a close duplication of stereotypes used to describe otaku in Japan, where some describe otaku as being some combination of socially deficient, unhealthily obsessive, concerned with childish things, and unconcerned about hygiene. "Socially deficient" may mean different things for Japanese versus American stereotypes of otaku, however. Japanese otaku are sometimes depicted as hopeless introverts who are seeking escape from the world so they can secretly indulge in their shameful hobbies, whereas American otaku (when "otaku" is used by some fans to mean the worst of fandom) are more often depicted as loud, obnoxious, and brazenly outgoing about their hobbies, interests, and fetishes—so much so that they are seen as invading the comfort zone and personal space of others.

When I present my otaku studies research to American anime fans at fan conventions, I remind them that "otaku" means many different things to many different people, whether they are in Japan, the United States, or elsewhere. No simple dichotomy allows us to say that there is a singular authoritative "Japanese definition of otaku" versus a singular "American definition of otaku." The otaku concept is wholly global now, existing at the confluence of cross-cultural "space of flows," as Castells (1996) might put it. American fans, at least subconsciously aware of the peculiar postmodern, and certainly postnational, nature of their activities, seem to understand this point immediately, even if they have not necessarily expressed it as such before. I also ask anime fans attending my talks how they feel about the word "otaku." These sentiments have changed through time, influenced by the mainstreaming of otaku culture in the United States and combined with fans' becoming more aware of the nuances surrounding the word and identity politics surrounding it.

Otaku culture has become more visible to the American mainstream through several different avenues. Started by fans in the mid-1990s, Otakon is a convention whose tagline, following *Otaku no Video*, is "Convention of Otaku Generation." With only a few hundred attendees in each of its first few years, Otakon has grown into the East Coast's largest annual gathering of American anime fans, boasting more than 25,000 attendees in 2008, occupying most of the Baltimore Convention Center, and bringing people from multiple states to Maryland for a weekend of fun, camaraderie, learning, consumption, and celebration. On the West Coast, Anime Expo remains the largest annual gathering of anime fans in the United States with more than 40,000 attendees in 2008, big enough to warrant a letter from Governor Arnold Schwarzenegger in the program book welcoming out-of-state attendees to California.

In the world of art and fashion, traditional-turned-pop-artist Takashi Murakami has brought otaku aesthetic sensibilities to international audiences previously undreamed of. While concepts such as Superflat, characters such as DOB, and Louis Vuitton handbags have remained off the radar of most American anime fans, Murakami's Kaikai Kiki studio continues to produce works that inspire serious and critical interest in anime and manga culture that lends an overall air of respectability (desired or not) to what everyday fans are interested in. Otaku collections of character figurines, for example, can be seen in a new light when one considers Murakami's "Miss Ko" statue—basically a life-size anime figure—selling for more than $500,000 at an auction by Christie's New York, the prestigious auction house.

Tour companies, such as Pop Japan Travel and Intermixi, have emerged to meet the new demand of American otaku who wish to visit Japan. These companies, often working in conjunction with Japan's tourist industry, offer otaku-oriented tours, promising visits to otaku hot spots such as Akihabara, anime and manga-related museums, and anime studios.

American anime fans encounter "otaku" as a cultural concept even at mainstream book retail stores. Bookstores that sell anime and manga-related merchandise will sometimes label that merchandise as being for otaku, and it is not uncommon to see young fans reading voraciously on the floor of the manga aisles. *Otaku USA* magazine, published bimonthly and covering topics such as anime, manga, video games, special-effects shows, and other topics of interest to American otaku, is also available at major bookstores around the country. A slogan of *Otaku USA*, displayed at its convention booths and on its *MySpace* page, is "It's not a sickness . . . it's an honor." The slogan highlights one of the prevalent negative stereotypes of otaku that American fans are often aware of, but it reclaims the word as a badge of honor.

With anime and manga both becoming increasingly mainstream in the United States, resistance to the usage of "otaku" appears to be decreasing among fans I have spoken to at conventions, with only a minority holding onto a strictly negative definition of the word. Certainly there are fans who use "otaku" casually to simply mean anime/manga fans, devoid of strongly negative or positive connotations. For my own studies, however, I have mostly been interested in the strategic ways people use "otaku" in negative or positive senses to bolster their self-identity and the communities to which they belong. Some proudly self-identify as otaku and use the term to characterize their community, while others distance themselves from otaku groups or use the term to refer to contamination of their community. In other cases, some people self-identify as otaku as a way of expressing shame in themselves and in their activities. I have never met such an individual in person, but I have seen expressions of otaku self-loathing online.

Since definitions of "otaku" are tied so closely to the self-image of American fans, they inevitably engender debates and mixed emotions. Some fans think that "otaku" is an inappropriate label for the fandom because of the negative connotation of the term, particularly in Japan. Among those who dislike the term, some not only want to avoid being called "otaku," but they also want to reserve that word for those fans they have encountered who exhibit stereotypically negative traits. Pushing "otaku" to the fringes of their subculture, those fans wish to express that they are the same as the rest of society in an attempt to defuse negative perceptions of anime and manga fandom—which can either be normal and healthy (them) or abnormal and unhealthy (everyone else). Other fans, however, use the term to refer generically to anime fans or seek to reclaim the word as a badge of honor. Being otaku can mean something more, something different, and also something positive—or at least potentially so.

IN SEARCH OF AN OTAKU ETHIC

Far too often, discussions of otaku culture have asked the question of whether being an otaku is bad. Even when people answer no, the next logical question—what makes being an otaku good?—is rarely asked. The negative aspects of being a fan, and fans who make other fans uncomfortable, are everyday concerns for anime fans. What I think is more worthwhile, however, is for fans to understand the significance and value of their activities in light of those who do not engage in such activities. Making such contrasts is especially important since otaku tend to be quite insular and tend to socialize within their specialized communities of interest. As otaku have had to insulate themselves against outsiders who would ostracize them for being different, one natural reaction for otaku is to reassert that they are just like everyone else, even though it is their differences that make them interesting.

As both an academic and someone whose identity formation was heavily influenced by the concept of otaku, I am interested in (a) the underlying factors behind otaku behaviors and (b) the broader implications of otaku culture on society. More specifically, as a scholar in the field of STS, I wanted to know what Otaku Studies had to offer our understandings of how publics use science (defined here as forms of knowledge and learning) and technology in everyday life, and how STS could help fandom scholars understand the significance of otaku. Other academics, notably scholars in Japan, have done an excellent job describing and theorizing the origins, meanings, and activities of otaku in Japan.[4]

But I wanted to understand otaku from a transnational perspective, in which otaku need not come from Japan nor even necessarily have an investment in Japanese cultural products. Otaku culture was first identified in Japan because of specific historical circumstances, and anime and manga became important products to Japanese otaku because of related circumstances, but those circumstances are not wholly unique to Japan; consequently, neither are otaku. My subcultural explorations are intended to speak with otaku and otaku scholars around the world.

Furthermore, I have a strong personal belief that otaku culture, at its best, has much to offer in terms of unique strategies of engagement with science and technology in the everyday lives of non-otaku. Being hard-core otaku is undoubtedly not for everyone, but for those who live in mass media–rich, heavily consumer-oriented societies, otaku philosophy and behaviors may offer some useful lessons and ideas to consider. For otaku themselves, I hope that sustained and evolving self-reflection on the (positive) meaning of their subculture will result in progress for otaku. I consider fans, therefore, to be a very important audience of my work, which is why I routinely speak at fan-oriented conventions and other events in addition to more formal venues. Just as Steven Levy (1984) offered a "hacker ethic" to delineate the hacker subculture, I offer an "otaku ethic" to highlight the values that inform otaku philosophy and practice.

THE OTAKU ETHIC

The otaku ethic is a list of items that I use to define, somewhat platonically, an idealized portrait of otaku culture. Otaku are likely to be described by my schema more or less—sometimes much more or much less. My demarcation of otaku is prescriptive, laying out a specific vision of otaku utopia. It is also descriptive, based upon my analysis of third-party descriptions of what otaku means and my own real-life experiences with otaku (Eng 2002). Documenting the otaku ethic was the necessary first step in my ethnographic study of otaku culture in the United States, the full results of which are documented elsewhere (Eng 2006). It served as the groundwork to define whom my informants were and what I needed to learn from them.

What I present below is a brief summary of the otaku ethic. Real people adhere to the otaku ethic in varying degrees, and the major lesson

I learned studying otaku in the real world is that the ratio of idealized "hard-core" otaku to those who adhere to parts of the otaku ethic in varying degrees is quite small, and it is possibly getting smaller through time as anime and manga are becoming more mainstream in the United States. While depictions of the few hard-core otaku might be entertaining and sensational, it is probably more accurate, useful, and fair to show how individual aspects of otaku culture have become important to people from various walks of life. The otaku ethic that I describe grows out of my observations of the U.S.-based anime fandom and how it localized the concept through specific cultural references and practices. Elements of the otaku ethic are shared with other U.S. fandoms and with otaku culture in Japan, but the otaku ethic is unique in representing a unique confluence of both. Unlike fandoms that surround domestic media, anime fandom requires a level of commitment and otaku "fannishness" that exceeds the more casual consumption possible with domestic media. Instead of merely representing a cultish engagement with a popular media form, otaku engagement represents a cultish engagement with a media form that is relatively inaccessible because of its foreign origin, or that is otherwise uncommon for other reasons. While it is beyond the scope of this chapter to do a full comparison with other forms of U.S. fandom, my description aims to elucidate what makes otakudom unique as a transnational and highly wired fan phenomenon.

Information is the most important thing, but information does not have fixed intrinsic value. The essence of information is secrecy; the utility of information comes from its movement.

The otaku concept of information is different from the hacker or cyberlibertarian notion that information is nonrival (meaning that its value is the same no matter how many people use it), and that it "wants to be (or should be) free." In contrast, otaku view information as having relative (as opposed to intrinsic) value, and otaku are most concerned with information that is valuable. Information value, following from Claude Shannon's definition (as summarized by Goonatilake 1991), is the statistically based difference between what is uncertain and what is already known or widely available. Therefore, that which is similar to what is already known or is predictable has low information value. Knowledge that describes the unknown and things that are rare have high information value. When information is freed and widely distributed, therefore, information value is necessarily lost. As such, otaku hoard information and do not share it indiscriminately. They share high-value information and goods only when there is an obvious benefit to them, whether in the form of monetary reward, increased recognition/reputation, or other information in exchange for what was shared. In summary, we might say that otaku trade more than they share.

Their focus on information value means that otaku care about trivia that others would ignore, and they create value where it did not previously exist. Otaku obsession with trivia is exemplified at anime conventions, where fans square off with each other to demonstrate their superior knowledge of anime and related subjects. It is not atypical for otaku conversations to be full of obscure references, in-jokes, and challenges. This obsessive attention to detail may help to explain the appeal of anime to American fans. In addition to theories about anime's containing familiar elements that Western fans can relate to but that are presented in novel ways, one may also consider the fact that anime contains incredible amounts of detail to be learned and remembered, especially because of the serial nature of some shows and franchises, such as *Mobile Suit Gundam*, which features a fictional universe of astounding scope and detail. American otaku, hungering for entertainment that sates their need for information, are drawn to such shows, and those shows deliver because many of them were created by otaku themselves.

Otaku draw connections between mundane products that others would not bother examining. Otaku also debate the significance of media products in ways that even the creators would never have imagined or expected. Non-otaku watch episodes of a television show and perhaps discuss them briefly with their friends or coworkers. Otaku, conversely, participate in forums to engage in long-running analyses of shows, even ones that are no longer being broadcast. Otaku create online resources dissecting every aspect of a show; cataloging things such as its creators, actors, and other staff; and creating databases to connect related works so that every show or episode can be examined in a larger context as opposed to being a single piece of ephemeral and disposable entertainment.

Otaku typically achieve information mastery through depth, knowing the deep details of a few things instead of focusing on the surface details of many things. Examples of this were some of the early "anime shrines" on the web, where a fan or group of fans would collect as much information as possible on a given anime, including the most trivial of details as well as deep analyses of the show, and publish massive amounts of media (images, videos, music, etc.) scanned from books, magazines, and other sources. Part of the motivation for this behavior, and a reason it is not as common today, is that anime was scarce in the United States in the early days of the web, so fans extracted the maximum amount of entertainment value from every show they could get their hands on, whereas modern otaku have a plethora of titles and other entertainment options available to them, making a depth-first approach less attractive than a wide-sampling approach. I call an otaku's decision to explore by going deep into a few things versus sampling widely, and how he or she optimizes that choice, the Otaku's Dilemma (Eng 2006). We also see otaku information philosophy expressed in the fansubbing and file-sharing activities of otaku, in which anime fans in the United States illegally share anime with each other, but with a relatively strict and highly nuanced ethic surrounding fansubs (see Chapter 8).

Appropriation is a valid strategy for information management, identity reconstruction, and resistance not only for marginalized groups but also for "reluctant insiders."

Otaku can also be understood as a culture of resistance, based on traditional understandings of subculture (such as described by Hebdige 1979). In particular, otaku present an interesting case study of a technologically engaged middle-class subculture. I characterize otaku as usually being middle class because being a *successful* otaku requires minimum access to resources and information, and that requires a certain amount of capital or disposable income. Certainly, one does not have to be middle class to be an otaku, to engage in otaku behaviors, or to espouse otaku ideals. Working-class otaku exist, but they do not necessarily have the abundant time or monetary resources to succeed in the competitive landscape that otaku inhabit. This situation may be changing, however, as the Internet (and increased access to it) makes more media and information free, or at least cheap. As such, otaku in the postscarcity society enabled by a cyberlibertarian sharing culture may look very different from otaku of previous generations.

Being middle class places otaku near the centers of society, and not at its margins, which leads to otaku resistance looking different from other forms of subcultural resistance, such as the resistance carried out by the marginalized. In particular, we may define otaku as "reluctant insiders" opposing the hegemony of inclusion as opposed to exclusion, and their resistance is oblique, based on appropriation rather than rejection of media and other technology that they fundamentally enjoy.[5]

Although otaku are not a free-information-sharing culture, they are not a shopping culture bound to mainstream markets and channels of consumption. Otaku do not rely on authorized sources of product information and distribution but have established their own self-defined networks of information and trade, placing value on products independently of "suggested retail price." For example, instead of acquiring goods at mainstream shopping malls (which are unlikely to carry the obscure items that otaku seek), otaku may frequent specialty stores, online auctions, or informal bazaarlike markets such as anime convention dealers' rooms. Instead of using advertising or traditional media to get information about products, otaku rely on word-of-mouth recommendations from people they trust in their social networks.

Furthermore, otaku appropriate ready-made products (often media related) and subvert them for their own ends. VCRs, computers, and the Internet are turned into potentially subversive tools for distribution of anime that was never intended for American consumption. Oftentimes, otaku avoid mass-market products altogether, and the subculture creates its own (often derivative) products, which it can trade for other products, money, or other forms of information both within the community and outside of it. Otaku-created derivative works, such as self-published comics known as *doujinshi*, use established characters in ways that might be wildly out of character (and are often sexually explicit, even when the source material is not). Anime shows are turned into music videos or fan parodies. Otaku, therefore, are not necessarily the target audience of the products they consume. American women obsess over shows intended for Japanese boys, and American men are proud fans of shows intended for Japanese girls. Finally, by interpreting culture in unauthorized and unexpected ways, otaku have developed nuanced and alternative positions on social issues that affect them (such as the depiction of sex in visual media).[6]

Networks can be used for personal (and collective) gain.

As already described briefly in this chapter, otaku use various networks heavily, so much so that I consider it a defining aspect of otakudom. If appropriation of media is one form of otaku resistance, so is their appropriation of networks. Other subcultures use networks of all sorts for information sharing and socializing, but otaku are a special case because their primary motivation, goal, and object of desire is information itself. Some subcultures can exist without information networks, but otaku cannot. To understand otaku in this context, it has been helpful to apply the lessons of Science Studies, whereupon it becomes clear that otaku have appropriated the structures and methods of science (which they may have learned from their schooling experiences) in addition to technology.

Although they are not part of the formal institutions of science, otaku adopt social practices of scientific culture in their everyday lives and as participants in an informal information economy—or ecology (Rosenberg 1997). Otaku are implicated in huge social networks of associations made possible by the development of communications network infrastructures such as the Internet, which are similar in many ways to networked scientific culture. Like scientists, otaku communicate via networks and use complex forms of rhetoric to establish information value and prestige (which distinguishes them from the old-school hacker ethic, which does not believe in information elitism). Bruno Latour (1987) makes the case that scientists cannot be successful without a network within which they can win over audiences and gain allies. Likewise, I would assert that otaku are also dependent on networks, whether those networks are formal, informal, based on close associations, based on loose associations, face-to-face, or online (in all kinds of venues). It is the community structures of otaku that allow their subculture to engender large-scale change. Otaku use of various networks will be discussed in more detail in Chapter 7.

OTAKU STUDIES EXPANDED

Through the schema described above, I have tried to understand otaku in terms of their norms and philosophies, their productive activities, their self-organization, and the ways in which they challenge orthodoxy—especially regarding information, consumption, and the role of fantasy in society. Japan is recognized as being important to the history and contemporary development of otaku culture, but I have refrained from defining otaku culture as being uniquely Japanese, instead emphasizing the ways in which otaku culture is transnational in scope. While the term "otaku" is undeniably of Japanese origin, just as with anime, the enthusiasm with which fans debate the term indicate how transnational the associated cultural referents are. As otaku scholars, we have the opportunity to seek out the places around the world where otaku culture emerged. By determining how and why that happened, we improve our understandings of otaku, giving us theories that address both the similarities between otaku in different places as well as the specific nuances brought about by cultural and geographic differences. A global perspective on otaku also helps us to move beyond culturally specific negative stereotypes, so that otaku might be viewed one day as liberatory and healing figures and not the causes or symptoms of societal ills.

Otaku culture and the underlying otaku ethic are tied to conditions found in media-saturated, highly networked, and ultramodern or postmodern societies. Japanese fan culture and anime provided a set of referents that mobilized a unique subcultural imagination in diverse locations around the world. In many ways, the otaku ethic is a proactive response to certain shared conditions that youth encounter in media-saturated contexts, a response that has given rise to a transnational subculture that is growing in size and scope. The spread of the otaku concept and ethic in the United States is an important case study in understanding the ways in which subcultures cohere across national boundaries given similar social and cultural conditions, paving the way toward understanding cultural and social movements that are both highly specialized and expansively transnational.

Notes

1. OAV stands for original animation video. It is used interchangeably with OVA. Both acronyms refer to direct-to-video anime.

2. Usenet is an Internet discussion system that predates the World Wide Web.

3. AnimeCon '91 is considered one of the first full-fledged anime conventions in the United States.

4. See, for example: Azuma (2001); Morikawa (2004); Okada (1996).

5. Otaku also are often seen as being marginalized, but given their typically middle-class position, I argue that otaku consciously make choices to self-marginalize in spite of the privileged circles they come from.

6. American anime fans have engaged in numerous debates regarding the ethical and legal implications of anime and manga depicting minors in sexual situations. Despite the sensitive nature of the topic, the viewpoints expressed by otaku in some of these debates have been surprisingly diverse, well stated, and cognizant of the complexities surrounding the issue.

References

Azuma, Hiroki. 2001. "Superflat Japanese postmodernity." hirokiazuma.com, www .hirokiazuma.com/en/texts/superflat_en1.html (retrieved April 28, 2009).

Castells, Manuel. 1996. *The rise of the network society.* Vol. 1 of *The information age: Economy, society and culture.* Malden, MA: Blackwell.

Christie's. 2003. "Lot 4/Sale 1232. Takashi Murakami (b. 1962) Miss ko2." Christie's, www.christies.com/LotFinder/lot_details.aspx?intObjectID=4101155 (retrieved January 5, 2011).

Conty, Enrique, and Hitoshi Doi. 1991. "Otaku No Video/Mikado." rec.arts.anime, http://groups.google.com/group/rec.arts.anime/browse_thread/thread/ 2f8ba581bf9e2da2?q=otaku (retrieved April 28, 2009).

Covington, Maiko. 1991. "WOTD—May 17, 1991 (the second one)." sci.lang.japan, http://groups.google.com/group/sci.lang.japan/msg/64e1619c8735b5e1?dmode= source (retrieved April 28, 2009).

Eng, Lawrence. 2002. "Otak-who? Technoculture, youth, consumption, and resistance. American representations of a Japanese youth subculture." Lawmune's Netspace, www.cjas.org/~leng/otaku.pdf (retrieved April 28, 2009).

———. 2006. "Otaku engagements: Subcultural appropriations of science and technology." PhD diss., Department of Science and Technology Studies, Rensselaer Polytechnic Institute, Troy, NY.

Gamboa, Noel. 1991. "AnimeCon '91." rec.arts.anime, http://groups.google.com/group/ rec.arts.anime/msg/171ea389c5eb2a5b?dmode=source (retrieved April 28, 2009).

Gibson, William. 2001. "Modern boys and mobile girls." Guardian.co.uk: *The Observer,* April 1. www.guardian.co.uk/books/2001/apr/01/sciencefictionfantasyandhorror .features (retrieved April 28, 2009).

Goonatilake, Susantha. 1991. *The evolution of information: Lineages in gene, culture and artefact.* London: Pinter.

Grassmuck, Volker. 1990. "'I'm alone, but not lonely': Japanese *Otaku*-kids colonize the realm of information and media: A tale of sex and crime from a faraway place." http:// waste.informatik.hu-berlin.de/grassmuck/texts/otaku.e.html (retrieved April 28, 2009).

Hebdige, Dick. 1979. *Subculture: The meaning of style.* London: Routledge.

Jenkins, Henry. 2006. *Fans, bloggers, and gamers.* New York: New York University Press.

Kinsella, Sharon. 2000. *Adult manga: Culture and power in contemporary Japanese society.* Honolulu: University of Hawaii Press.

Kitagawa, Masahiro. 1990. "Re: Ignorance of foreign cultures." soc.culture.japan, http://groups.google.com/group/soc.culture.japan/msg/aee97126c799d1bf?dmode= source (retrieved April 28, 2009).

Latour, Bruno. 1987. *Science in action.* Cambridge, MA: Harvard University Press.

Leo, John. 1990. "Which portable is best for you? (LONG)." rec.games.video, http://groups.google.com/group/rec.games.video/msg/6c211477c3e4e1ed?dmode=source (retrieved April 28, 2009).

Levy, Steven. 1984. *Hackers.* New York: Penguin Books.

Morikawa, Kaichiro. 2004. *OTAKU: persona = space = city.* Tokyo: Tosho Print.

Mou, David. 1991. "Otaku no video/Mikado." rec.arts.anime, http://groups.google.com/group/rec.arts.anime/msg/1229c8d67c560752?dmode=source (retrieved April 28, 2009).

Newitz, Annalee. 1994. "Anime otaku: Japanese animation fans outside Japan." *Bad Subjects,* http://bad.eserver.org/issues/1994/13/newitz.html (retrieved April 28, 2009).

Okada, Toshio. 1996. "International university of otaku." International OTAKU University, www.netcity.or.jp/OTAKU/univ/aisatsu.html#e (retrieved April 28, 2009).

Patten, Fred. 2004. *Watching anime, reading manga.* Berkeley, CA: Stone Bridge Press.

Rosenberg, Charles. 1997. "Toward an ecology of knowledge: On discipline, context, and history." In *No other gods: On science and American social thought,* 2nd ed., 225–239. Baltimore: Johns Hopkins University Press.

Takeda, Yasuhiro. 2002. *The Notenki memoirs.* Canada: A. D. Vision.

Terry, Edith. 1994. "Japan logs on to the Internet." CNNMoney.com: *Fortune,* http://money.cnn.com/magazines/fortune/fortune_archive/1994/09/05/79729/index.htm (retrieved April 28, 2009).

II

INFRASTRUCTURE AND PLACE

5

Comic Market as Space for Self-Expression in Otaku Culture

....

HIROAKI TAMAGAWA

INTRODUCTION

This chapter describes conventions centered on *doujin*—fan-created manga—as spheres of activity for otaku. A significant share of otaku activity in Japan is rooted in doujin culture, and doujin events, where these amateur works are bought and sold, are the centers of commerce for this scene. The driving force behind the creation of the doujin culture has been Comic Market, the oldest doujin market in Japan, first convened in 1975 and continuing to maintain its status as the largest otaku event in the world.[1] Even before the term "otaku" was established in the culture, fans of anime and manga congregated at the Comic Market to traffic in doujin.[2]

I will analyze the doujin universe as a place of otaku activity, using Comic Market as the primary lens. The format of a doujin event such as Comic Market is fundamentally different from the typical fan convention organized in the United States and Europe. Only a handful of doujin market events like Comic Market exist overseas. Unlike general-purpose fan conventions, doujin markets are organized primarily for the distribution of doujin, not for panels, viewing anime, or trafficking in other kinds of merchandise. In order to describe the role of doujin market events in otaku culture, this chapter will take a historical approach, drawing on interviews and documents to trace the emergence and evolution of the Comic Market.[3] In addition, the chapter will draw on quantitative analysis of survey data on current Comic Market attendees to offer a snapshot of the current state of this event, which has been running now for more than thirty years.

This chapter focuses on the history of the doujin content-distribution network from the late 1970s to the present, examining the infrastructure supporting fan activity and how it has evolved through time. It builds on previous studies of fandom that have focused primarily on the personalities of fans, the community structure, and the content of fan-created works. This focus on fan infrastructure and distribution also addresses the dearth of research on the commerce of self-published works in Japan after the *minicomi* ("mini-communications," or niche publishing) boom of the 1970s. Current research on publication in Japan focuses almost exclusively on the commercial publishing world, which has resulted in the neglect of self-publishing and noncommercial markets.

THE MISSION OF DOUJIN MARKET EVENTS

Definition of Doujin

I define doujin as self-financed, self-published works created by an individual or collaboration between individuals. In Japan, it is difficult for individuals to gain access to commercial distribution without going through a publisher, so self-published works go through alternative channels of distribution.[4] In other words, doujin publication is a kind of amateur publication outside the professional commercial market. Doujin publication is not limited to print media, and it includes doujin software published in other media formats such as floppy discs, CD-ROMs, and DVDs.[5] Artists bring their work for the purpose of display and distribution.

The Comic Market requires that all works sold at the event be self-produced and self-published. "Comic Market is an exhibition and market for amateurs. Participation by commercial and professional organizations is excluded as a rule" (Comic Market Preparations Committee 2008, 1). Although the rules for participation in Comic Market stipulate that all works must be created by amateurs, it does not exclude authors who have been professionally published. Even authors who publish in commercial publications may participate in Comic Market with their self-published works. In other words, technically doujin refers to self-financed works that are created for noncommercial purposes. This chapter defines doujin culture as the subculture centered on these non-commercial works.

Analytical Perspective and Purpose

Previous studies have examined Comic Market and doujin activity through the lenses of social, cultural, and gender studies. For example, Kobayashi (1996) reflected on the pitfalls of conducting ethnographic research on Comic Market and analyzed doujin creation activities from anthropological and folklore perspectives. Natou (2007) drew on interviews and surveys to analyze the network of women who engage in the creation of derivative works through doujin. Ishida (2007) conducted ethnographic interviews of doujin artists in her analysis of doujin community substantiation. This earlier research characterizes Comic Market as a space for communication and self-expression and focuses on types of communication, doujin creation processes, and doujin content, particularly the *yaoi* genres that feature the recasting of male manga and anime characters into homoerotic narratives.

Related research on science fiction fandom overseas employs similar analytical frameworks. For example, in his analysis of how science fictions fans "poach" from existing texts, Jenkins (1992) focused on slash fiction—the repurposing of existing works into a homosexual narrative.[6]

In contrast, the analytical focus of this chapter is on otaku infrastructure and place rather than on the content of the communication and expression. Otaku activity occurs in a multitude of places, such as the Internet, otaku specialty shops, and events. Morikawa (see Chapter 6) adopts a similar approach in his analysis of Akihabara's transition from an electronics shopping district to an otaku town, and Aida (2006) analyzed maid cafés (where waitresses dress up as anime fantasy maid characters) as spaces of desire for otaku culture. Some previous work on Comic Market employing a similar approach is Hiejima's 2003 study of how the Comic Market Preparations Committee introduced corporate booths at the event, and my own 2007 study of these same committee members and their work in creating a space for fan activity.

Some previous research on fan culture abroad also acknowledges the importance of place. For example, Bacon-Smith (1992) identified fan clubs and conventions as places where fans can meet other fans. Pustz (1999), who does research on comics fans, analyzed the Internet, comics shops, and conventions as the underlying infrastructure for fan activity. Although these conventions are similar in providing the infrastructure for fan activity, they are not exact analogues of Comic Market in Japan.

San Diego Comic-Con and Anime Expo are central events for comics and anime fans in the United States. Unlike Comic Market, these events do not focus on a narrow range of activities, instead showcasing a broad spectrum of offerings such as inviting professional authors and musicians to participate in autograph sessions, concerts, lectures, corporate vendor exhibits, and panel discussions. Booths for fans to exhibit and distribute their doujin and fanzines comprise but one facet of the overall event in a section called Artist Alley (Pustz 1999).[7] In addition to this piece of the event that centers on fan-produced work, there is a dealers' room where comics, merchandise, secondhand books, and other items are sold. In other words, American conventions do not specialize in doujin or any one specialized medium for otaku self-expression (see Chapter 7).

As with Comic Market, fans with common interests established and organized these American fan events, but the event content markedly differs. I distinguish between the two types by referring to the tenor of these overseas events, with their broad range of content, as "convention style," and that of Comic Market and other events focusing on the exhibition and sale of doujin as "doujin market style." Now I turn to a description of Comic Market as an exemplar of doujin market–style events and examine the event through a historical look at surveys, documents, and interviews.

FROM THE BIRTH OF COMIC MARKET TO THE RISE OF PARODY DOUJIN

Achieving Independence from Fan Conventions

Long before Comic Market's inception, manga artists created doujin. Ajima (2004) has pinned the origins of manga doujin to before World War II. Here, I begin my overview approximately ten years before the first Comic Market.

In 1966 the Mushi Pro Corporation published the first issue of a serial title, *COM*, based on works from the Astro Boy Club, a fan club for the manga artist Osamu Tezuka.[8] The issue included a section titled "Guracon" (Grand Companion) that solicited reader submissions and listed announcements and recruitment ads from doujin "circles" (publishing groups).[9] Regional chapters of circles in Hokkaido, Kansai, and Kyushu emerged. Manga societies became widespread, with members creating and publishing doujin. This movement came to a close, however, when *COM* ceased publication in 1971.

In the post-*COM* era, manga fans found new ways to congregate through conventions such as Manga Communication and Nihon Manga Taikai (Japan Manga Convention). Manga Communication sought to foster a manga fan community by organizing sleepover events, sessions, and newsletters. It was the spiritual successor of *COM* and created a medium through which manga fans could communicate with each other. Nihon Manga Taikai primarily organized lectures by manga artists and screenings of anime: "[The events organized by Nihon Manga Taikai] included Fanzine Booth, where about 20 circles sold doujin. . . . Some university manga clubs sold doujin at campus festivals, but back then, most doujin were limited to circulation within the clubs. So this event presented the first opportunity for external distribution of manga doujin through sales" (Yonezawa 2000, 9). According to Yonezawa, the inclusion of doujin sales booths at Nihon Manga Taikai served as a precursor to the Comic Market.

In addition to Nihon Manga Taikai, other fan events such as Shojo Manga Taikai and Manga Fan Festival were already being held during the early 1970s. These events were modeled after Western fan conventions.[10] Shimotsuki (2008) describes how the first Nihon Manga Taikai planned debates, fan group introductions, manuscript exhibits, fanzine introductions, anime screenings, secondhand books and fanzine sales, auctions, raffles, and social events with artists.[11] It invited professional artists to give talks, sign autographs, and preside over screenings but also included a section for distributing doujin. In other words, Nihon Manga Taikai followed a similar format as present-day anime and comics conventions in the United States.

The first Comic Market was held in December 1975, with thirty-two circles and approximately 700 participants. Compared to today's numbers, it was very small in scale. However, from its very first occurrence,

Comic Market distinguished itself from other manga-related events by being an exclusively doujin market event. The event was founded despite the fact that Nihon Manga Taikai had already established the convention-style fan event genre. A woman who has been a participant in Comic Market since its inception explains why organizers designed an event that split from Nihon Manga Taikai:

> The organizers of Manga Taikai were elitist. It wasn't just Meikyu [Labyrinth] members who felt this way; other participants did too. People wanted other options for connecting with each other. (female, in her fifties)[12]

According to this informant, participants resented the Nihon Manga Taikai organizers for having exclusive decision-making power for events and guests.

By inviting professionals to their events, conventions establish a hierarchy between the commercial artists and the fans. With an event that is exclusively for doujin creators, however, the distinction between professionals and fan creators is blurred. Both are in a sense peers, seeking to share their creativity. Singling out the doujin sale section and excluding professionals eliminated the basis for conflict and hierarchical distinction and allowed all participants to see themselves as peers.

An additional motivation for starting a new event was a desire to expand the space devoted to distributing doujin.

> The main events at Nihon Manga Taikai were screenings and talks, so the doujin market was in a small room. [At Comic Market], we wanted to focus more on distributing [doujin] rather than invite authors to hold talks and autograph sessions. (female, in her fifties)

There was growing demand from the doujin community for a space to present their work.

In his 2008 memoir, Shimotsuki describes how Nihon Manga Taikai barred Meikyu and other circles affiliated with the group from participating in its event, sparking a confrontation between convention organizers and participants. The disagreement over the organizers' practices led Meikyu and other groups to seek new directions that were focused on doujin.

The sequence of events that led to the founding of Comic Market defined it as a gathering explicitly differentiated from existing fan events and focusing on the creation of a doujin distribution market. "The function of Comiket, or Comic Market, as a market is the single defining characteristic that distinguishes it from other manga conventions" (Comic Market Preparations Committee 2005, 32). Initially, however, Comic Market did include some elements that it had purportedly chosen to exclude, such as screenings. C1 included a Dynavision screening of *November Gymnasium*; C2 held an exhibit of Fumiko Okada's drawings and events other than the sale of doujin.[13] These events were peripheral, however, and intended as supporting elements to the core mission of the market.

> Since there were few circles at the time, there wasn't much to do in the afternoons. So [these events] were a way for participants to linger at the event until closing time. (female, in her fifties)

As the number of participating circles grew, these peripheral events gradually disappeared, making their last appearance at C16 as a screening of the 8-mm film *Paper Wars*. Around the time of C18, a splinter group created Comic Square (initially titled New Comic Market) because of disagreements that were at least in part over the nature of events permitted at Comic Market. During a published interview reflecting on the split, Yonezawa, still president of Comic Market at the time, described how anime events were the source of the conflict within the preparations committee:

> Yonezawa: Pro-anime members wanted to invite voice actors for concerts and do tie-up screenings with recording companies.
> Bell: Autograph sessions, too.[14]
> Yonezawa: We kept saying that sort of thing doesn't fit what Comiket's about.
> (Comic Market Preparations Committee 2005, 96)

Staff members who split to form Comic Square sought events that included elements from the professional industry. In a way, this represented a return to the Manga Taikai era of fan events that Comic Market had rejected at its inception. After the split, Comic Market made a formal decision to exclude events other than the doujin market.[15]

Beyond Derivative Creations and Fanzines

Comic Market attracted flocks of doujin artists because it was an event dedicated to doujin. Participating circles in the early days represented a diverse mix, including circles publishing original works, manga review circles, fan clubs of professional manga artists, and university manga societies. The lineup contrasts with that of Nihon Manga Taikai, which positioned fans as the audience of professionals. Comic Market attracted individuals engaged in acts of self-expression around doujin, including creation and critique of manga:

> SF Taikai served as a meeting point for professionals and fans. But Comiket and other manga events were more about putting professionals and amateurs on equal footing, more doujin than fanzine. (male, in his fifties)

This Comic Market participant, who identifies himself as a science fiction fan, indicates how the doujin at Comic Market did not fit the mold of fanzines, which were created by fans of professionals and their work. In contrast to fan conventions, where participants called professionals *sensei* (teacher/professor/author) out of respect, Comic Market had a more democratic and nonhierarchical culture. At the time, the term "otaku" was not in wide use, and the term "fans" was a general-purpose term. Not all fans engaged in appropriating commercial works and creating derivative works, and many fans were simply enthusiastic about manga culture.

"Parody" doujin that draw from commercial works now dominate the doujin genre, so it is tempting to characterize doujin culture as belonging to a fan audience of professional artists. However, at the time of Comic Market's inception, doujin were also a medium for amateurs to create works outside of the realm of commercial publications. In addition to circles specializing in original works, some university manga societies also sought to produce original work. Other circles were dedicated to publishing doujin that reviewed and commented on manga, and their members aimed to further the art of self-expression in manga through critique rather than through celebration of particular works:

> Though it manifested in different ways, [during that time, otaku] shared a common goal to "make manga independent" and "liberate manga from the dominance of text." If they published critique in writing, it

would have been viewed in the same light as literature. That's why Meikyu used manga to critique manga. (male, in his fifties)

For example, one of the core series in *Meikyu's Manga Shin Hihyou Taikei* (New Series of Manga Critique) was *The Poru Family*, a critique-as-parody work of Moto Hagio's *The Poe Family* (Comic Market Preparations Committee 2005).

During Comic Market's formative years, in addition to *COM's* legacy of creating original works, the high popularity of the *shojo* (girls') manga genre (in part aided by the debut of rising stars such as Moto Hagio) exerted a strong influence. Original shojo manga flourished in the doujin scene. Manga criticism embodied a critique of existing genres of literary criticism and an intention to drive manga expression, and university manga-society newsletters serialized original manga drawn by their members. In this period, when original works were central to the doujin scene, participants were manga fans who wished to advance the art of self-expression in manga by creating their own works and critique.

From Self-Expression to Parody

Given this history, how was it that the Comic Market came to be established as a place for fans to congregate around derivative works? The derivative works and parodies that dominate Comic Market today are constructed using characters, setting, and backstory from an existing work and then creating narratives of the doujin artists' choosing in the form of manga and novels. Fans create these derivative doujin by appropriating professional work.

During Comic Market's early years, original works constituted the majority of doujin. Even back then, however, circles included fan clubs that embodied the traditional relationship between fans and professionals. Fan club doujin functioned both as newsletters and as venues for presenting collaboratively produced work by club members. The tenor of the fan club doujin was different from the parody doujin of today and resembled fanzines produced by Western science fiction fans. Fan club doujin contained information about the author (for example, bibliography and recent updates), reviews and information about the author's specific works, illustrations, and manga. Two fans describe the situation in these initial years of the Comic Market:

Manga Shin Hihyou Taikei had manga critique in the form of parody, but there weren't a lot of fan manga that were actual parodies. (male, in his fifties)

Anime fandom was initially a part of science fiction and manga fandoms. Fans would debate things like whether the Wave Motion Gun in *Yamato* would ever exist. They wouldn't make parody doujin based on one work because of printing costs. Several people would contribute to one, so it'd be a compilation based on different works [that contributors wanted to use]. By the time *Combattler V* and *Deimos* came out, groups of people who liked one work formed their own circles. Before then, it was normal to both read and draw manga, but around 1978, '79, there were more people who just read manga. (female, in her fifties)

Eventually, parody in doujin arose naturally from the kinds of critiques that groups such as Meikyu and fan and manga clubs engaged in. Today's doujin, however, are not focused on criticism and consist almost entirely of derivative works, generally derived from a single series. Anime played a large role in these developments.

The number of anime-oriented circles began to increase around 1977 because of *Space Battleship Yamato*'s popularity. By the time C11 was held in April 1979, the event space was split between anime circles and manga circles. Around this time, parody doujin focused on a specific series began to gain prominence, joining the ranks of more "traditional" fanzines (containing reviews and information about professional works) and fan club newsletter–style doujin (containing manga, illustrations, and articles contributed by members). Anime magazines influenced this shift in anime doujin content: "Commercial fan magazines, like *OUT*, *Animage*, and *Animec* were founded, focused on the kind of anime series that had been the topic of doujin. These magazines created a huge market, too. Not surprisingly, the magazines were a more commercialized, expanded version of anime doujin at Comiket" (Yonezawa 1997, 288). Information previously available only through doujin thus became widely available through commercial magazines, undermining the role that fanzines had played in providing information.[16] This pushed anime doujin to shift toward parody doujin.

By accepting the inclusion of parody content, Comic Market continued to expand. It adopted an open-door policy to doujin by not setting any content requirements, providing a space for fans to circulate derivative works. However, the shift was accompanied by the attempt to privilege original works through the creation of an original works–only market called Manga Gallery and Market (MGM). One of Meikyu's core members, Jun Aniwa, became the leader of MGM. MGM was based on another event, Mini Market, which Meikyu had sponsored in 1980 as a means of restoring a more intimate space for communication between circles and readers that had become increasingly elusive with Comic Market's rapid growth.

In other words, two contrasting events emerged from Comic Market: Comic Square, which sought to provide a fan event for professionals and the industry, and MGM, which sought to continue to provide a venue for original works in opposition to the growing dominance of parody. These two offshoots were an indicator of Comic Market's goals to chart a middle path. The decision to be ecumenical laid the groundwork for explosive growth.

While the content of the market was diversifying, Comic Market's foundations solidified in the early 1980s. As Comic Market gained clarity of purpose, it needed to unify its participants' mind-sets. This led to the publication of *Comic Market Manual*, an informational pamphlet, in 1982. The manual is now integrated into the participant application form for circles.

Comic Market Manual contains a section titled "Mission and Purpose of Comic Market." With only minor edits through the years, it shows that Comic Market's basic stance has remained the same since the very beginning: honoring the equality of its participants, providing a place for freedom of expression, maintaining this space, and supporting the participant community. This mission is carried out for participants by the Comic Market Preparations Committee that organizes the event. The *Comic Market Manual* and mission statement have had very few changes, indicating both the flexibility and the core resilience of the mission. "Comic Market is but a framework: its contents change continuously depending on the participants and circumstance" (Comic Market Preparations Committee 2005, 355). By accepting every mode of self-expression, Comic Market looks to the circles and broader cultural shifts as mechanisms for change. In turn, Comic Market has come to define itself through its function of providing a space for doujin dissemination. "Whatever the form, Comiket must go on indefinitely as long as manga and anime fans need Comiket" (Comic Market

Preparations Committee 2005, 355). During its thirty-year history, although there have been changes necessitated by expansion, such as changes to the Preparations Committee, inclusion of printers and transport companies, and corporate booths, the overall stance has remained consistent. Comic Market continues to strive for the maintenance of Comic Market and its founding principles.

EXPANSION OF SPACES FOR SELF-EXPRESSION AND DISTRIBUTION

Proliferation of Markets

By the early 1980s, the basic form and structure of Comic Market was established. During the 1980s, the *lolicon* ("Lolita complex" genres featuring preadolescent girls) boom held sway among men, and *Captain Tsubasa* was popular among women. While doujin trends continued to shift, Comic Market simply continued its steady expansion. During this period, non-Comic Market infrastructures for sharing doujin were sites of new kinds of activity. In addition to doujin market events, consignment bookstores represented another means of distributing doujin. I will begin by briefly summarizing the history of each.

As Comic Market participants grew in number, the doujin market gained recognition as a specific event style and spread nationwide. Initially, the spread of manga doujin markets came from nonmanga doujin markets, such as when Minicomi Fair (Mini-Communication Fair) added manga doujin to its lineup (Shimotsuki 2008). This initial trend was followed by a second wave, when events focused on manga cropped up across Japan, imitating Comic Market.

> Regional university manga societies took the initiative—places like Iwate University, Matsuyama University, and Nagoya University began organizing regional markets. (female, in her fifties)

These new markets included Iwate's Iwa-Man, Nagoya's Comic Carnival (COMICA), Osaka's Comic Bazaar (Comiiru), Matsuyama's Manga Sale, and Kobe's Comic Street, among others.[17]

In tandem with these fan-organized events, commercial companies also began to organize doujin markets. Tokyo Bungei Publishing and Akaboo Communications began organizing Comic City (and Super Comic City); Tokyo Bungei Publishing organized Doujin Minicomi

Fair; and Studio YOU, Comic Live.[18] Although Comic Market has been a nonprofit operation staffed by volunteers, other doujin markets gradually began to make corporate ties.

> When industry events started showing up, we just thought it was a good thing to have more events because there were so few at the time. [Comic Market] had just expanded to [being held] twice a year, so we felt that more opportunities and establishing a broader base were good developments. (female, in her fifties)

Given that opportunities to distribute doujin were limited, participants did not seem to object to having for-profit corporations organize doujin markets.

As market events grew and became massive, fans started organizing "only events" specializing in one doujin genre. The MGM event specializing in original works is one example of an early only event. Another original-works-only event, Comitia, was established in Tokyo in 1984. Within the broader parody genre, fans and corporations began organizing events limited to parodies of a specific series.

> "Only events" existed even back in *Captain Tsubasa* times, maybe even earlier. But in events for a single genre, I think it started around *Captain Tsubasa*. Before, none of the existing works had a large enough following to support an only event. The Wing Market organized by Akaboo Communications helped popularize *Captain Tsubasa*. (male, in his forties)

With the increase of specialized circles, only events became more common. In addition to corporations such as Akaboo organizing only events, established and well-known circles within a particular genre banded together, and fan volunteers also began to organize only events. In this way, general-purpose markets and only events began to be held across the nation. Many of them, such as Comic City, Comic Live, Comitia, and Gataket, continue to be held today.

Bookstore Distribution

Consignment bookstores present an alternative means of distributing doujin. In Japan, the majority of printed works are routed by the publisher through third-party wholesale distributors before reaching bookstores and then consumers. Because doujin circles cannot negotiate with distributors, circles cannot plug into the typical distribution network. However, circles can negotiate with individual bookstores and shops to carry their doujin. Minicomi, which became popular from the late 1960s onward, were self-published informational magazines that were sold in bookstores, cafés, and record stores through consignment. Some bookstores sold manga doujin through similar arrangements and functioned as distribution outlets before Comic Market was formed.[19]

Through time, the distribution avenues for doujin manga differentiated themselves from other forms of self-published works such as literary fanzines, hobby zines, and local newsletters geared for a less specialized audience. What I could glean from the limited remaining documents from this period was that the only kind of stores that focused on the sale of doujin manga were stores that sold manga as well as doujin.

During the early 1980s, doujin were sold at the offices of *Puff* and *Comic Box*—magazines featuring information on doujin and commercial manga. However, an article published in the 1985 September issue of *Lemon People* announced the following: "Earlier this month, Free Space, which was a permanent doujin market maintained by *Comic Box*, closed. By August, *Puff*'s Comic In will also close down. This means there will be no more permanent markets for doujin" (Ajima 2004, 80). This indicates that storefront doujin sales were difficult to maintain. However, by the late 1980s, some manga specialty bookstores set aside space for selling doujin:

> By the late eighties, doujin were a valid sale category, so manga specialty stores in Tokyo like Manga no Mori, Takaoka Shoten, and Shosen Book Mart started stocking doujin. Doujin of several dozen circles could be found on the basement floor of Manga no Mori. Shoen [Book Mart] had about the same amount, about two shelves' worth. (male, in his forties)

Despite the trend, given that bookstores and circles had to negotiate individually, the number of circles that even manga specialty scores could accommodate was limited. In 1990, police raided bookstores such as Shosen Book Mart and filed obscenity charges against doujin with mature content, leading to the decline of consignment practices during the early 1990s.

The bookstore consignment system for distributing doujin remained in a secondary role until the late 1990s. The shift was tied to the emergence and growth of new bookstores such as Tora no Ana (established

1994) and K-Books (established 1992) that aggressively pursued consignment doujin sales. As these stores grew into chains, doujin distribution networks expanded concomitantly, allowing circles to reach audiences in regions beyond their immediate spheres of distribution.

At the time of writing, in 2009, bookstores were selling doujin by consignment in every region of Japan. One chain, Tora no Ana, had fifteen stores nationwide and an online sales site. Several different sales statistics of the doujin market exist, and it is difficult to discern which are correct. *Otaku Sangyo Hakusho 2008* (2008 Otaku Industry White Paper) values the bookstore consignment-sales market at 13.45 billion yen (approximately US$135 million), which exceeds the share of doujin market-event sales. Thus, the bookstore consignment distribution system has emerged as the more permanent alternative to the event-based, face-to-face distribution system of doujin markets.

THREE DECADES LATER: COMIC MARKET AND THE DOUJIN WORLD

Comic Market as a Market

In the previous section, I drew on documents and interviews to analyze the birth and development of the doujin market from the 1970s onward. In this section, I turn to a survey conducted to mark the thirty-year anniversary of Comic Market and examine its current status through a quantitative lens. I analyze the event's development through the past three decades.

The thirtieth anniversary survey was conducted between 2003 and 2005 through a collaboration of the Comic Market Preparations Committee and researchers who were part of the Comic Culture Research Society. In this section, I will draw on survey results based on answers given by participating circles at Comic Market. This survey was distributed to 52,000 circles participating in C66 and asked questions about the groups' activity during the year 2003 and their participation in C65 (held December 2003).[20]

During the three days C65 was held, 35,000 circles participated and distributed their works. As seen in Figure 5.1, distribution statistics (including printed matter and software) indicate that during a single Comic Market event the greatest share of circles (35.3 percent) distributed 0 to 49 copies, 20.9 percent of circles distributed 50 to 99 units, and

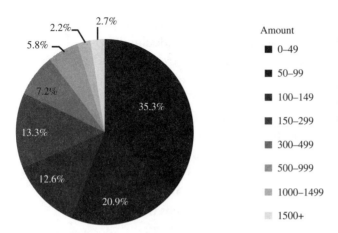

Figure 5.1. Volume of doujin distributed by percentage of participating circles ($n = 24638$) during C65. Credit: *Comic Market 30th Anniversary Survey* (Sugiyama 2008).

Amount
- 0–49
- 50–99
- 100–149
- 150–299
- 300–499
- 500–999
- 1000–1499
- 1500+

12.6 percent distributed 100 to 149 copies. In other words, few circles were able to distribute large quantities of their work. Furthermore, only 2.7 percent of participating circles distributed more than 1,500 copies. Extrapolating the actual number of circles from participant statistics reveals that nearly 1,000 circles succeeded in distributing more than 1,500 copies of their work during a single Comic Market event. Thus, despite the variance in distribution statistics, overall Comic Market constitutes a sizeable market for doujin. According to the survey report, the total number of doujin distributed during C65 was estimated as being 7,136,000.

Statistics that indicate whether circles participated in other doujin markets and consignment bookstores are shown in Tables 5.1 and 5.2. Only 27.2 percent of circles limited their participation to Comic Market, roughly three-quarters of all participating circles attended other doujin markets, and 24.9 percent stated that they distributed more doujin at other doujin markets than at Comic Market. Only 13 percent of circles used consignment book stores. Of these, 2.2 percent stated that they distributed about the same amount of doujin through consignment as through doujin markets, and 3 percent stated that they distributed more doujin through consignment than through doujin markets. The two response categories comprised approximately 40 percent of circles using consignment bookstores, indicating that consignment represented a valuable means of distribution among circles who did use consignment bookstores.

Table 5.1 Participation in doujin markets other than Comic Market during 2003

Response	% Participating circles ($n = 36780$)
Did not participate in other doujin markets.	27.2
Was able to distribute more work at Comic Market than at other markets.	27.0
Was able to distribute about the same amount at Comic Market and other markets.	20.9
Was able to distribute more work at other markets.	24.9

Source: Comic Market 30th Anniversary Survey (Sugiyama 2008)

Table 5.2 Use of consignment bookstores and comparison of distribution amount with doujin markets during 2003

Response	% Participating circles ($n = 37731$)
Did not use consignment bookstores.	87.0
Was able to distribute more work through doujin markets than through consignment.	7.8
Was able to distribute about the same amount through consignment and doujin markets.	2.2
Was able to distribute more work through consignment than through doujin markets.	3.0

Source: Comic Market 30th Anniversary Survey (Sugiyama 2008)

All of these statistics indicate how Comic Market has become a massive market. Other doujin markets and consignment bookstores also function as alternative spaces for doujin distribution. At the time of the 2003 survey, Japan's market for commercially published manga was 254.9 billion yen (approximately US$2.6 billion) and 528.33 million units in sales (Zenkoku shupan kyokai, Shupan kagaku kenkyujo 2008). The doujin market is small in comparison but not insignificant.

The oppositional relationship between doujin and commercial publications is apparent in how Comic Market was framed as a rebellion against Nihon Manga Taikai. Dissatisfaction about commercial publications, particularly manga serials, was a driving force behind Comic Market's inception. "The once-innovative *seinen* [young men] manga serials had become insular. Serials like *Shonen Magazine*, which had always tried to evolve and stay cutting-edge, scaled back its content for younger readers. Even *Garo*, which used to surprise readers with fresh content, stagnated. Manga had become all about sports and action, and it felt as though manga's potential was becoming stifled" (Comic Market Preparations Committee 2005, 26). In an interview, former Comic Market President Yonezawa describes how he was attracted to doujin because they embodied potential that no longer existed in commercial publications: "Above all, I wanted to create a self-made distribution network that would displace [existing commercial distribution networks like] Tohan and Nippan so [important doujin works] would be able to circulate. . . . As for how I'd make that happen, I just thought, well, if I could organize a market and a network of markets would spread nationwide, that'd be it" (Sugiyama 2008, 125). Thus, the goal was to further doujin's creative potential by constructing a self-made publication distribution network that would replace distributors supporting commercial publications.

Thirty years later, it is clear from comparing the relative scale of distribution of doujin and commercial publications that doujin have not displaced commercial publications. That was not the goal, however, of Yonezawa and other Comic Market founders. Their goal was to distribute works that would not get distributed via commercially published manga and to create a space for new ways of self-expression through manga.

Given the focus on the pursuit of self-expression through manga, original works might be considered the core genre of doujin. The first Comic Market president, Teruo Harada, also stated the following when reflecting on his retirement as president in 1979: "I have no intention of repudiating fan clubs and cosplay, but I had wanted to see circles creating original works flourish. Instead, it's all about other types of circles and trends. Even circles doing original works are mostly recasting commercial works. Once I realized that, my hopes for doujin to become a wellspring of new imaginings shriveled" (Shimotsuki 2008, 182). In the C65 survey conducted approximately twenty years later (see Table 5.3), circles producing original works comprise 12.9 percent of the total, and the rest are circles parodying anime or other

Table 5.3 Circle applicants' stated genre in C65

Genre	% Participating circles ($n = 28288$)
Original work	12.9
Doujin software, gal games	9.7
Games	15.7
Fan clubs/circles (*Shonen Jump* works)	18.3
Anime	7.4
Fan clubs/circles (novels and other)	8.5
Celebrity	10.4
Fan clubs (manga)	8.9
Male-oriented	8.3

Note: Derived by author from statistics in *Comic Market 30th Anniversary Survey* (Sugiyama 2008).

works such as those in *Weekly Shonen Jump*.[21] Overall, parody doujin and derivative works have become the norm in Comic Market.

However, the pursuit of self-expression through manga is not the sole province of original works. Parody manga can give rise to new works and forms of expression, and many doujin artists who draw parodies also draw original works. Despite the current dominance of parodies and derivative works in Comic Market, the pursuit of self-expression has not been abandoned. As previously indicated in Yonezawa's interviews, Comic Market was needed as a means for distribution, but its underlying purpose was to maintain the diversity of manga.

The survey also asked participating circles about their experience with commercial publications. Among the respondents, 14.4 percent said they had experience in commercial publication, indicating that there is no clear distinction between commercial publication and doujin publication. We cannot assume a tidy correlation between amateurs and doujin and between professionals and commercial publication. Of those who did not have experience with commercial publication, 11.7 percent responded that they would like to publish commercially, which means that some doujin artists seek to participate in the commercial market (see Table 5.4).

In fact, many professional manga artists began as doujin artists and achieved success in commercial publications, including notable artists such as Yun Koga, CLAMP, and many others. In addition, there

Table 5.4 Experience with, and attitude toward, publishing in commercial magazines (% participating circles, $n = 37219$)

No experience with commercial magazines			Experience with commercial magazines	
Would not want to publish in commercial magazines (30.8%)	Would want to publish in commercial magazines, if given opportunity (43.1%)	Really want to publish in commercial magazines (11.7%)	Have experience, but not main source of income (9.9%)	Main source of income (4.5%)

are works that began in doujin and transitioned to commercial publications such as *Gunslinger Girl, Tsukihime*, and *When They Cry*. Entire genres such as lolicon and yaoi, which are linked intimately with Comic Market, have been incorporated into commercial publications and now wield enormous influence over otaku culture.

Harada comments on Comic Market's strengthening its ties to commercial publication rather than providing a growing market for original doujin. "From Meikyu's standpoint, Comic Market was not founded to nurture professionals, but rather to provide a place for doujin artists who would never gain entry into commercial publications" (Shimotsuki 2008, 180). Comic Market has, however, succeeded in serving both functions.

In the survey, 30.8 percent of respondents stated that they have no desire to publish in commercial magazines. Thus, roughly a third of all circles in Comic Market participate for the purpose of creating doujin without the goal of transitioning to commercial publications. Comic Market participants include professional manga artists who make their living through commercial publications, doujin artists aspiring to commercial success, and doujin artists who have no desire to publish commercially. Although created in opposition to commercial distribution, the Comic Market and the doujin industry cannot be understood by simple dichotomies between professionals and amateurs or between commercialism and free artistic expression.

As commercial publishers have come to actively seek out doujin artists, they have incorporated not only individual artists but also certain kinds of works and trends that exemplify doujin. Commercial and doujin publications have become intertwined. Doujin markets do not exist solely to provide manga artists for commercial publications nor purely to provide a space for derivative works. Comic Market is a space allowing a wide variety of circles to present and distribute their works. It does not discriminate, and everyone is equal.

The Ethos of Creating Diverse Alternative Media

The construction of Comic Market as a space valuing diversity and minimizing hierarchies owes its success in large part to the circumstances leading to the creation of the Comic Market Preparations Committee and its ethos.

Because of its objections to Nihon Manga Taikai, the Comic Market Preparations Committee rejected convention-style events and ensured that all participating circles had maximum freedom and equality. To that end, the committee does not discriminate against any doujin content and tries to provide each circle a fair chance at participation. Instead of privileging circles with strong sales or of a certain genre, the committee tries to equalize each circle's odds of getting into Comic Market within each genre. The committee's emphasis on diversity means it sometimes "gives [special] consideration to circles that are sole representatives of a genre [so that they may participate]" (Comic Market Preparations Committee 2008, 5). Furthermore, as Morikawa (2003) surmised, the committee's decision to avoid positioning booths in accordance to the status of the circle also reflects the committee's principles of equality and sets Comic Market apart from corporate events.

Comic Market draws heavily on the term "participant" (*sankasha*). Organizers are called staff participants, attending circles are called circle participants, visitors are called general participants, and attending industries are called corporate participants. By insisting on the term "participant," the committee instills a sense that all attendees are contributing to the construction of the place, and nobody identifies as a "customer." All participants are also equal; staff participants are not superior to the rest. Staff participant positions are open to general and circle participants. When participants opt to become staff participants, they leave behind their identities as fans of specific works and act for the good of Comic Market as a whole, to contribute to its operations (Tamagawa 2007).

The commitment to minimize discrimination, hierarchy, and authority and to ensure diversity embodies the core principle created by Comic Market, and it is now shared among doujin markets. The principle is embodied not only in the committee's mission statement but also in the participation policies for circles, the concept of "participant," spatial layout, and other tacit forms of rules and policies.[22]

This style of doujin market event replaced the earlier convention style and became one of the most familiar styles for otaku in Japan. Although it would be meaningless to claim that one style is superior to the other, it is arguable that the doujin market style played a significant role in the development of doujin culture in Japan in a way that set doujin apart from fanzines overseas.

In addition to Comic Market, other means of doujin distribution have proliferated through the years, such as other doujin markets, consignment bookstores, and online sales. From a distribution standpoint, Comic Market's founding goal of constructing a self-made distribution network has been realized.

Doujin also evolved into a medium not only for original works and new means of self-expression in manga but also for various forms of expression in otaku culture such as parody doujin, games, and music. This evolution of doujin as a multicontent medium was not enabled and nurtured through the power of a distribution infrastructure alone but through the creativity of doujin artists and the consumers, the otaku. As a distribution infrastructure, Comic Market maintains an open stance to all content and allows circle and general participants to shape the evolution of doujin content. Under the auspices of this approach, which differs markedly from commercial marketing, many artists and works have been born and have advanced doujin culture.

With a clear purpose from its inception, Comic Market succeeded in concretizing its mission into a rational system and in cultivating a distinct doujin market style. Comic Market's operations embody the principles and goals of its founders thirty years ago. Within that space for self-expression, approximately 35,000 circles gather twice a year to distribute doujin in massive quantities. Comic Market built an alternative market system that maintains diversity and provides otaku with an easy means of self-expression. It provides otaku media for otaku by otaku.

CONCLUSION: FROM FAN TO OTAKU

In previous research on fanzines and doujin, the analysis tends to cast fan participation as resisting the mainstream and poaching from commercial media (Jenkins 1992). This is in many ways a natural outcome of treating fans and otaku as members of an audience. However, Comic Market's history makes clear the limitations of defining doujin culture as the actions of an audience poaching and appropriating commercial media.

Shifting the analytical lens away from fans as an audience of commercial media and toward conceptualizing otaku as its own tribe with its own cultural practices makes it clear that Comic Market and doujin culture are not limited to creating parodies of specific works. A diverse group of artists create works as fans of anime, manga, and games. Comic Market and doujin constitute one of the infrastructures necessary for the community's activities. The processes of content creation and re-creation intertwine in complex ways between the twin spheres of commercial media and doujin culture. From this, we see that otaku cannot be boxed into the categories of anime and manga consumers, of a fan audience. We must reconceptualize otaku beyond the confines of being mere members of an audience.

Notes

1. Comic Market is widely known by its abbreviated monikers, Comiket and Comike. The event will be referred to by its full name for consistency in this chapter unless abbreviated forms are used by informants in direct quotes.

2. This chapter examines events before the term "otaku" came into widespread use. Comic Market organizers describe the convention as an "event for fans." Many of the works cited in this chapter also use the term "fan" rather than "otaku." I will use both the terms "otaku" and "fan" to refer to participants of Comic Market and, more specifically, the term "fan" to describe those who identify strongly with a particular media work.

3. I conducted individual interviews in 2008 and 2009 with people who attended Comic Market during the 1970s and 1980s. The interviews were unstructured, and they ranged from one to four hours. Informants included three men and one woman. Two participated in the event as staff and one as a member of a group producing doujin. Quotes from the interviews will specify the informant's gender and approximate age at the time of the interview.

4. There are some established means of self-funded publication wherein the author contracts a commercial publisher in Japan. I do not consider these kinds of publications doujin for the purposes of this chapter.

5. In this chapter, I use the term "doujin" in its broad sense to include not only printed media but also other formats, including doujin software.

6. Slash fiction is the American fan culture equivalent for yaoi and "boys' love," in which fans recast characters from their favorite works in homosexual relationships.

7. Artist Alley provides a space for both amateur and professional creators (writers, manga artists, illustrators, etc.) to exhibit and sell their own work. In contrast, the space provided for the sale of videos, published books, and products by retailers and resellers is called the Dealers' Room. The latter space is populated by specialty stores, industries, and individuals seeking to sell off their stock. Consequently, it does not serve as an outlet for an individual's creative output.

8. Mushi Pro Corporation was a subsidiary of Mushi Production, an anime studio established by Osamu Tezuka. Established in 1966, Mushi Pro Corporation dealt in publications but declared bankruptcy in 1973.

9. "Circles" refer to doujin publishing groups. Originally, circles published compilations of works created by groups of individuals such as fan clubs. Today, even an individual author is called a circle.

10. Nihon Manga Taikai modeled itself after SF Taikai, a Japanese convention for science fiction fans. SF Taikai was itself influenced by World Con, an international science fiction fan convention. SF Taikai is credited with introducing the convention style to Japan.

11. Takanaka Shimotsuki is the nom de plume of Teruo Harada, Comic Market's first president. In this chapter, some of his writings and comments are attributed to his actual name, depending on the author attribution.

12. Meikyu was a critics' circle that also served as a managing body of Comic Market during the event's early years. Many of the key figures involved in Comic Market were also members of this group.

13. From this point on, I will follow the Comic Market Preparations Committee's convention of referring to specific Comic Market events with the notation C[number of event].

14. Vice president of Comic Market Preparations Committee at time of interview (2005).

15. After changing venues to Tokyo Big Site, Comic Market decided to permit corporate booths, thus reinstating some of the boundaries inherent between professionals and fans (see Hiejima 2003).

16. See Yoshimoto (2009) for an in-depth overview of commercially published informational anime magazines.

17. Of the regional markets listed, Comic Carnival, which began in 1978, and Comiiru have a long history. Refer to *Puff*'s 1979 November/December special issue on *National Manga Doujin Map* for detailed information.

18. Akaboo Communications is a subsidiary brand name used by Kei Corporation when organizing doujin markets. At present, the name is used to organize Comic City.

19. Shimotsuki (2008) indicates that he also used minicomi centers (bookstores devoted to amateur and noncommercial publications) to distribute doujin during that time.

20. I am a member of the Comic Culture Research Society and am involved with ongoing analysis. For this section, I am referencing a report on the study (Sugiyama 2008). All references to the survey are drawn from the report unless otherwise stated. The circle participant survey forms were distributed alongside C66 application forms; 37,620 completed forms were collected, comprising an overall response rate of approximately 72.3 percent.

21. Percentages were derived by matching circles' genre codes on application forms to the code key provided by the Comic Market Preparations Committee and grouping genres into the nine categories as seen in Table 5.3.

22. Because of continued expansion, some evidence shows that hereto tacit understandings are no longer being shared by all participants. Some Comic Market Preparations Committee publications cite offenders who do not know or follow the rules.

References

Aida, Miho. 2006. Moeru kukan: Maid cafe ni kansuru syakaigaku teki kosatsu. *Studies in the Humanities and Science* 47: 193–219.

Ajima, Shun. 2004. *Manga doujinshi etcetera '82–'98: Jokyoron to review de yomu Otaku shi*. Tokyo: Kuboshoten.

Bacon-Smith, Camille. 1992. *Enterprising women: Television fandom and the creation of popular myth*. Philadelphia: University of Pennsylvania Press.

Comic Market Junbikai. 2005. *Comic market 30's file*. Tokyo: Yugengaisha Comiket.

———. 2008. *Comic market manual 75*. Tokyo: Yugengaisha Comiket.

———. 2008. *Comic market 75 circle sanka moushikomi set*. Tokyo: Yugengaisha Comiket.

Hiejima, Takeshi. 2003. Comic market no yukue: Aru "bunka undo" ni miru rinen to genjitsu no kankei ni tsuite no kosatsu. *Social and Cultural Studies* 14: 115–127.

Ishida, Kimi. 2007. Dokusha comunity no kochiku: Doujinshi community ni thuite no katari no bunseki kara. *The Science of Reading* 50 (3/4): 94–104.

Jenkins, Henry. 1992. *Textual poachers: Television fans and participatory culture*. New York: Routledge.

Kobayashi, Yoshihiro. 1996. From folk to filk-mitsuryo teki bunka arui wa kusanone no souzou. *Japan Association for Lifology* 1: 97–106.

Media Create Souken. 2008. *Otaku sangyo hakusho 2008*. Tokyo: Media Create Souken.

Morikawa, Kaichiro. 2003. *Shuto no tanjo: Moeru toshi Akihabara*. Tokyo: Gentousha.

Natou, Takako. 2007. "Nijisosaku" katsudo to sono network ni tsuite. In *Sorezore no fan kenkyu: I am a fan*, 55–117. Tokyo: Fujinsha.

Puff. 1979. *Tokushu: Zenkoku manga doujinshi chizu*. Tokyo: Seisuisha.

Pustz, Matthew. 1999. *Comic book culture: Fanboy and true believers*. Jackson: University Press of Mississippi.

Shimotsuki, Takanaka. 2008. *Comic Market soseiki*. Tokyo: Asahi Shinbun Shuppan.

Sugiyama, Akashi, ed. 2008. *"Comic market" no bunka shakaigaku teki kenkyu*. Kagaku kenkyuhi hojokin kenkyu chosa hokokusho. Fukuoka: Akashi Sugihama.

Tamagawa, Hiroaki. 2007. Fandom no ba wo tsukuru to iu koto: Comic market no staff katsudo. In *Sorezore no fan kenkyu: I am a fan*, 11–53. Tokyo: Fujinsha.

Yonezawa, Yoshihiro. 1997. Comike bunka no 20 nen: Ryukou wo sakidori shite kita comic market. In *Chuokoron* 1357, 276–283. Tokyo: Chuokoronsha.

———. 2000. Manga doujinshi no rekishi no gairyaku wo saguru: Comic market jyunbikai daihyo, Yonezawa Yoshihiro shi interview. *Comic Fan* 10. Tokyo: Zassousha.

Yoshimoto, Taimatsu. 2009. *Otaku no kigen*. Tokyo: NTT Shuppan.

Zenkoku shuppan kyokai, Shuppan kagaku kenkyujo. 2008. *2008 Syuppan shihyo nenpo*. Tokyo: Zenkoku shuppan kyokai, Shuppan kagaku kenkyujo.

6

Otaku and the City:
The Rebirth of Akihabara

· ·

KAICHIRO MORIKAWA

TOWARD AKIHABARA

In the past few years, I have taken foreign students on guided tours of the district of Tokyo known as Akihabara. The students' majors varied across many disciplines, including urban planning, media studies, and cultural studies. But they all had one thing in common: they were not going to Akihabara to buy electronics.

In the postwar period of economic growth in the 1970s and 1980s, Akihabara was established as the primary electronics district in Tokyo, where both families and technology enthusiasts would flock to buy appliances and electronics. From the late 1990s onward, Akihabara was dramatically transformed into the epicenter of otaku taste, represented in specialties such as fanzines (*doujinshi*) and anime figurines. Akihabara station is now cluttered with billboards featuring girls drawn in anime style and advertisements for stores that specialize in manga. The main street is lined with posters and life-sized cardboard signs of anime girls promoting dating sims.

"Why are there so many anime drawings of immature-looking girls here?" is the first question the visiting students ask me. I was initially hard-pressed to come up with an explanation. To say that Akihabara has many enthusiasts of prepubescent girls would invite too many misunderstandings, and it would not explain why those who favor such artwork congregate in Akihabara in such large numbers. The students' question is essentially a question about the significance of the ongoing transformation of Akihabara.

From the mid-1990s, Akihabara was rapidly transformed from an electronics district into Japan's epicenter for otaku. It seemed as though there was a massively capitalized, organized effort to transform the district. In quick succession, the electronics stores of yore were replaced by specialty stores geared to otaku, while characters from anime and games began to dominate the urban landscape to an unprecedented degree. It was as if the stereotypical otaku bedroom, plastered with anime posters, had been blown up and recreated in the heart of the city. For the first time in history, a non-mainstream taste was driving urban development, independently from any political or corporate power.

In this chapter, I will examine the transformation of Akihabara and the underlying factors that led to this transformation. Specifically, I will describe the process by which the otaku demographic converged in Akihabara and ultimately converted it into an "otaku town."

AKIHABARA'S CONVERSION INTO AN OTAKU TOWN

> Akihabara is in your neighborhood, Sato Musen
> Akihabara with lots of electronics, Ono Den
>
> Come to Ishimaru Denki for electronics, Ishimaru Denki is in Akihabara
> (advertising jingles for electronics stores)

Through the 1980s, Akihabara was devoted to household appliances. Just as in the commercials for the major electronics stores, young married couples, giddy at the prospect of improving their lifestyles, shopped for new refrigerators and camcorders with their adorable children in tow (see Figure 6.1). At that point, Akihabara still embodied the illusion of domestic perfection that the Doubling National Income Plan had promoted throughout the economic boom.

Beginning around the late 1980s, however, as the economic bubble burst, Akihabara began to lose its market share to the mass retail chains such as Yamada Denki that were cropping up in suburban areas. The price of household appliances dropped, and shoppers living in Tokyo's commuter towns began opting to drive to mass retail stores in suburban strip malls instead of spending money on expensive train tickets so their families could visit Akihabara. Buying new appliances no lon-

Figure 6.1. Screen shots from an Ishimaru Electronics Commercial that ran in the 1980s. Credit: Kaichiro Morikawa.

ger inspired the excitement that had once justified the excursion to specialty shops in the electronics district.

FROM FAMILY TOWN TO OTAKU TOWN: THE GEOGRAPHIC CONCENTRATION OF PERSONALITY

Robbed of their household appliance consumers, Akihabara's electronics stores began shifting their focus to personal computers. LAOX's six-story-tall building devoted to personal computers marked a turning point when it opened in 1990, just as other big-name electronic chains were creating specialized "MS-DOS," "Mac," or "mobile computing" branches. This development was accompanied by a shift in Akihabara's consumer demographics, as families looking for household appliances were replaced by young male computer geeks.

Of course, Akihabara had always had its share of geek customers. Even in the early days of the electronics district, there were those who came to rummage through electronic parts to use in their personal projects, and audiophiles came in droves during the 1970s when home audio systems became all the rage. However, the mainstays of Akihabara's existence as an electronics district were postwar modern families seeking what the popular media dubbed the "three sacred treasures" of household appliances—TV, refrigerator, and washing machine—as well as other major appliances such as the air conditioner. In other words, the "normal" consumers who now typically flock to suburban mass retail stores constituted the core consumer base of Akihabara. In the 1990s, however, as Akihabara's retail outlets became focused on computer electronics and specialty stores, its core consumer base also shifted to enthusiasts seeking specialized goods.

This shift was unique in that it was not simply a shift in age or gender demographics. Before Windows 98 or even Windows 95 made their debuts, not many suburban strip-mall mass retailers had personal computer sections. Because of this, computer aficionados grew loyal to Akihabara in that period, and the city began to attract these customers from greater distances. Eventually this influx of computer geeks became part of an urban personality drift. The impact of this drift extended well beyond the move to personal computers and ultimately triggered a much greater transformation of Akihabara.

THE MODELING OF TASTE: GARAGE KITS

"Garage kits" are well known among model enthusiasts (see Figure 6.2). The model kits sold by big-name manufacturers such as Tamiya and Hasegawa are intended for mass production on the order of thousands and tens of thousands, and only the models of relatively popular vehicles are merchandised. However, the most enthusiastic model hobbyists tend to favor model types that are not commercially produced.

Figure 6.2. Robot (left) and Bishojo (right) garage kits, typical of today's genres.
Credit: Kaichiro Morikawa.

Craftspeople within the hobbyist community design and create their own models based on photos and drawings. Some go a step further by cast-copying original models they have designed, creating parts, and selling the resulting kits to their fellow enthusiasts, partly for bragging rights and partly to get some money back. Garage kits developed from this practice, and their name reflects their origins in the handmade contexts of personal hobbyist workshops. Initially, they mostly consisted of military models.

I say initially because the nature of the domestic garage-kit market began to change during the mid-1980s. Small companies operating out of family-run factories that had previously manufactured models for museums and events began making forays into garage kits as a mail-order business, placing ads in magazines for model hobbyists. As a result, although the market continued to target enthusiasts, it expanded from its grassroots origins to a national scale. By the late 1980s, manufacturers had begun to create their own retail showrooms, and the first specialty stores for garage-kit enthusiasts had emerged.

These small-scale manufacturers hired enthusiasts who were creating garage kits as a hobby or working part-time for model hobbyist magazines to serve as model designers. The hobby became professionalized. At the same time, the demand for specific garage-kit motifs attracted increasing attention, prompting a shift away from sci-fi and monsters to characters from anime and games that were popular among otaku. By the 1990s, the majority of these kits consisted of models representing anime girls and giant robots, and garage kits came to be associated with a proliferating range of models that catered to otaku and were produced on a small scale.

The shift to anime character models was market driven, but garage-kit makers have not abandoned their commitment to niche fans. They continue to create models of minor characters that large model manufacturers would hesitate to merchandise. In the case of popular characters, several different model designers will often create models that reflect their personal interpretations and preferences, thus going well beyond a simple effort at fidelity. This kind of meticulous connoisseurship is what makes garage kits such a distinctive product.

After 1997, stores specializing in garage kits exhibited an interesting distribution pattern. Until that time, garage-kit stores were not tied to specific areas or towns, nor were their factories based in a specific area, as with the large model manufacturers, who were concentrated in Shizuoka. In the greater Tokyo region, for example, stores tended to be scattered through districts popular among youth, such as Kichijoji, Shibuya, Yokohama, and Shinjuku. However, during the short three-year period from 1997 to 2000, almost all the stores relocated to Akihabara or established new branches there. Previously devoid of garage-kit stores, Akihabara suddenly emerged as Japan's central place for garage kits.

This concentration of garage-kit stores is just one facet of the transformation that Akihabara underwent during those three years. Other specialty stores featuring products related to manga, anime, and games—doujinshi, cosplay items, trading cards, dolls, and anime merchandise, for example—also became concentrated in Akihabara, with the trend increasing into the twenty-first century. As with garage-kit stores, these establishments had originally been scattered throughout youth-centered districts such as Shibuya and Kichijoji.

Of course, even before this shift, Akihabara had ties to anime and games. Electronics stores with VCRs, laser disc players, computers, and gaming consoles also sold software, including anime and games. However, the business model and distribution channels of the electronics stores were fundamentally different. The slew of new specialty stores in Akihabara were not offshoots of electronics stores that were now expanding their horizons into related markets. These specialty stores already existed in major shopping districts such as Shibuya and Kichi-joji. Their rapid expansion into Akihabara created a megacenter for otaku personality and taste—an otaku *personapolis*—within a few years, beginning in 1997—a transformation so incredible that one might think some very powerful forces were involved.

OTAKU MEN AND WOMEN: THE URBAN DIVIDE

Even while Akihabara was transformed from a town of home ap-pliances to a town of computer enthusiasts, it did not initially receive much attention from otaku. Before otaku specialty stores converged in Akihabara, East Ikebukuro had been the primary otaku district. And the case of East Ikebukuro illustrates how Akihabara's evolution into a particular kind of hobby town was related to cultural trends in other areas of Tokyo, specifically gender-based distinctions.

East Ikebukuro is now favored by female otaku. From the begin-ning of the twenty-first century, specialty stores catering to women who read boys' love and *yaoi* (see Chapter 9) began to concentrate in East Ikebukuro. As Akihabara became a gathering spot for male otaku, East Ikebukuro became its female counterpart.

It is difficult to gauge the number of bookstores that cater to women, not just those that specialize in yaoi literature. However, it is clearly un-usual to have a concentration of ten such bookstores in one area. Nor-mally bookstores have separate areas that cater to women and men. For example, in the case of manga, bookstores are clearly divided into shelves targeting female readers on the one hand and those targeting male readers on the other. And this in-store divide has been duplicated on a larger, urban scale in Akihabara and East Ikebukuro. For example, many otaku specialty stores have branches in both Akihabara and Ikebukuro, and each branch features the same kinds of products, in particular manga, doujinshi, anime DVDs, and character merchandise. However, the customers in the Akihabara branch are primarily male, while the customers in the East Ikebukuro branch are primarily female.

What is behind this urban divide between otaku men and women? Specialty stores featuring manga and anime-related goods were actu-ally in business in East Ikebukuro long before they ever opened in Aki-habara. Their history can be traced to the early 1980s, when Animate, an anime goods store, opened across from the Sunshine 60 building in

March 1983. Garage-kit stores did not begin converging in Akihabara and driving the city's transformation into an otaku town until after 1997. Furthermore, Messe San-oh, a game software store considered a forerunner of Akihabara's turn to otaku, began selling doujinshi only around 1993. In other words, East Ikebukuro had a ten-year head start on Akihabara.

Akihabara's transformation began in the 1990s with game software stores. By contrast, East Ikebukuro's transformation began with anime goods stores that rode the anime boom of the early 1980s. These disparate starting points may have had some influence over the two districts' subsequent development. At the time, PC gamers were mostly male, whereas in the anime arena, female fans were more prominent.

Nonetheless, while East Ikebukuro enjoyed a concentration of otaku stores before Akihabara did, those stores were not specifically female-oriented during the 1980s and 1990s. Until Akihabara's transformation began in the late 1990s, otaku stores in East Ikebukuro apparently catered to both genders.

From 2000 on, however, East Ikebukuro's manga and anime stores began shifting their product lineups heavily toward women. In 2000 alone, several new stores that catered specifically to women otaku opened, including KAC Shop, a store specializing in new doujinshi targeting women; Volks, a doll specialty store; and Aqua House, which admits only female customers. Other stores specializing in character goods and doujinshi targeting women followed, and the area was even dubbed Otome Road, or Girl's Road.

One of the factors behind this shift was that the district of Ikebukuro had always enjoyed a relatively high number of female shoppers. Another was the presence of Animate, which was at the core of East Ikebukuro's specialty stores, and which had been relatively favored by female otaku. After renovating to occupy an entire eight-story building in 2000, it began organizing frequent events for fans.

When the demand for goods catering to male otaku became concentrated in Akihabara in 1997, East Ikebukuro stores had to adjust their inventories, sending employees who specialized in products favored by male otaku to their Akihabara branches. Consequently, as the stores became less populated by male otaku, the shopping environment of Otome Road turned more and more comforting to female otaku, and female customers increasingly flocked to the area. In a sense, Akihabara and East Ikebukuro's Otome Road are like siblings.

The two otaku towns share a common history. A decisive segregation of customer gender identity was generated on a citywide scale, accelerating the concentration and expansion of subcultures in the respective areas. Otaku culture evolves and advances when members of the opposite sex are absent. It is unusual for male and female otaku to develop a romantic interest in each other by watching anime, playing games, and going to specialty stores together. Even if they share interests, they differ on the specifics. This conflict between men and women in their tastes perhaps played a role in East Ikebukuro's transformation from a place where both male and female otaku congregated into an overwhelmingly female Otome Road.

OTAKU STORES REMAKE THE "BIRTHPLACE OF PERSONAL COMPUTERS"

Now that I have provided some context on Akihabara's development in relation to that of East Ikebukuro, I would like to return to the transformation of Akihabara into an otaku town.

The Radio Kaikan building was at the leading edge of Akihabara's transformation from an electronics district to an otaku town. Situated right outside Akihabara station's "Electric Town Exit," the building used to be crammed with specialty stores featuring Akihabara's core product offerings, such as home electronics, audio equipment, and computer supplies. As a result of its location and its offerings, its symbolic importance is similar to that of the Rockefeller Center in Manhattan.

The seventh floor of the Radio Kaikan building features a plaque designating the building as Japan's "Birthplace of Personal Computers." The plaque marks the spot formerly occupied by the first shop to sell the personal computer's precursor, the microcomputer kit. Masayoshi Son, the CEO of Softbank, Kazuhiko Nishi, founder of ASCII, and others who went on to become leaders of the domestic PC industry frequented the shop as teenagers.

No stores in the Radio Kaikan building specialized in manga or garage kits until 1998. The first two floors consisted mostly of home appliance stores, followed by two floors of audio equipment stores and a floor devoted to personal computing, as though the building's floors were geological strata showing the sedimentation of Akihabara's core products through the years.

Starting in March 1998, however, the building's tenants underwent a rapid change, as though a large-scale buyout or massive rent increase had occurred. By the end of the year 2000, approximately half of the Radio Kaikan's available retail space was taken up by new otaku specialty stores (see Table 6.1). During the course of approximately three years, electronics stores closed one after another and were replaced by manga and garage-kit stores. Occupying prime real estate in front of the train station, the building had once embodied Akihabara's identity as an electronics district. By 2001, the famous NEC showroom that

Table 6.1 Timetable: Expansion of otaku specialty stores into the Radio Kaikan building between 1998 and 2002

1998	March	King Star opens, second floor
	April	Kei Books (specializing in manga, doujinshi, and anime goods) opens, third floor (takes up half the floor space); Kaiyodo (garage-kit manufacturer) opens retail store, fourth floor
	July	Volks (garage-kit manufacturer) opens retail store, sixth floor
1999	January	Yellow Submarine opens branch specializing in trading cards, seventh floor
	July	Volks expands floor space by one-half, sixth floor
	October	Yellow Submarine opens branch specializing in models and garage kits, fourth floor
2000	August	Yellow Submarine's trading-card branch expands floor space
	September	Yellow Submarine opens branch specializing in scale models, seventh floor
	October	Kei Books expands floor space to entire floor, third floor
	December	Kaiyodo opens branch specializing in "freebie" toys packaged with junk food, second floor; Yellow Submarine's garage-kit branch expands floor space, fourth floor
2001	September	Volks opens branch featuring rental showcases, seventh floor
2002	June	Eihodou, previously a video electronics store, reopens as a specialty store of dating sim games, second floor

Figure 6.3. Storefront of a garage-kit seller. Credit: Kaichiro Morikawa.

had been dubbed the "Birthplace of Personal Computers" had been replaced by a garage-kit manufacturer's retail store (see Figure 6.3). Where computers were once on display, there are now anime character figurines.

The rapid change to the Radio Kaikan building is striking, and it might appear as though it were the result of an aggressive strategy on the part of management to attract otaku businesses. After I conducted fieldwork, however, it became clear to me that no such strategy was at play. In fact, building tenants and neighboring stores indicated that the management staff are rather old-fashioned and had not wanted the building to become the new nexus of otaku-centered Akihabara. Some storekeepers I spoke to suggested that the management would want to save face vis-à-vis other electronics stores in the area and thus would not want to be interviewed about any strategy they might have. And in fact, I was unable to interview the management about the reasons for the changing nature of the building's tenants.

The management leases retail space by the month and does not take a commission on sales. Some storekeepers pointed out that as a result, the management has little incentive to lure stores with robust sales or to draw up a marketing strategy. The small size of the individual stores involved also makes it unlikely that the new tenants formed a cabal intent on a hostile takeover of the building. Some of the newcomers used existing connections to begin their talks with the management, but these connections were apparently limited to helping them get a foot in the door and never were used to broker deals to evict existing tenants.

The reality was that the management grudgingly gave business to otaku stores when stores selling home appliances and audio equipment went into the red and downsized or left the building. This created the impression that the Radio Kaikan building's rapid transformation was the result of a well-executed business strategy. It was actually a result of specialty stores' proactively and aggressively expanding into Akihabara. What motivated this phenomenon?

NICHE DEMAND FLOWS INTO AKIHABARA: GOOD NEWS, COURTESY OF *EVANGELION*

The relocation of Kaiyodo, a well-known garage-kit store, is one indicator of how otaku stores relocated and concentrated in Akihabara. The Osaka-based company's Tokyo store had been situated in Shibuya since 1986. In 1997, it moved that store to a building on the banks of Kanda River in Akihabara and then to the fourth floor in the Radio Kaikan building in 1998. Here is an excerpt from an interview with Kaiyodo's senior managing director, Shuichi Miyawaki:

> We don't really employ a strategy based on merchandising and research when we pick cities. It's almost all about whim and about what looks fun. When we first moved into Tokyo in 1984, we were initially in Kayabacho for two and a half years. There wasn't any special reason for picking that location. We chose that spot just because it was close to Tokyo station and easy to get to from Osaka and outside of Tokyo. At the time, we thought that as long as we had good quality, the customers would come to us no matter where we were. It was a "come to us if you want to come" type of mentality.
>
> But after two years or so in Tokyo, we knew all too well that Kayabacho was no good and that it wasn't very convenient for us either. For example, if we wanted to grab a bite to eat during the weekend, we were in a ghost town because it's a business district.
>
> So we moved on to Shibuya. One of the biggest reasons we moved there was because there was a Tokyu Hands there.[1] At the time, there weren't as many Tokyu Hands around as there are now, so Shibuya was the place to go if you wanted to go to Tokyu Hands. We'd often stop by Tokyu Hands if we were in Tokyo for work from Osaka. Another rea-

son was that the lifestyle standards of people living in Shibuya and western parts of Tokyo seemed to be higher. Garage kits are expensive, so they kind of choose their customers. Also, it's something you probably hear often, but another reason was that Shibuya was often featured in magazines and had a reputation for being a trendsetter in youth culture.

We were in Shibuya for a long time, from 1986 till our move in 1997. While we were there, parts of Shibuya had this otaku-town ambiance, and that became part of its image. We had Volks and Yellow Submarine come in, a cosplay store, and Manga no Mori too. After we went to Shibuya, a lot of different otaku stores came, so we kind of felt that we called them to Shibuya.

There were times then when our motivation went down. Around 1992, we felt we'd done everything and run out of ideas. Our resin kits and soft vinyl kits had reached a point where we didn't have any more innovation. We could maybe increase the number of parts from 10 to 11, minor things like that. Some were starting to suggest that we close up shop. But stopping requires energy too, so in a way we kind of just kept dragging things out.

Then in 1995 and 1996, we got the *Evangelion* boom and the garage-kit industry really expanded businesswise.[2] Back then, initial production numbers were in the two thousands and three thousands. Now, we celebrate if we can get three hundred sold. In the garage-kit business, there aren't many models that'll sell over three hundred. Thanks to the boom, we gained some energy, but we could tell that the *Evangelion* effect would be over by around 1997. *Evangelion* burned out the otaku market. It was different from *Gundam* and the other *mecha* [piloted robot] stuff because they ended *Evangelion* on a very final note and made it clear it wasn't going to continue. So when we were thinking about what to do next, our store manager started saying that if we were going to do anything at all, we'd have to move into Akihabara.

Akihabara had come up in conversations a lot from before. Before, when our model designers came out to Tokyo for a Comiket [Comic Market; see Chapter 5] or a garage-kit wholesale event, they would first go the day before the opening day of Comiket to Jimbocho. To otaku, even the act of casually buying manga has more prestige if they go to a specialty store like Manga no Mori and Comic Takaoka. From there, they'd go to Akihabara to get laser discs and then to Comiket to get doujinshi, but all those kinds of stores were starting to converge in Akihabara. Even back then, we already had the porno-doujinshi stores showing up in Akihabara.

The store manager was a really sharp man, and this got his attention. Kaiyodo's the type of company to go right along with one guy's idea as long as it seems right, so we just decided, with no particular plan, to go to Akihabara. We knew we weren't going anywhere the way things were, so we decided to use the relocation to Akihabara to motivate ourselves.

The first year, we set up shop in a building next to the Kanda River. We occupied the basement floor and the first floor, but it was only around four hundred square feet. Also, there was some internal stuff going on, so we weren't very focused on doing business that year [see Miyawaki 2002]. The store manager had quit too, so we were trying to start up the shop without our core staff. But people came and we had sales despite all that. That was when I personally felt Akihabara's power. It was like even though we weren't doing anything, we were getting customers.

So toward the end of 1997, we decided to actually give things a serious try, so we asked a broker to find us a spot. He told us that there was a vacancy in this Radio Kaikan place. At the time the rent was a bit steep for us so it was an adventure for an otaku shop. Businesses like ours that deal with otaku are, well, underground, like bugs under a rock. We don't like being exposed to the sun. We used to think it's kind of embarrassing to be seen by normal people. But we started thinking that coming out of the shadows and going to a sunlit place like the fourth floor of a building in front of a train station might actually be fun.

Right around the time we moved to Akihabara, we were in a place called "America Town" in the Parco department store in Osaka. It's ground zero for Osaka youth culture, and you won't find anything otaku-related there, but in part because of the *Evangelion* subculture boom, it was fashionable at the time to buy anime figurines. So, our successes in Osaka and in Akihabara had made us confident. We thought we could do it, so we rented about fourteen hundred square feet in the Radio Kaikan building. (December 22, 2000, at Kaiyodo's Osaka headquarters)

Although the case is in many ways idiosyncratic, the example of Kaiyodo indicates how *Evangelion*'s success motivated its relocation to Akihabara. *Neon Genesis Evangelion* (produced by Gainax and directed by Hideaki Anno) was a TV series that aired between 1995 and 1996. It garnered tremendous acclaim from otaku, caught the attention of the general youth demographic during reruns, and enjoyed a huge popularity boom in multiple media by the time the two movies spun out from the series hit theaters in 1997. Licensed merchandise was developed in multiple formats, with an emphasis on books, laser discs, games, and figurines. *Evangelion* is estimated to have generated 30 billion yen (approximately US$30 million). Mainstream bookstores nationwide had *Evangelion* sections, and there were so many doujinshi about the series that a huge section was set aside for it at doujinshi conventions. As stated in the excerpt above, *Evangelion* even expanded the garage-kit market by an order of magnitude. Life-sized figures were being sold for an unprecedented price of 380,000 yen (approximately US$3,800) each. And in addition to generating a huge market for the series, *Evangelion* was also a central factor in the subculture boom that followed, creating demand for anime and American comic-book character merchandise among the general public.

The *Evangelion* boom lent the energy and thrust necessary for the expansion of specialty stores into Akihabara's prime real estate. The timing of the boom and the expansion were in sync. The stores involved in that period of transition were all businesses that benefited from the *Evangelion* boom. The dam broke once other stores saw that the initial wave of stores was raking in more profits than expected.

BUILDING THE ARCHITECTURE OF OTAKU TASTE

Otaku visiting from the provinces had generally followed a specific route on their pilgrimages to Tokyo. They would visit a manga store in Jinbocho, buy laser discs in Akihabara, and buy doujinshi in manga conventions in Makuhari and Ariake. These disparate pilgrimage spots converged in Akihabara. Project EVA, the consortium that had put up the money for *Evangelion*, was a joint venture with businesses dealing in laser discs (King Records), manga (Kadokawa Shoten), and games (Sega Enterprises, now Sega Corporation). Both the pilgrimage route and the relation between different media enterprises are grounded in the same structure of otaku interests as the multiple media forms.

Those who like anime enough to collect laser discs also will tend to like games, doujinshi, and garage kits. This "architecture" of otaku taste links the numerous specialty stores that moved into the Radio Kaikan building from 1998 on. Although stores moved in individually in a piecemeal fashion, they developed a synergistic relationship to one another, eventually taking over entire buildings with a patchwork of related otaku interests.

The store Gamers, another forerunner of the city's turn to otaku culture, opened a character merchandise store in May 1997. By November 1999, it had opened a seven-story building as its main store on the main avenue in Akihabara. With character goods on the first floor, games on the second, manga on the third, anime DVDs and CDs on the fourth, trading cards on the fifth, garage kits and models on the sixth, and a trading-card gaming room doubling as a café on the seventh, the building's floors constituted a cross-section of otaku taste. This is an architecture of otaku taste in bricks and mortar.

Other stores began opening otaku department stores: LAOX's hobby building in November 1999; Comic Tora no Ana Building No. 1 in November 2000; Animate Akihabara in April 2001; Gamers Main Building No. 2 in July 2002; and Asobit City in October 2002 (see Figures 6.4 and 6.5). In addition, Akihabara Department Store in the Akihabara station renovated all three floors in March 2002, restructuring its store lineup from suits and shoes to otaku merchandise such as manga, games, figures, anime DVDs, and model trains and even setting aside a special section for *Gundam* character goods. Employees who had previously sold suits were initially hesitant about being transferred

Figure 6.4. Otaku department stores. Credit: Kaichiro Morikawa

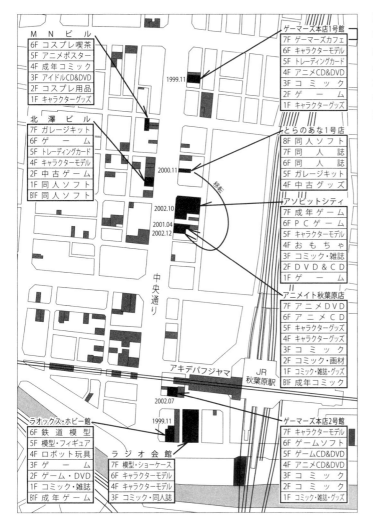

Figure 6.5. Distribution of manga, anime, and game specialty stores in Akihabara as of January 2003.
Credit: Map by Kaichiro Morikawa.

to these new stores. The otaku interest framework had even overtaken a fifty-year-old department store.

The connection between manga, anime, games, and character models, which I referred to as the architecture of otaku taste, is nothing new and has been widely recognized. Given this, it may seem natural that such stores converged in Akihabara. After all, Akihabara already had an otaku atmosphere, so the new stores fit right in.

However, in terms of the shaping of a city district, the phenomenon was extremely new. A different influence was at work, different from those that had driven other urban developments. The extent of this difference becomes clear once it is seen in the context of Akihabara's initial emergence as an electronics district.

AMERICAN INTERVENTION IN THE BIRTH OF THE ELECTRONICS DISTRICT

Two major factors lay behind the formation of the electronics district. First, right after World War II ended, students at the nearby Electrical Manufacturing Technical School (now Tokyo Denki University) took up side jobs of making and selling radios. The immense popularity of these handmade radios induced street vendors dealing in electronic parts to migrate to the area. However, in 1949, the General Headquarters of the occupying forces issued an eviction order to the vendors in order to broaden the streets, and the small black market was faced with extinction. After the vendor association submitted a petition, the prefecture and the national railway company provided an alternative location under the train tracks of Akihabara station, and all the vendors were squeezed into that space. By initiating the first concentration of radio stores and centers in the station area, these developments led to the establishment of the electronics district.

Another important catalyst was the positioning of the Hirose Shokai Corporation, an Akihabara old-timer from the prewar period with networks that extended to the provinces. Retailers and distributors would come from around the country to Akihabara to stock up. As a result, Akihabara gained a reputation for being inexpensive, and its location as a transportation hub began to attract the general public. By the 1970s, the postwar home-appliance boom brought about by the Doubling National Income Plan and the "three sacred treasures" of home appliances transformed Akihabara into Japan's premier electronics district. An area measuring less than one square kilometer was home to 10 percent of Japan's household appliance market.

During the economic boom, Akihabara was a place where manufacturers offered exceptional price cuts and also experimented in order to obtain feedback from their customers. Company technicians were sent in droves to stand in front of retail stores as salesmen with specialized knowledge. Numerous big-name home-appliance manufacturers gave their full support to the development of Akihabara (Yamashita 1999).

In sum, the birth of the electronics district can be attributed to a combination of factors. Akihabara was historically a downtown district, it was close to a technical school for electronics, it had the history of the vendor-eviction order, and it had a plethora of textbook advantages such as distribution networks and transportation. Particularly notable is the way the vendor-eviction order provided direct momentum for the electronics district's formation. The subsequent concentration of electronic-parts vendors under the train tracks was accomplished by order of the American occupation.

By contrast, the post-1997 transformation did not involve any policies or distribution channels. The changes were not brought about by administrative policies but by a single televised anime series. It is worth noting again that there was no organized development by real estate or big-name investors. Nor was there an effort by a conglomerate of manufacturers such as *Evangelion*'s sponsor to remake Akihabara into a town for otaku. Akihabara's turn to otaku is fundamentally different from the way in which Shibuya and Ikebukuro were developed, with capital from railway corporations such as Tokyu and Seibu.

The recurring theme I encountered while investigating established electronics stores and newcomer otaku stores was that Akihabara's transformation into an otaku town was spontaneous and demand driven. As demonstrated by Kaiyodo's immediate and unexpected success upon relocation, this urban phenomenon did not require the involvement of big corporations.

REALITY MIMICS CYBERSPACE

Why then did such a large demand for otaku products emerge—without any organized corporate or government effort—in Akihabara in particular? Although the *Evangelion* boom was the catalyst, it would not have triggered a change unless there was an existing demand for otaku culture in the area. As mentioned previously, Shibuya and Kichijoji already had more specialty stores than did Akihabara. Why did neither of those districts nor Jinbocho become an otaku district? The answer to this question is key to understanding Akihabara's transformation into an otaku town—and it relates to Akihabara's unique urban personality traits.

As mentioned in the beginning of this chapter, this personality derived from Akihabara's concentration of computer enthusiasts, or geeks. Geeks tend to like anime-style characters, anime, games, and garage kits. This architecture of otaku taste replaced traditional principles and powers involved in urban development such as historical context and government policy, shaping the transformation of Akihabara in new ways.

One idea that has attracted considerable attention in the e-business field is the idea of communities of interest (Fischer 2001). Propelled by the spread of the Internet, communities of interest that do not depend on shared geographical locations or blood ties are growing in numbers and influence. These communities manifest themselves in various forms, including online portal sites and web forums devoted to particular interests and tastes (see Chapter 3).

Simply put, in the case of Akihabara, an urban district was recreated by an architecture of tastes and interests as though the structure of the web manifested in real space. Computers are by nature machines that specialize in mimicking reality. Akihabara points in the opposite direction, where reality mimics the cyberspace created by computers. So what does it look like when an online community or structure of taste manifests in reality?

EXTENSION OF PRIVATE ROOMS TO URBAN SPACE

The former Gamers main building No. 1 had been known as the Digiko building because its mascot from a TV anime series, *Digiko* (Digi-girl), was prominently displayed on the building's rooftop sign.[3] Displaying anime characters on store signs is not unusual in Japan, but in Akihabara, the sheer density of anime imagery is intense, with posters cluttering walls, sidewalk signs, and life-sized cardboard cutouts. These images are particularly prominent in game-shop storefronts, which brazenly display posters of dating sims while exhibiting the female characters as life-sized figures or body-pillow covers on the bustling sidewalks of Akihabara's main avenue (see Figure 6.6). It has recently even become common to see female anime and game characters in special advertisements embedded in the floor in the front of the train station's ticket gates. Such images have spilled over from the stores on the main avenue, infiltrating even the floor of the extremely public space of the station (see Figure 6.7).

Figure 6.6. Game shops on Chuo-dori (Main Street).
Credit: Kaichiro Morikawa.

Figure 6.7. Advertisement for a pornographic game on the floor of the JR Akihabara station.
Credit: Kaichiro Morikawa.

Is this explosion of kitschy icons any different from the vigorous commercial development during the economic boom or the efforts by municipal authorities to revitalize their cities by turning hometowns into theme parks? If developments in Akihabara are the same as these other trends in urban development, then for answers to this question we can rely on the main critical analyses of the consumer society and urbanism that developed in the 1980s (for example, Nakagawa 1996). Or is there something fundamentally different happening in Akihabara that cannot be reduced to economic expansion?

I would also like to pose another question. I have been emphasizing the personality traits of Akihabara's user base, but cities having their own distinct populations and ambience are nothing new. Otemachi is a city of suit-clad businessmen, and Harajuku was once the dancing grounds of the harem-suited *takenoko-zoku*.[4] Is the concentration of otaku in Akihabara any different from what we saw in these other districts?

Businessmen gather in office districts because of their social status and roles. The takenoko-zoku were performers using Harajuku as their stage; they did not continue acting out their roles once they went home. The phenomenon in Akihabara, by contrast, represents the extension of private into public spaces, personal rooms into cities.

The characters that are engulfing Akihabara exhibit the same graphic style that characterizes Japanese anime: large eyes and childlike features. The similarities are immediately visible when you look around in Akihabara, and they are now so prominent that the aesthetic has come to represent Akihabara. Depending on whom you ask, there are subcategories such as "*moe* style" and "*puni* style," but for the sake of clarity, I will use "anime style" to refer to all of them (see Chapter 2).

As an icon of otaku taste, anime style has long lurked in the private rooms of otaku or within the confines of back-alley store walls in consumer districts such as Shibuya and Kichijoji. Mass consumer industries have worked to control people's tastes and interests by appealing to issues of social status and upward mobility. However, the otaku, being resistant by nature to such social pressures, had no choice but to feel like outsiders or minorities in urban areas that had been commercially developed by advertising agencies. Both otaku stores and their customers wanted to avoid attracting attention, but like a tribe seeking self-determination, they flocked to Akihabara under the banner of their shared interest in computers.

The concentration of a marginal personality type in an urban district has exposed the previously hidden interests of otaku in Akihabara to the extent that it transformed urban space. The otaku's private space has become connected to public space. The otaku's stance outside the mainstream, their understanding of themselves as a marginal subculture, is the most significant characteristic that distinguishes Akihabara's transformation from earlier commercially driven urban developments.

At the birthplace of personal computers in the Radio Kaikan building, we can now see the most purified and cutting-edge manifestation of this phenomenon. The hobby store Volks, which had been in the building since 1998, opened a new type of store there in 2001. Called Rental Showcase, the store's interior is lined with rows of strange shelves that resemble transparent lockers (see Figures 6.8 and 6.9).

The store is a type of flea market. People who have something to sell rent a locker for 2,000 to 5,000 yen a month (approximately US$20–50), depending on size and location. Renters tag and arrange their own wares, and the store takes 15 percent in fees for successful sales. The cases are lined up as if they were rooms in a building.

The cases contain various treasures from various tastes: old models that are no longer in production, with assembled and colored figurines,

Figure 6.8. Volks's Rental Showcase store in the Radio Kaikan building. Credit: Kaichiro Morikawa.

Figure 6.9. Items of interest displayed at Rental Showcase. Credit: Kaichiro Morikawa.

prizes from "UFO catcher" games, photos of pop idols, items whose value may be known only by those in the know, and even some unidentifiable objects. Each case is a private shop as well as a private room that contains a concentrated version of the merchant's taste. In that sense, the store resembles a cross-section of a giant apartment complex. Perhaps this scene foreshadows Akihabara's future landscape.

Many say that Japan's cities are losing their individuality and becoming uniform. The nature of capital, which standardizes everything it touches, has repainted the face of historic cities in tandem with commercialization. However, Akihabara has begun to spontaneously recapture a distinctive urban individualism, and it has done this through a decentralized, demand-driven cultural mechanism that departs from traditional organized urban planning.

Notes

1. Tokyu Hands is a large department store carrying a wide range of hardware, craft, and hobby supplies.

2. *Evangelion* is a popular cult anime series featuring a coming-of-age story of an adolescent boy and fighting robots. Many consider the series to epitomize key dimensions of otaku culture and that it marked the beginning of a rapid spread and partial mainstreaming of otaku culture.

3. The Dijiko building was closed April 6, 2003, and main building No. 2 became the new Gamers main store.

4. *Takenoko-zoku* were youth who dressed up in colorful robes and danced in the streets of Harajuku on Sundays during the economic boom years of the 1980s.

References

Fischer, Gerhard. 2001. External and shareable artifacts as opportunities for social creativity in communities of interest. In J. S. Gero and M. L. Maher, eds., *Proceedings of the fifth international conference on computational and cognitive models of creative design*, 67–89. Sydney: Key Center of Design Computing and Cognition, University of Sydney.

Miyawaki, Shuichi. 2002. *Ideas from Kaiyodo: A group of modelers*. Tokyo: Kobunsha.

Nakagawa, Osamu. 1996. *Japan's camouflage: The Disneyland-fication of public facilities*. Tokyo: Shokokusha.

Yamashita, Yuko. 1999. The rise and fall of discount shops: Akihabara as commercial accumulation. In *The era of marketing revolution: Revolutions in sales and distribution*, 77–120. Tokyo: Yuhikakku.

7

Anime and Manga Fandom as Networked Culture

LAWRENCE ENG

Otaku are drawn to anime, manga, science fiction, and computers because they are subjects that are dense and information rich, enabling otaku to immerse themselves in a rich knowledge economy. Otaku knowledge requires immersion in not only information and media but also in ongoing social exchange about topics of interest. Particularly for overseas fans, much of their knowledge and media content is gained through contact with other fans instead of or in addition to commercial or professional sources. This was certainly the case in the early years of the fandom, directly influencing the landscape of fandom in the present day. Contrary to the stereotypical image of the otaku as socially isolated, anime fan communities are highly social and networked, relying on a combination of online and offline connections. This chapter describes the ways in which the U.S. anime and manga fandom originated and evolved from the 1960s to the present, focusing on the social networks and exchanges among fans that have been the bedrock of this evolving fan scene. After first outlining a history of the anime fandom in the United States, the chapter focuses on the current state of otaku networks that include local networks, online networks, and conventions.

A BRIEF HISTORY OF ANIME, FANDOM, AND OTAKU IN THE UNITED STATES

To understand American otaku identity and subculture, we must first explore the intertwined histories of the growth of fandom and the rise of anime as an entertainment medium in the United States. Although U.S. fans have not been central to the creation of anime itself, they have had a strong influence on how the medium is distributed, appreciated, and consumed in this country. Various books (Patten 2004), documentaries (*Otaku Unite* 2004), and websites (Right Stuf 1998) have cataloged with great detail the anime television shows and films that were seen by early fans of the medium in the United States, whether they were shown on American television, at convention video rooms, or on traded videocassettes. A surprisingly large amount of history has been recorded by early fans such as Fred Patten, a founder of the Cartoon/Fantasy Organization (or C/FO) and a seminal figure in the birth of organized anime fandom in the United States. The C/FO is considered by many to be the first anime club in the country, with numerous branches all across the United States. Patten, in addition to highlighting the specific titles that made an impact on early American audiences of anime, kept detailed records of fan activities from the late 1970s, into the 1980s, and beyond.[1] Drawing from the work of Patten and others, here I provide a historical overview of the growth of anime fandom in the United States.

Anime Makes Its Debut in the United States

Anime made its debut in the United States in the early 1960s, with titles such as *Astroboy* (*Tetsuwan Atom*), *Speed Racer* (*Mach Go Go Go*), and *Simba the White Lion* (*Jungle Taitei*), capturing the imagination of children (and adults) who watched the shows with little awareness that they were actually created in Japan specifically for Japanese audiences. Knowledge of and interest in Japanese animation gradually spread, primarily by word of mouth, among the already large and active science fiction fandom in the United States. In 1975, the first consumer videocassette recorder was made available to the public, opening new opportunities for the medium to spread as American anime enthusiasts traded tapes with each other and with contacts in Japan. Eventually, these well-connected anime fans began hosting anime-only video rooms at science fiction conventions.

Among early audiences in America, anime was commonly referred to as "Japanimation," highlighting the foreign origins of the medium. Anime was clearly identified as cult media consumed by a cult fandom in the United States; it was being enjoyed by U.S. fans despite the fact that it was not officially available to, marketed to, or intended for non-Japanese viewers. It is unsurprising, therefore, that anime gained early traction among members of the American science fiction fandom. This is a community heavily invested in cult media outside of mainstream media distribution, such as shows that are off the air and not being distributed or shows published overseas (such as anime or British television).

The C/FO was founded in Los Angeles in 1977. Other chapters of the C/FO were formed in other parts of the country, including the East Coast. Anime and information about anime was difficult to come by for that first generation of American fans, so clubs such as the C/FO relied heavily on personal contacts to acquire new shows and information. According to my informants, some of whom were intimately involved in this early American anime fandom, anime fans from all over the country would communicate with each other by fairly primitive means, sending hard-copy documents containing anime information such as synopses, reviews, and translations to each other. Club members also gathered to attend screenings of Japanese television shows and films that would have been extremely difficult for them to acquire on their own. At some club meetings, members would also chain VCRs together for mass copying of tapes. Although electronic networks of communication were still in their infancy, some fans from those early days think that the anime community was more close-knit then than now, because people had to make personal connections with people all around the country to get the information they needed.

The Establishment of a U.S. Anime Fan Scene

Through the late 1970s and into the early and mid-1980s, more and more anime titles were shown on American television, and the Japanese origins of those shows became more evident because of the growing awareness of Japanese pop culture in the United States. The popularity of Hello Kitty, karate, and ninja movies coincided with the American business world's interest in Japan's economic successes in the 1980s. Despite the growing awareness and interest, however, Japanese animation was still not easy to acquire in the United States.

One of the earliest anime licensing and distribution companies was Streamline Pictures, headed by the late Carl Macek, who brought anime to the masses in the mid-1980s through *Robotech*, a mashup of three separate and narratively unrelated anime titles.[2] Streamline had an advantage of being early to market, capitalizing on the fandom's desire to have easy access to anime. Streamline titles were much easier to find, less expensive, and more easily understandable than Japanese imports. They ultimately failed, however, to win the loyalty and enthusiasm of the new generation of American anime fandom that was gaining more access to anime and anime information than ever before through other means.

What was Streamline up against? In addition to having more access (more shows on television, more information in mainstream publications, etc.), the new generation of fans also had higher standards. While the older fans were happy about having any Japanese animation to watch, and they did not always object to English-dubbed works, newer fans often thought that the works were best in their original language with as little tampering as possible. This attitude was probably spurred by poor translations and adaptations that were not true to the original storylines, along with a growing appreciation of anime as a uniquely Japanese cultural product.[3]

Additionally, starting in the mid-1980s, technology became available for fans to start adding their own subtitles to existing video, so that translations of anime could now be seen on screen instead of just being printed or read aloud during showings. The proliferation of fan-subtitled anime (or "fansubs") helped spread the appreciation of the works in their original language, even to the point where American fans became knowledgeable enthusiasts of particular Japanese voice actors and actresses (see Chapter 8). Finally, the new generation of fans was dissatisfied by the lack of variety of anime available to them commercially. Streamline and other early anime-distribution companies developed a reputation for releasing only the most provocatively violent or sexually explicit anime, which fans thought hurt the reputation of anime in the United States.

Fan Clubs and the Expansion of Fandom

Anime fandom continued to expand and evolve in the late 1980s and early 1990s. The children who watched anime on television grew older and continued to nurture their enthusiasm for the medium when they entered college. As a result, this period saw an explosion in anime clubs being formed on college campuses. Anime clubs provided fans

with several things. The availability of anime in mainstream retail outlets was still limited, and clubs enabled fans to pool their resources so
that they could see anime that was too difficult or expensive to acquire
on their own. They also allowed fans to share information with each
other. Most important, fandom was still nascent enough in the United
States that finding like-minded fans in one's hometown could be a
challenge. Therefore, college clubs represented the first opportunity
for some fans to make friends with other fans, in person.

Anime had become somewhat easier to obtain by the late 1980s.
With the rise of companies such as Streamline Pictures, US Rendi-
tions, and Animeigo, commercially available anime was just getting its
start in the United States. The latter two companies are notable for
being the first ones to release unedited anime with the original Japanese dialogue intact, along with English subtitles. College and university anime clubs showed many of these commercially available titles,
but they also had growing access to informally distributed anime from
Japan, whether it came from somebody's Japanese pen pal who sent
tapes in the mail, U.S. servicemen and women stationed in Japan who
brought tapes to the United States, Japanese video stores in California,
or local television broadcasts intended for the Japanese population of
Hawaii. The availability of Japanese import videotapes and laser discs
was growing as well, and some anime fans would pay premium prices
to acquire them.

However, most otaku who attended college anime clubs did not have
easy access to Japanese pen pals, Japanese rental stores in California,
or laser discs. Instead, they belonged to a tape-trading network. These
networks would grow even larger as the practice of fansubbing evolved.
While individuals could request and obtain fansubs in the mail, anime
clubs were often given priority when it came to getting fansubs first.
Fans believed that, when circulated via clubs, fansubs helped educate
people about anime but did not harm the industry because only a few
people owned them. A single fansub could benefit an entire club of
twenty to one hundred members, as opposed to every one of those
members owning a bootleg tape. Before the advent of Internet fansub
distribution in the late 1990s, college anime clubs were the primary
place to see the latest anime from Japan. These clubs, in addition to
providing a fun and social atmosphere where fans could watch anime

together, played an important role in educating the fandom about the diversity of anime beyond what was commercially available. By doing so, the clubs helped generate demand for varied, high-quality, unedited, and well-translated anime in the United States. College anime clubs typically avoided showing violent and sexually explicit titles that dominated the commercially available anime in the United States in these early years. Instead, they screened a large variety of anime in multiple genres, helping to create the diverse market we see today.

Members of some of the early anime clubs would go on to work in the anime industry or to organize major conventions. Some members of Cal-Animage Alpha, the University of California, Berkeley, anime club, would eventually found Anime Expo, one of the largest anime trade conventions in the United States (Anime Expo 2009). Animeigo got its start after the founders of the company attended meetings of the Cornell Japanimation Society (CJS) and realized there was a market for unedited anime in the United States.[4] The club's founder and first president, Masaki Takai, would become a founding member and translator for Animeigo.

For many, college clubs provided the first opportunity to socialize with other fans. Watching anime became a social event, along with club administrative meetings, informal anime showings, and other get-togethers that might include video gaming or other activities not necessarily associated with anime. Some of the more time-intensive activities that anime clubs were involved with included hosting screening marathons, creating music videos, creating parody videos, and hosting their own anime conventions (which are mostly fan organized and volunteer driven to this day). High school clubs would emerge a bit later as American anime fandom became younger and more diverse, a consequence of anime's becoming more mainstream and readily available.

Fandom Moves Online

While the VCR and postal mail were the primary technologies employed by the first generation of American anime fans, the new generation of fans in the early 1990s relied increasingly on the Internet.[5] Some even used earlier information networks such as CompuServe and GEnie to connect with other fans. In addition, anime bulletin board services (or BBSes) allowed fans to share scripts, synopses, and images with each other. However, because of the high cost of calling BBSes long-distance, this pre-Internet electronic network was not widely used by the fandom.

The Internet succeeded where BBSes did not because it was a large network spanning the entire United States and beyond, and much of the best and earliest Internet access in the United States could be found at universities. College-going anime fans colonized this new electronic frontier quickly, forming anime-related newsgroups on Usenet, establishing electronic mailing lists to replace the old postal mail newsletters, and setting up FTP and Gopher sites to share media.[6] On FTP repositories such as Venice, anime fans could download hundreds of scanned images from anime-related books and other promotional materials, as well as translated scripts, media files, and other information. Gopher sites provided primarily textual information. Usenet, a bulletin board–like system, was the primary venue where anime fans engaged in discussions with each other. In the mid-1990s, the most important Usenet "group" for anime fans was rec.arts.anime, which later became rec.arts.anime.misc.[7]

With the advent of Usenet groups such as rec.arts.anime, anime fandom in the United States and beyond had a single electronic discussion system that was free and accessible for those with Internet access. Because of its role as a central electronic meeting place for anime fans, rec.arts.anime attracted some of the most active anime otaku in the United States, including convention organizers, members and organizers of anime clubs, and members of the fledgling American anime and manga licensing and distribution industry. By actively sharing information, asking useful questions, providing insightful answers, participating in heated debates, and by sheer force of personality, the first anime fan Internet celebrities emerged. For example, in March 1996, Enrique Conty posted to rec.arts.anime a total of 158 times (Tsurugi 1996). Usenet users took their identities and reputations very seriously, crafting complex ASCII art signatures to place at the bottom of all their posts. Anime fandom grew rapidly during this period, but it was still small enough that there were a few personalities and resources that most Internet-connected anime fans knew about.

Until the debut of Deja News, a service that published archives of Usenet activity, Usenet messages were ephemeral except in cases in which an individual user saved them to his or her computer. In the absence of archived messages, certain questions would appear on newsgroups over and over again. In response, people would write frequently asked questions (FAQs) to answer common questions and instruct new users to read the FAQs before posting to the group. These documents provided some of the earliest formal and authoritative knowledge among anime fans online, and as such, the FAQ authors themselves became more authoritative and well known within the fandom.

The rise of the web in the 2000s and more accessible means of self-publishing offered new ways for fans to express themselves to other fans, and this communication has continued to evolve in tandem with changing technical capabilities. With improved bandwidth and sophisticated compression algorithms, anime itself could be distributed online, and anime fans were some of the earliest, most prolific, and most sophisticated video-file sharers on the Internet. This easy and free availability of anime changed the dynamic of fandom significantly, altering the role of anime clubs, anime-related websites, and even conventions.[8] On the commercial side of things, more anime than ever is available at mainstream retail outlets, and the explosion in popularity of manga has created an audience of Japanese pop culture consumers that is younger and includes more female fans.

FAN NETWORKS TODAY

Anime fandom continues to evolve and expand as communication and network infrastructures become more ubiquitous and sophisticated. Today's fandom is more massive and diverse than the early fans in the C/FO days probably could have imagined, but there is still historical continuity. Many of the commitments to what I have called an "otaku ethic" (see Chapter 4) continue to pervade the fandom, even as it has broadened, and many anime fans share certain tendencies in their engagement with social and technical networks that were evident even in the early years. In the remainder of this chapter, I describe the ways in which today's fans communicate and connect in terms of their commitment to certain forms of networked culture.

Local Networks

While stereotypes of anime otaku portray them as being socially isolated and rarely meeting anyone face to face, most anime fans actually get their start in fandom via face-to-face interactions. Among my research informants, most were exposed to anime broadcast on television. Their first interactions with other people who also enjoyed anime tended to be close to them to begin with, such as best friends, siblings, or cousins. Later, their circle might expand to include people they met at school who shared an interest in anime. Very few of my informants preferred to watch anime completely alone. Most liked watching it in the presence of friends or even with strangers who were also anime fans. The importance of anime as a social activity was repeated by most of my informants. Ben Spigel, one of my interview subjects, had been an anime fan since he was thirteen or fourteen years old, and when I asked whether he ever watched anime alone, he responded: "Nah, I still don't. I still see it as more a communal activity. We usually talk and laugh above the show so much that even when we watch dubs of animes, we turn on the subtitles so that we can still talk loud."

Most of my informants typically had a small circle of friends who shared their hobby, and some would even organize anime clubs of their own at the college or high school they attended. Having local friends who are also anime fans means sharing the cost burden of buying anime, a substantial benefit given how expensive anime titles are. Beyond the financial benefit, however, most anime otaku also enjoy the social aspect of being fans, laughing and talking about the shows they like and being moved by the same emotional scenes. Some otaku expand the scope of their fandom by participating in other shared activities, such as creating fan art, fansubbing, interacting with fans online, attending conventions, or forming anime clubs.

While most anime clubs are centered on watching anime, they often include secondary activities, and the role of the anime fan club has changed through time. Today, anime clubs still exist at colleges, universities, and elsewhere, but their importance has diminished somewhat now that a wide variety of unedited anime is so readily available at major retailers and on the Internet.[9] They have had to redefine themselves, shifting focus away from showing anime to other activities such as group shopping trips, costume making and cosplay events, group video gaming, anime lending libraries, and convention organizing.[10]

Online Networks

The most profound change affecting anime otaku networks has been the development and growth of the Internet, which has allowed an unprecedented number of people with shared interests to interact with each other—expressing their opinions, asking and answering questions, doing research, exchanging and publishing information, and organizing events. As described earlier, the prior generation of Internet platforms such as FTP, Gopher, and newsgroups provided connection points for geographically dispersed fans, but it was the World Wide Web that allowed fandom to spread and expand through the 1990s and beyond.

More specifically, the web allowed users to cheaply publish persistent content online.[11] Fans had total control over what was published on their websites, and they typically provided links to other sites with related information. In the early days of the web, publishers of anime sites promoted their sites by mentioning them on Usenet and on electronic mailing lists and by submitting them to directories such as Yahoo! and specialized directories of anime websites such as the Anime and Manga Resources List and the Anime Turnpike.[12] A site might include information on an anime's staff and cast, episodes summaries, scanned images, character descriptions, merchandise lists, multimedia files, and related links. In the 1990s, information on many anime titles was not easy to come by, so website creators sought to fill a niche by providing that information. Provisioning high-quality information required research, and sites varied in quality depending on web design as well as on how much information the site owner was able to uncover. Anime site owners would try to make their sites stand out by using the best graphics, user interface, cutting-edge design, and content. There were also different types of specialist websites, such as sites covering specific anime creators, genres, voice actors and actresses, merchandise, and characters.[13] The vast majority of sites, however, were those dedicated to single anime titles. In addition to providing information to other fans, the sites allowed their creators to express their devotion toward their favorite shows and to enhance their own reputation as anime experts.

When there were only a few anime websites, there was not much competition between them, but now many sites compete to be the most popular and authoritative.[14] In addition to needing compelling content, getting attention for one's site required listing the site on popular directories and getting the site noticed by the right people. For example, in the early days of the web, various organizations gave out "awards" to certain websites to recognize high-quality content on the web. In addition to getting noticed by those organizations, some fans also took pride in their sites' getting informal awards from other fans, and they would include a section on their websites listing all the awards they had received. Another strategy would be to create one's own award and give it to related sites. In doing so, one indicated good taste in websites, established oneself as being authoritative enough to be a judge of other people's content, and managed to get other website owners to place a link on their sites back to the awarder's website.

For a period in the mid- to late 1990s, anime-related sites made by individuals were trendy and commonplace. Free web-hosting services such as Geocities and Angelfire made it very easy for even younger anime fans to host their own websites. While dedicated otaku made the most of the web and produced information-rich sites, most were casually constructed, did not contain much content, and did not offer anything new. These sites were almost never updated and only rarely removed, since it is so inexpensive to keep sites up. As the total number of sites grew, it became increasingly difficult for directory sites to maintain usable lists of links—lists that were growing ever larger and more unwieldy. Ultimately, methods of trying to organize and rank the ever-growing number of sites on the web were replaced by a new paradigm: web search. Google, with its PageRank technology, helped to usher in a new era, in which sites are organized and presented to searchers based upon their popularity—not decided upon by a human editor but based on analyzing aggregate human behavior. Sites that are linked to the most often gain the most authority, thereby upping the ante for anime otaku who wanted to become the established expert on their topic of choice.

With the advent of search and the growing abundance of anime overseas, the landscape of the online fandom has shifted away from personally maintained sites about particular series toward general-purpose sites that aggregate information about anime. In the past, when the availability of anime was much lower, otaku spent more time learning and writing about a single show. Websites about moderately popular or even unpopular anime used to have a built-in audience because of the fact that anime fans (without much to choose from) were likely to see those anime and spend time learning more about them. Now, when one show is completed, fans have plenty of new shows to move on to, and otaku are spending less time analyzing and probing deeply into specific titles. Only the most popular shows have a large enough audience to sustain websites that garner a high number of repeat visitors and that merit constant updating of content and the maintenance of a community and forum. Professionally produced anime-related magazines such as *Otaku USA* (first published in 2007) have further reduced the need for highly detailed, niche information on the Internet regarding specific anime titles. Instead, we see the online anime scene now dominated by large generalist sites, commercial sites, and web forums.

GENERALIST SITES   Generalist anime websites—containing information on a large number of anime titles or related information—are the current dominant form of anime site. To make sense of the massive amounts of information related to their hobby, anime fans are increasingly looking for sites that aggregate and organize that information for them. Coupled with advances in web database technology, sites such as AnimeNfo.com allow anime fans to quickly look up basic information on a large number of shows.[15] Each entry on that site is part of a larger database so that one can also look up other shows that came out in the same year, belong to the same genre, or were produced by the same studio. Entries also contain brief summaries and user ratings to help users decide whether they actually want to watch that particular anime title. AnimeNfo.com also contains a large database of voice actors and actresses for those fans who like to keep track of that and use such information to help them choose which anime to watch next. Another feature of the site is that it has its own self-contained community in the form of an Internet relay chat (IRC) channel and web forum.

Anime News Network, focused on anime and manga news, is another important website for anime fans online.[16] On any given day, half a dozen or so news items may appear, encouraging fans to visit the site daily to keep up with the latest happenings in the world of anime and fandom. Anime News Network has an editorial staff, but anyone can send in news item submissions. News items typically include announcements regarding new anime titles being broadcast on television or released on home video, special guests appearing at anime conventions, links to external articles talking about anime and the anime industry, and links to external articles talking about anime fans. The site also contains reviews, articles, editorials, and convention reports. The community on Anime News Network is one of the most active on the web, with registered users posting on dozens of topics on any given day, with even more guest users reading the content.[17] Perhaps the most significant feature of Anime News Network, however, is its "encyclopedia."

The Anime News Network encyclopedia includes a lexicon explaining the meanings of various Japanese words commonly heard in anime and also anime- and fan-related jargon. Even more impressive is its database of anime (and manga) titles, similar to the AnimeNfo.com database but with important differences. Like AnimeNfo.com, encyclopedia entries on Anime News Network describe a show's genre, provide a basic summary, list staff and cast members (voice actors and actresses), and show user ratings. Unlike AnimeNfo.com, however, the database is based on a crowdsourced model and is open to registered users, so that people with information on a show can add it to the database. As such, having a large number of users on the site with a collectively broad range of knowledge on anime allows the encyclopedia's database to be very rich in detail.

As mentioned earlier, websites devoted to less popular anime have become less common. For many reasons, the incentive to create such sites has decreased. However, articles on many of these anime have appeared on Wikipedia, the open online encyclopedia. Instead of hosting an independent site on an anime that few people care or know about, it is easier to publish similar information on Wikipedia instead. A major difference, of course, is that authorship credit is not considered as important on Wikipedia since anyone can contribute to and edit articles. Wikipedia articles are similar to the entries in the Anime News Network encyclopedia in that user contributions are possible, but one can also remove and edit content on Wikipedia and even create brand-new articles. Also, the format of Wikipedia articles tends to be more text oriented and descriptive, whereas Anime News Network encyclopedia entries are more database oriented (fields of information instead of long narrative descriptions). Wikipedia's ubiquity and ease of use, combined with its high popularity and Google rank, have made it a very common source of information for anime fans. The downside is that Wikipedia articles have often appropriated content from and in some cases replaced the need for independent fan sites covering the same content, and encyclopedias cannot fully replicate the type of original analysis, information gathering, and diversity of opinions that were prevalent on fan sites.

Following Web 2.0 trends in general, fan activities online are now more likely to include daily journal entries, photo and video albums, and republishing of easily digestible news articles. Image boards (such as those found on 4chan)—sites that mainly exist so users can submit and download images—exemplify the ephemeral nature of current popular web content.[18]

COMMERCIAL SITES   Commercial websites are also an important component of today's otaku network landscape. Companies that distribute anime in the United States, such as Media Blasters, Animeigo, and Funimation, all have sites to promote the titles they sell. In the early days of the web, official sites for specific anime titles were not generally considered good information resources, but as the industry grew and evolved, the quality of those sites improved.

Retail websites are also important in that one can buy the largest variety of anime and anime-related products online. Anime specialty stores exist, but they are fairly uncommon or exist only in major metropolitan areas such as Los Angeles, San Francisco, and New York City. Many comic book stores carry anime, but only as a secondary product. Major brick-and-mortar retailers and video stores have begun to carry more anime titles, but their selection is limited by shelf space, so less popular and older titles are harder to find in such stores, and they rarely carry secondary merchandise such as anime-related books, posters, and toys.

Animenation.com, in particular, is a well-known retail site that also hosts a vibrant and well-populated web forum community.[19] AnimeOnDVD.com was created near the beginning of the DVD boom.[20]

Renamed Mania.com after the original owner of the site sold it, it continues to be one of the most popular anime sites on the web. Although AnimeOnDVD.com was not a commercial website at first, it was heavily related to commerce because it focuses on a single type of commercial product. In addition to hosting reviews of just about every anime DVD that is commercially available in the United States, the website posts news regarding new releases and license acquisitions. Mania.com continues to host a popular web forum community, focused heavily on anime DVDs and other issues surrounding the anime industry but also containing broader topics of discussion.

WEB FORUMS   Just as the amount of anime-related information grew online and sources of that information became dispersed through time before coalescing again in generalist websites, a similar phenomenon occurred around anime-related online communities. Rec.arts.anime was a centralized online place for English-speaking anime fans to interact with each other. As the Internet became more popular, however, more people began using Usenet, which made the content of groups such as rec.arts.anime very chaotic. New anime fans on Usenet had to be constantly instructed to read the relevant FAQs before posting questions that many others had already asked repeatedly. The crippling blow to Usenet, however, came when advertisers began to "spam" Usenet groups with unsolicited and off-topic messages. Anime fans who used to read rec.arts.anime and related newsgroups eventually migrated to the web, and new anime fans who came about after the web boom neglected Usenet altogether. Many younger fans do not even know what Usenet is.

Early anime websites about specific anime titles would often include simple forums to allow communities to form around their published content. For the most part, those early forums were not successful because any given show had several websites devoted to it, and many of those hosted similar—and therefore redundant—forums. Except for extremely popular sites, such as those dedicated to the most popular shows, few of the niche forums were able to create sufficient critical mass to form an active community with a constant stream of new posts. Anime-related communities on the web did not take off until more generalist sites appeared. These included discussion sites with subforums devoted to anime in general in addition to specific titles, and forums hosted by other generalist sites such as Anime News Network, Anime Nation, and Anime on DVD. These large sites have attracted enough participants to make them bona fide online communities.

Anime Conventions

Most anime otaku conduct their daily anime-related activities on the Internet. They also tend to have a small circle of local friends with whom they watch anime, and in some cases, they also have access to local anime clubs. The ultimate events for anime otaku, however, are anime conventions. Anime conventions are large fan gatherings that have multiple tracks of programming to keep anime fans occupied and entertained for two to four days, usually running over the weekend. The vast majority of anime conventions are run by fans themselves, though different conventions have different levels of industry participation. Anime conventions trace their history to science fiction and comic book conventions, where members of the fledgling anime fan community would get together informally in their hotel rooms to show off the latest anime they had acquired. Later, science fiction conventions such as Baycon in the late 1980s would include official anime screening rooms. Even at this time, most of the anime screened was not translated, but hard-copy summaries were made available to the convention attendees.

Although any gathering of anime fans might be considered a convention, anime conventions are generally distinguished from more informal gatherings by virtue of their size, broad advertisement, annual occurrence, and multiple forms of programming. What counts as the first true anime convention might vary depending on one's definitions, but one of the most notable early conventions was AnimeCon '91 held in San Jose, California, considered the first international anime convention because it hosted guests of honor from Japan. Anime-Con evolved into Anime Expo, still one of the largest anime conventions in the United States. The largest conventions are the ones that have been around the longest, including Anime Expo (which moved to Southern California); Project A-Kon in Dallas, Texas; and Otakon in Baltimore, Maryland. While anime conventions got their start in major metropolitan areas, one can now find multiple anime conventions in most states all throughout the year. The increase in anime conventions can be linked to the overall growth in anime fandom as online networks have expanded. Most anime conventions advertise heavily on the Internet, have their own websites, and host their own web forums and mailing lists so that convention organizers and prospective attendees can talk to each other and plan their convention experiences.

Of the various otaku I spoke with and interviewed, most had attended anime conventions or planned to. Of those otaku who had attended conventions, most have particular things they like to do as attendees. For example, some enjoy shopping for merchandise in the dealers' room, where vendors sell anime and anime-related goods. Others like watching new anime in the multiple video and film rooms. Still others browse or staff tables at the artist alley where fan art is sold, or they attend the art show, which displays fan art that one can often buy or bid on. Costuming (or "cosplay") is also a major part of anime conventions (see Chapter 10). Most attendees do not wear costumes, but a significant and apparently growing number of fans do enjoy dressing up as their favorite anime and video game characters, getting their pictures taken by admiring fans, and participating in the masquerade featuring humorous skits or musical acts. Frequently, cosplay is done in groups, with multiple people portraying several characters from the same anime or game.

For those otaku who want to show off their obsessive knowledge, conventions often hold game shows. Otakon, for example, runs an annual game show in which contestants compete against each other using their knowledge of anime trivia. Other information-related programming at conventions includes professional and fan-run panels. Professional panels are generally run by members of the anime industry who give eager fans details about upcoming releases and future projects. These panels give fans and anime companies an opportunity to directly interact during question-and-answer sessions. Given that many in the anime industry used to be amateur fans themselves and continue to be fans of the products they distribute, the atmosphere is generally positive (unless the topic of discussion is controversial—for example, illegally copied anime). Other professional panels include those held by Japanese guests of honor who talk about their work and allow fans to ask them questions. Fan-run panels are diverse and the most likely place to find die-hard otaku sharing information on their favorite anime or the various creative activities they do as fans. They cover a wide range of topics, including cosplay tips, Japanese culture, learning the Japanese language, how to write fan fiction, how to draw anime, how to make anime music videos, website creation, anime cels, anime toys, manga, how to run anime clubs, and panels talking about specific anime shows or particular genres of anime. Many of these panelists also have a significant online presence, either through a website of their own or through their active participation in an online community. Some anime fans attend panels to see and meet panelists who are essentially minor online celebrities.

All of the anime fans I spoke to who attended conventions agreed that they enjoyed them as places to socialize with other anime fans. Ben Spigel explains: "The great thing about cons, I find, that because everyone knows that you have common interests, it's easy to start conversations with people randomly and have something to talk about." Some attend with local friends, and others use the occasion to meet up with friends who live elsewhere. Many use conventions as a way of meeting up with friends whom they know only from online interactions. For example, participants on a web forum might organize a forum meet-up, such as going out to share a meal during the convention. A couple of interviewees told me that they like talking to total strangers at anime conventions, just casually interacting and talking about their shared interest in the medium. For some attendees, the line between socializing and work is blurred. My informant Pinguino, an independent comic book creator, explained to me that she spends almost all of her time at conventions meeting friends. When I asked her about the people she meets at conventions, she said, "I'm friends with half the people who make independent comics, I think. A lot of people say that I'm the most connected person they know. So I'm meeting friends, but that's work too 'cuz I'm tracking info for *Flippersmack*, so I know when to interview them and stuff."[21]

It is not uncommon for otaku to use conventions to strengthen the online and offline networks they already have. They also use conventions to acquire information and material goods they cannot easily find elsewhere. Finally, for otaku who cosplay, run their own panels, or organize and staff the conventions, anime conventions are a place where they can show off their skills and expertise. Conventions are a place to have fun and socialize, but they are also a place where otaku can promote themselves. Being a well-known anime otaku, for example, can lead to increased access to other networks, information, and goods. In other words, becoming well connected or well known within otaku circles allows one to engage with the community at a high level.

CONCLUSION

The U.S. anime and manga fandom represents a case of network culture that has made full use of peer-based knowledge networks and media distribution to create a unique cult fandom. In many ways, overseas fans were an early prototype of peer-to-peer network culture even before the advent of the Internet. With the rise of online networks, the fandom expanded dramatically—the cultural norms of anime fans meshing seamlessly with the affordances granted by those networks. The evolving commercial market for anime and manga in the United States has been closely intertwined with the growth of the fan base and fan networks. Even as anime and manga have turned into highly successful forms of commercial media in the United States, fan peer networks, online sites, and events continue to be highly robust and central to the experience and consumption of anime.

Notes

1. Patten's archive of records can be found in the Eaton Collection of Science Fiction, Fantasy, Horror, and Utopian Literature at the University of California, Riverside, library.

2. Those anime titles were *Super Dimensional Fortress Macross* (1982), *Super Dimensional Cavalry Southern Cross* (1984), and *Genesis Climber MOSPEADA* (1983).

3. See, for example, *Warriors of the Wind*, widely considered to be a conspicuously poor adaptation of *Nausicaä of the Valley of the Wind* (1984).

4. Animeigo released *Madox-01: Metal Skin Panic* in 1990 (Woodhead 1990). CJS would later be renamed CJAS (the Cornell Japanese Animation Society), which I joined as a Cornell undergraduate in 1994 (Eng 1998).

5. Pinguino, one of my informants, told me that she spends an average of seventeen hours a day on the computer (fourteen hours on Tuesdays and Thursdays), sleeping four to eight hours a night.

6. FTP stands for file transfer protocol. Gopher is a pre-web information-sharing protocol that uses text menus arranged in hierarchies.

7. Usenet is a highly distributed Internet discussion system that was popular in the 1990s. Organizations such as colleges, universities, and Internet service providers (ISPs) operate Usenet servers that copy and propagate user-posted messages

widely so that any given newsgroup will have the same content regardless of the location and time. Usenet groups tend to have much more activity than do e-mail lists, and conversations between users can go on for a very long time.

8. The role of conventions in anime fandom will be discussed later in this chapter. What constitutes an "anime convention" is up for debate and colors discussions of what counts as the first American anime convention, but early and generally show-specific conventions took place in the mid-1980s, followed by a wave of non-show-specific anime-focused conventions that started in the early 1990s. This does not include anime video rooms that various fans hosted in science fiction conventions around the country.

9. At the time of this writing, http://animesuki.com, a major listing of anime fansubs, lists more than 800 anime titles (not counting individual episodes or installments) available for free download.

10. The Rensselaer Polytechnic Institute anime club, RSFA (Rensselaer Science Fiction and Anime club), holds an annual science fiction/gaming/anime convention called Genericon.

11. Or rather, more or less persistent, since a user could decide at any time to stop publishing his or her content.

12. Anime and Manga Resources List: http://csclub.uwaterloo.ca/u/mlvanbie/anime-list; Anime Turnpike: www.anipike.com

13. Sites devoted to specific characters were sometimes known as "shrines," though that term can also be applied to any site devoted to a specific subject, such as a single anime television series.

14. I fondly remember when I knew *every* anime-related website that one could visit, something that is impossible to do now.

15. www.animenfo.com

16. www.animenewsnetwork.com

17. Users who read content on a virtual community site but do not post are known as "lurkers."

18. www.4chan.org

19. www.animenation.com

20. www.animeondvd.com

21. *Flippersmack* is Pinguino's online fanzine.

References

Anime Expo. 2009. "Anime Expo® 2009 continues to hold the title of nation's largest anime and manga event with a record number of over 44,000 in attendance." www.anime-expo.org/2009/07/05/anime-exporeg-2009-continues-to-hold-the-title-of-nations-largest-anime-and-manga-event-with-a-record-number-of-over-44000-in-attendance (retrieved July 10, 2009).

Anime News Network. 2005. "How many anime conventions a year do you go to?" www.animenewsnetwork.com/poll.php?id=58 (retrieved July 10, 2009).

Eng, Lawrence. 1998. "10 years of decadence, CJAS-style (another CJAS history article)." www.cjas.org/history/cjas-10th-anniversary (retrieved July 10, 2009).

Otaku unite. 2004. Central Park Media.

Patten, Fred. 2004. *Watching anime, reading manga.* Berkeley, CA: Stone Bridge Press.

Right Stuf. 1998. History of anime in the US. In *Anime resources.* Grimes, IA: The Right Stuf International. www.rightstuf.com/rssite/main/animeResources/usHistory/part1 (retrieved April 27, 2009).

Tsurugi. 1996. "Stats." rec.arts.anime.misc, http://groups.google.co.uk/group/rec.arts.anime.misc/msg/fce2ab32676a29b1 (retrieved July 10, 2009).

Woodhead, Robert J. 1990. "MADOX-01 SHIPS!!!" rec.arts.anime, http://groups.google.com/group/rec.arts.anime/msg/40a832cd154aa717 (retrieved July 10, 2009).

8

Contributors versus Leechers:
Fansubbing Ethics and a Hybrid Public Culture

MIZUKO ITO

Today's massive international anime and manga audiences have been built through the energies of teams of highly dedicated fans who have localized and distributed Japanese content in diverse languages and regions. Beginning with the activities of anime clubs in the 1980s, fansubbing (fan subtitling) has been a core practice of overseas fans, a necessary condition for access to the foreign cult media of anime. In the absence of commercial distribution overseas, the fan-to-fan traffic in fansubbed VHS tapes is credited for creating markets and audiences outside of Japan. With the growing availability of digital production tools and Internet distribution, fansubbing, and its sister practice of scanlation (scanning and translating manga), have become a vehicle for large-scale distribution of anime and manga, dwarfing commercial efforts at localization and overseas distribution. The relationship between the anime industry and fansubbing is both symbiotic and antagonistic; each requires the other for its survival, and yet they compete to capture the attentions of a growing audience of anime viewers.

The case of fansubbing offers a window into the complex negotiations between media industries and fans as they navigate their entry into a networked and digital age. Complicated by issues of transnational localization and flows, fansubbing provides a unique twist to the ongoing wrangling over intellectual property, peer-to-peer distribution, and noncommercial appropriation of digital content. A self-consciously noncommercial practice, fansubbing is driven by diverse motives, including the demand for high-quality localized content, a desire to contribute to the international fandom, and opportunities for learning, fame, and recognition. Although highly contested, fansubbing and "leeching" (downloading and viewing of fansubs) is framed by a set of ethical guidelines that dictate how fans should "give back to the industry" and what content is appropriate for subbing and distribution. These practices and norms surrounding fansubbing offer a model for a public culture that values both amateur noncommercial and professional commercial contributions.

This chapter draws from ethnographic research on fansubbing, part of a broader study of the English-language anime fandom. In the period from 2005 to 2008, my research team and I interviewed fifty-six North American fans, of whom fifteen had contributed to fansubbing in some capacity.[1] With only two exceptions, all fans we spoke to engaged in leeching, though to varying degrees. In addition to the interviews, we participated in major conventions, including Anime Expo, Fanime, Anime Weekend Atlanta, and Anime-LA, and conducted ongoing observations on online forums and Internet relay chat (IRC) channels related to fansubbing and fansubbed content. The chapter begins by laying out a conceptual framework for understanding hybrid commercial/noncommercial forms of public culture in relation to online fan practice and then provides some background on the history and current practices of fansubbing. The final section of the chapter focuses on the norms and ethics of fansubbing and leeching, examining both in turn before concluding with an analysis of how fansubbing suggests a model for a new kind of hybrid public culture.

PUBLIC CULTURE IN A NETWORKED AGE

In the inaugural issue of *Public Culture*, Arjun Appadurai and Carol Breckenridge suggest that "the world of the late twentieth century is increasingly a cosmopolitan world. More people are widely travelled, are catholic in their tastes, are more inclusive in the range of cuisines they consume, are attentive to world wide news, are exposed to global media-covered events, and are influenced by universal trends in fashion" (1988, 5). They suggest the term "public culture" as a way of referencing an arena of cosmopolitan cultural forms and public life that lie at the intersection of the accelerating flows of people and media. From the vantage point of 2010, this view from 1988 appears prescient; as mobile phones and the Internet have become an everyday presence in the lives of many across the globe, the nature of publicity and sociability are deeply implicated in the flow of media and communications across various spatial boundaries. Today's networked publics are a site of ongoing struggle over the meanings of publicity, property, and common culture in a transnational arena (Russell et al. 2008; Varnelis 2008).

One of the defining struggles in our transition to a digitally networked public culture has centered on the tension between intellectual property regimes and the public domain. As amateurs and regular folks have gained status as producers and distributors of media online, media industries have fought to retain control of their intellectual property and distribution channels. I will not replay the legal battles over file sharing, derivative works, and intellectual property, which deserve their own studied treatment in relation to the fansub case (Hatcher 2005; Leonard 2005). What I would like to focus on is the broader sociocultural context of the sometimes synergistic and often hostile codependency between media fans and industries. In his book *Convergence Culture*, Henry Jenkins (2006) describes instances of relative success in achieving synergy in the industry-fan relations defining the *Survivor*, *American Idol*, and *Matrix* franchises. These examples provide a counterpoint to hostile battles over file sharing and the lawsuits that media industries have brought to their listeners, viewers, and fan creators.

Today's industry-fan relations surface foundational questions about the appropriate roles and norms for varied types of media makers and distributors in a reconfigured public culture. Although this debate has often been framed as a polarized fight between free-culture activists and greedy capitalists, the reality of everyday culture and practice is not so black and white. Most people inhabit a murky and ambivalent gray zone that values the output of professional cultural production while also appreciating the opportunities for peer-to-peer social sharing and amateur creativity that digital media offer us. Lawrence Lessig, a spokesperson for a cultural commons and a less oppressive copyright regime, has focused in his most recent book on hybrid models, such as Craigslist and Second Life, that integrate sharing and commercial economies (Lessig 2008).

We are still in the early stages of defining what these hybrid models might look like. Although we have a long history of studying the incentives of commercial actors, we know much less about what drives what Lessig describes as the "sharing economy" (2008) or what Yochai Benkler (2006) has called "commons-based peer production." A small but growing body of research has been looking at the motivations and incentives that drive participation in voluntary, open, amateur, and non-commercial forms of work (Hippel 2005; Leadbeater 2004; Shirky 2010). Research on cases such as Wikipedia (Giles 2005; Swartz 2006), open source software (Feller et al. 2005; Weber 2004), and game modding (Kow and Nardi 2010; Postigo 2010; Scacchi 2010; Sotamaa 2007) have indicated that these forms of production rely on motivations and norms that not only differ from financially driven ones but are often actually hostile to them. We are beginning to arrive at a more nuanced picture of the diversity of forms of participation in noncommercial production and collectives. For example, Lakhani and Wolf (2005) have noted that some of the key ingredients of open and distributed innovation are the voluntary nature of participation and the diversity of motivations that contributors bring to the activity, varying from skills development, a sense of mission, competency display, and the desire for social connection. Sharing economies and amateur production foreground incentives and motivations that center on learning, self-actualization, and reputation rather than financial rewards.

Within this broader body of examples of networked, digital, and noncommercial production, fan production raises unique issues. Unlike groups that center on fully open content, such as open source software or Wikipedia, fan culture begins with the love of professional media content. While fans can irk the industry with practices such as unauthorized distribution and modification, they are fundamentally enthusiasts and evangelists for commercial media. Successful examples of industry-fan synergy have tapped into this fannish enthusiasm and the desire for legitimization by the industry. For example, game industries have organized modding competitions where they reward the most devoted and skilled game modders with prizes and recognition (Sotamaa 2007). Fansubbing may look at first blush as if it is simply robbing commercial production and localization of their revenue streams, but the practice is framed by fans as an act of evangelism in the service of expansion of commercial markets for anime. Fans actively seek intimacy with and recognition by the industry while simultaneously being motivated by a fundamentally different set of incentives that they hold in common with other forms of noncommercial production.

Put differently, fan production is not technically what Benkler (2006) has described as commons-based peer production but instead relies on a hybridized vision of intellectual property that lies within the gray zone between proprietary and open regimes. What this suggests is not only a consideration of diverse motivations for production and participation but also a less singular vision of the commons or public domain. If we consider today's public culture as a space that includes the circulation of both commercial and noncommercial forms of culture, otaku culture inhabits the zone of translation and integration of the two. This zone has been fraught with tension, but it is also the site of generative new models that cannot be reduced to either a purely open commons-based model or a purely proprietary commercial one (Condry 2010).

Fansubbing arose to fill an unmet consumer demand not being served by commercial industries. Fans assumed the costs of localization, distribution, and marketing, converting commercial media into a noncommercial peer-to-peer regime out of necessity and passion. Gradually, fansubbing and distribution have taken on a life of their own, deeply integrated in the community and social practices of contemporary wired fans. In the remainder of this chapter, I describe the history and current practices of fansubbing in more depth, as well as the norms, ethics, and motivations on the fan side of the equation. I conclude by revisiting the issues of industry-fan relations encountered at this nexus between commercial and noncommercial culture, and I suggest that a hybrid version of public culture can provide a model for mediating the tensions between commons-based and proprietary markets.

GENERATIONS OF FANSUBBING

The practices of fansubbing originated in the mid-1980s with the advent of technology that enabled amateur subtitling.[2] Before this period, fans exchanged print versions of translated scripts and VHS tapes through a growing network of anime clubs in the United States. Initially, distribution was restricted to small networks of clubs and convention screenings, and there was a relatively close relationship between the leadership in the U.S. fandom and the Japanese industry. For example, anime studios provided fans with material to show at conventions, and they would review the work of fansubbers. Several fans I spoke to noted that many of those involved in the early fansub scene went on to work in the licensing and localization industries for anime.

Gilles Poitras, a prominent fan who was involved in these early years, describes how the VHS fansubbing days were characterized by a strong desire to support the anime industry and not compete with the commercial releases. "Back in the days of VHS, I met many people who had a little [anime] on VHS that they had fansubbed that they just adored. So what they would do is they would go and buy a copy of the Japanese release so they'd have the Japanese release and . . . then they would have their fansub. It was their way of supporting the industry." It was during this period that fansubbers established ethical guidelines that signaled their support of the industry and their noncompetitive intent. They defined their work as strictly noncommercial, and they would stop fansubbing and distribution as soon as a series was licensed for the U.S. market. Fansubbers justified their work as an effort to build and test an audience for new series in the United States to encourage commercial release outside of Japan.

By the mid-1990s, VHS tapes of fansubbed anime had begun circulating more broadly through peer-based fan networks, and by the late 1990s, fans began turning to the Internet for anime distribution through sites such as eDonkey or IRC channels. This shift to online distribution happened in tandem with the growth of digisubbing through the use of accessible digital subtitling programs. The shift to digital production and distribution dramatically expanded the scope of both fansubbing contributors and leechers. With the advent of BitTorrent in the early 2000s, the distribution of fansubbed anime exploded, and we saw the birth of the contemporary digisubbing ecology. Fans involved in the early VHS years see the new generation of digisubbers as an entirely new breed. XStylus, who once timed scripts for VHS fansubbing, emphasizes that "there can be absolutely zero comparison between the VHS days of fansubbing and the digisubbing of today. . . . The anime club I went to was actually a subbing group, but they did not distribute what they subbed. . . . They would actually buy a show from overseas and translate it themselves."[3] In contrast to those early years, today's fansubbing teams are highly dispersed and organize online through IRC, and they see their mission as broad distribution.

Anime industries began to take note, and occasional cease-and-desist letters were sent to groups, requesting that they stop subbing a series. For the most part, however, anime studios and localization companies have continued to turn a blind eye toward fansubbing practice.

While the scale and nature of the fansub scene have changed and expanded dramatically in the past decade, today's fansubbers still recognize many of the norms and ethical guidelines established in the early years of the practice. Among both fansubbers and leechers, almost everyone acknowledged the importance of "giving back to the industry" through the purchase of DVDs. Every fansubber I spoke to referenced the norm of dropping a series after licensing, though not all groups actually adhered to that norm. Many argued that they are continuing in the tradition of opening and testing markets for anime overseas. In turn, the generation of subbers who came of age in the first wave of digisubbing complains about the new generation of subbers who have lax ethical standards and fansub series that are already licensed and released on DVD.

As the technology and culture of fansubbing continue to evolve, we can expect to see ongoing generational differences between subbers who came of age during different moments in the scene. Despite the various discontinuities in fansubbing through the years, the practice has steadily developed an increasingly robust and efficient set of infrastructures for the peer-to-peer traffic of anime across national boundaries. The expansion of the fansub scene online was closely tied to the growing popularity of Japanese popular culture overseas (see Introduction). Gradually expanding into multiple regions and languages, fansubbing continues in its mission to make diverse and otherwise unavailable anime accessible to fans around the world. And despite each generation's complaints about the eroding ethics and discipline of the newer generation, the work ethic of fansubbing is remarkably robust. I turn now to the fansubbing work process and discipline in today's digisubbing scene.

THE FANSUBBER'S WORK

Anyone who has had a glimpse of the work of fansubbing cannot help but be impressed by the discipline and dedication of teams who turn out subtitled episodes week after week as a purely volunteer endeavor. The way that teams and work processes are organized varies by group, but certain kinds of jobs and workflow have become fairly standardized in the scene. The process begins with the work of the raw capper, who captures the "raw" untranslated episode via television broadcast or through a Japanese file-sharing site. The process then moves to the translator, who listens to the episode and generates an English script. One or sometimes two editors or translation checkers will check the script and then turn it over to the timer, who segments it and times how long each segment should appear on-screen. The typesetter then chooses fonts and creates any signs or special effects, such as karaoke effects for songs. After the typesetting is complete, an encoder prepares an initial video for quality checking (QC). Most groups then put the episode through one or more rounds of QC and revision before turning it over to the encoder for a final encode and then to the distribution team, which releases the episode on IRC and through BitTorrent.

Because team members are dependent on one another to complete the finished project, groups generally have a high degree of camaraderie and coordination. As members finish their jobs on a particular episode, they coordinate handoffs. Often there is an expectation of turnaround within a certain amount of time. One timer, razz, describes how the expectation for the series he is now timing is a turnaround of three to four hours after he receives the finished script. Sai, a translator in another group, notes a somewhat more relaxed but still demanding temporality: "We know that quality check is actually demanding because of time constraints. You're expected to quality check within one or two days. That's very taxing. Translators, we get two or three days." Team members are generally logged onto a closed "staff" IRC channel to coordinate these handoffs, as well as onto an open channel where leechers congregate and await announcements about new releases and staff openings.

This collaborative and high-pressure work situation requires effective coordination and management and also leads to tensions and politics within and between groups. A few of the fansubbers I spoke to had founded their own groups or were part of the founding of groups. They described how groups were started with a spirit of fun and experimentation, gradually developing into more formally organized work teams. Even as he worked for other large groups in the scene, as a high schooler Kurechan started a group with his girlfriend, who was fluent in Japanese, as a fun project to do together. Akira also started a group when he was in high school, after he fansubbed an episode on his own and released it on an IRC channel he hung out in. People in the channel volunteered to help out with new releases, and a new fansub group coalesced. "At first our quality wasn't actually that great, but of late . . . we've cleaned up everything." At the time I interviewed him, his group was a high-functioning work team that turned around quality episodes within days of release in Japan. He described his group as "family," with a strong sense of social cohesion and a disciplined work ethic.

Many of my interviewees also described the scene as "full of drama" and "highly political," as people move in and out of different roles and groups, and different fansub groups compete for recognition. Still in college at the time, Sai describes how the leader of her group was feuding with another group leader. "So they would be doing 15-year-old things like 'you suck' and 'moron' and kick banning [excluding] each other from the [IRC] channels. . . . I felt really old already at the time but I was like, 'Can you guys just talk to each other and apologize?' and they were like, 'What are you talking about? This is war!'" Sai also describes the turmoil in her startup group as they worked to establish standards for membership and get rid of underperforming staff. She moved into a leadership role in the group when she stepped up to fire an underperforming translator. Eventually Sai instituted a new process for admitting staff, including formalizing the QC process and admitting QC staff into the staff channel after a trial period. Although some groups have a very strictly hierarchical structure, leadership is more commonly negotiated in these more ad hoc and fluid ways. More established groups have formal recruitment procedures, including tests designed for each specialty and trial periods before a new member is admitted as staff.

Different fansub groups have specialties and different emphases. Most groups have a reputation for subbing particular genres of anime. Some of the groups that fansub the most popular anime have set a standard that they will turn an episode around within twenty-four or even eighteen hours of broadcast in Japan. One group has described how it achieves this by having team members in different time zones to keep the workflow on a twenty-four-hour cycle. These groups are often described pejoratively as "speed sub" groups by fansubbers who subscribe to a more methodical pace and process. By contrast, "quality" groups will generally make an effort to keep up with the weekly broadcast schedule of a series, but they might take much longer, attributing delays to a more careful translation, typesetting, and QC process. The best of both types of groups work to exacting standards and are under constant scrutiny by peers, competitors, and audiences. Discussions in online forums and on fansub comparison sites pick apart the differences in the quality and approaches of different groups, particularly when there are multiple groups fansubbing a single series. Comparison sites post multiple screen shots from the same episode done by different groups, which highlight differences in typesetting, translation, editing, and encoding (see Figure 8.1).

When different groups are subbing the same series, they compete to produce the quickest or the highest-quality releases to attract leechers. Groups make their decisions about which series to sub based on their personal tastes as well as whether they want to compete with the groups who have already signed on with a series. Playing out in both private and public forums online, groups can be highly critical of the quality of the releases of their competitors. Groups will keep track of the BitTorrent download numbers through trackers that they publicize on their sites. The slower, quality-oriented groups will distinguish themselves

Figure 8.1. Screen captures of titles and typesetting of different fansub groups from the Jimaku Hikaku fansub comparison site. Credit: Screen capture by Mizuko Ito.

by the high quality of their translations and the effort they put into typesetting. Typesetters from these groups will create custom titles and signs that closely mimic the on-screen text of the original episode, customizing text for storefronts, product labels, and other text that appears on screen. They also develop elaborate karaoke-style effects so that people can follow the timing of both the Japanese and the English translation of songs. Fansubbers I spoke to noted with pride that this kind of attention to detail far exceeds the industry standard of simply going with one default font regardless of its appropriateness for the series or scene.

Fansubbers frequently suffer from burnout, and most groups are relatively short-lived. Five years is considered a very well-established group, and only a handful of groups have survived for longer. Among the active fansubbers whom I interviewed, in the two- or more year span between then and this writing, most have dropped out of the scene though they continue to be part of the anime fandom. Zalas describes how most groups "fizzle out" rather than going through a formal breakup process. The Internet is littered with fansub group sites that show no evidence of new activity in years, but new groups are constantly cropping up to take their place in the scene. The ecology of fansubbing is maintained through these processes in which new entrants can start or join new groups, develop new practices and standards, and then eventually retire from the scene. The scene also depends on a diverse set of motives for participation, both for contributing fansubbers and leechers. I turn now to a closer look at the specific motivations and ethics that fansubbers bring to their participation and then contrast these dynamics with how leechers define and frame their participation and ethics.

CONTRIBUTORS

In my interviews with fansubbers, one of the first social distinctions that I was introduced to was that between "contributors" and "leechers." Put simply, contributors are those who contribute labor and expertise to the process of fansubbing, and leechers are consumers who download and view fansubbed works. People involved in distribution lie in the middle of this spectrum. Although they contribute bandwidth and storage space to the infrastructure of fansubbing, because they do not contribute human labor and expertise, they are not generally included among the ranks of "full staff," and they are relegated to a separate "distro" channel. While the motivations that leechers bring to fansubbing are relatively uncomplicated—they want access to anime— the motivations of contributors are a bit more complex. The level of commitment that fansubbers devote to what is often grinding and boring work cannot be fully captured by either notions of altruistic volunteerism nor by the creative passions of the hobbyist.

Yochai Benkler in *Wealth of Networks* identifies new forms of noncommercial "peer production" as people have gained access to the processing power of computers and networks to connect, collaborate, and publicize. He notes that people have always had a diverse set of motives to produce culture and knowledge, only some that rely on market and financial incentives. On the nonmarket side, motivations and social practices are highly diverse and include governmental and educational institutions committed to public knowledge, as well as individual writers and creators "who play to 'immortality' rather than seek to maximize the revenue from their creation" (Benkler 2006, 47). More recently, Clay Shirky (2010) has suggested that we are living in a time when the world's "cognitive surplus" is being mobilized in new ways because of the networked and participatory nature of the online world. "Back when coordinating group action was hard, most amateur groups stayed small and informal. Now that we have the tools that let groups of people find one another and share their thought and actions, we are seeing a strange new hybrid: large, public, amateur groups."

Studies examining the motivations for participation in Wikipedia, open source software development, and game modding have described different motives for participation, puzzling over why people would contribute effort and expertise with little or no financial rewards (Kow and Nardi 2010; Lakhani and Wolf 2005; Sotamaa 2007; Swartz 2006; Weber 2004). Though these groups differ on many details, research findings suggest a general pattern that participation in these groups is tied to a sense of autonomy and efficacy, which is in turn tied to the voluntary nature of the activity. Fansubbers, even while expressing a high degree of commitment and sense of obligation to their team and audiences, also underscored that it was "a hobby" that they did "for fun." Further, this body of work also indicates that reasons for participation are diverse but cluster roughly around ideals about contributing to a shared collective vision or resource, learning and self-actualization, and status and social belonging. I have also seen these motivations at play in the case of the fansubbers I spoke to, and I touch on each set of motivations in turn.

Becoming a Contributor

When I queried fansubbers about what motivated them to start subbing, all of them cited some desire to "contribute" to the fandom. Most fansubbers started off as leechers and decided to become contributors after discovering some form of value they could provide to the scene. For example, zalas describes how he discovered the online fandom, started leeching, and eventually went on to start making anime music videos (AMVs). His AMV making led him to a pursuit of raw video files. "And eventually, I got a very good hang of it, and I was like, 'Maybe I should try to contribute back to these fansubbers. I can offer my services downloading raws for people.'" Similarly, Aren describes how he was part of the eDonkey file-sharing scene when he was thirteen years old, downloading anime through a modem connection. "I thought maybe I should contribute something to the communities . . . so I wasn't only downloading the stuff with my old modem but also contributing." Although his parents allowed him only two hours a day of modem time, he contributed this limited bandwidth by helping distribute anime. "It doesn't seem exciting watching something uploading, but it was kind of exciting to contribute something to the community because it was like oh, if they just keep leeching stuff it won't contribute to the community. Anime faces extinction." Moving on from these early experiences at contributing, zalas and Aren both went on to found their own fansub groups and become active participants in the fansub scene.

As is evident with Aren and zalas, fansubbers' sense of contribution was not generally framed in terms of the ethic of "giving back" to the anime industry per se, but more in terms of adding value to the anime fandom as a whole, a fandom that includes the interests of fansubbers, leechers, and the commercial industry. Razz says, "I enjoy bringing anime that's hot off the presses to people around the world." Similarly, Akira says that he subs "to be nice I suppose. . . . Just a community to contribute to because stuff we sub hundreds of thousands of people watch." As part of this broader sense of contribution, many

fansubbers also noted the benefits to the industry: that they were opening new markets and recruiting new audiences for anime. Lantis ties
his motivations to this ethic. "I just feel so good when I can release
something that conforms to my standards and make it available to the
world of anime the same way that fansubbers did back in the VHS
days."

Lantis notes that his drive to contribute was also motivated by the
desire to maintain the quality of fansubbing. He discovered fansubs
when he was in high school and began following particular groups that
he thought had high-quality editing. When one of his favorite groups
advertised for a staff position, he immediately applied. Razz was motivated to take on the job of timer for a group because he noticed "bleeds"
when a subtitle continues to be displayed on-screen after a scene change.
"You won't see this kind of intricacy on any anime DVD, but [among
fansubbers] it is generally considered an eyesore." Upon hearing his
complaints, the leader of the group invited him to take on the job.
After running his own group for many years, zalas has transitioned to
a position of fansub critic for the scene and is involved in quality
checking the translations of a game that he cares a lot about. "I want to
give back to the community, kind of an ethical motivation I guess. . . . I
tend to be a stickler over whether things are translated properly. . . . I feel
like I'm this critic guy who looks over and makes sure things aren't
screwed up."

These motivations that center on a sense of contributing to a broader
good and community were also tied to the ethical positions that fansubbers took in their relationships with the anime industry. The long-
standing ethic that groups should drop a series after licensing can run
into conflict with the interests of leechers and the quality standards of
fansub groups. For example, when a series is licensed midseason, fansubbers must make the call about whether they will drop the series or
complete it for their viewers. They see their decision to start subbing a
series as an ethical obligation to their viewers, and they are reluctant
not to deliver on a completed season. Sai explains, "The argument of
'Well it's licensed but it won't get released for N many more months so
it wouldn't be fair to the fans to make them wait.'" Groups that drop
midseason get a negative reputation among leechers. Fansubbers also
feel committed to upholding the quality standards that they have established. Leechers and fansubbers alike acknowledge that high-

quality fansubs are more accurate, better executed, and truer to the original Japanese source than their commercial versions. When a quality group drops a series, it means depriving audiences of a more high-quality viewing experience.

Some groups have modified the previous norm and have decided to stop subbing only after the DVD is actually released in their region. After licensing or after receiving a cease-and-desist letter, some groups have taken the remainder of the season underground, releasing under a different name so they can retain the ethical pedigree for their more public group identity. A few prominent groups that sub very popular and long-running series such as *One Piece*, *Naruto*, and *Inuyasha* have continued openly subbing and releasing even after licensing and broadcast in the United States, arguing that it is unreasonable to expect fans to wait for the industry to catch up on more than one hundred episodes that have already been fansubbed. Fans from the VHS days look askance at this shifting ethical landscape. Gilles Poitras argues, "I had to wait 10 years for *Nadia*. They can wait." XStylus also takes issue with fans who insist on access to fansubbed versions. "If a show does get licensed, the companies get bitched out because now the fansubs for that show cease. . . . The fans do not know how lucky they've got it. Unlike the big lawsuit-happy assholes in Hollywood, the anime companies DO care, and do listen."

Although different fans and fansub groups take different positions on the ethics of when to stop subbing and distributing, all the fans I spoke to are united in their commitment to support the anime fandom. The debates boil down to differences in how they perceive the value of their contributions and the relative priority they give to different constituents in this hybrid public culture that includes both commercial and noncommercial interests. While fans from the VHS era see their interests in closer alignment with those of the anime industry and position themselves more as traditional media consumers, the newer generations of fans tend to align with a more fluid and hybrid networked public culture in which the industry does not have as privileged a position.

Learning and Self-Actualization

In addition to the values surrounding their sense of contributing to and improving the fandom, fansubbers also describe being motivated by a sense of learning, self-actualization, and pleasure in creative work. In this, they share participatory motivations similar to what we see with other amateur creative and fan groups. All the fansubbers I spoke to took pride in the quality of their work and valued fansubbing as an activity that helped them acquire skills and expertise. For example, Sai started fansubbing as a translator specifically to improve her Japanese. Having grown up in Japan, she was fully bilingual but was concerned about losing her Japanese after going to the United States for college.

Other subbers described how as they got involved in the scene they became attracted to certain specialties that they found intellectually or creatively stimulating. Aren moved from the German fansubbing scene to the U.S. one, met other encoders who were much more accomplished than he was, and began to learn from them. "It just got interesting because other encoders were like 'Here are some tips and tricks' . . . so it got pretty interesting." Unlike the kind of learning that these young people were experiencing in school, learning within the fansub scene is embedded in an authentic set of work practices, in which they are able to connect with and learn from more experienced peers who share their passionate and specialized interests (Ito et al. 2009). This kind of learning and skills development is highly motivating and tied to a sense of autonomy and self-actualization. Kurechan got more involved in the scene as he was mentored by more experienced fansubbers in different specialties. "My tsing [typesetting] was *really* bad at first . . . but I worked hard and learned from the masters of the time. And I hung out @ doom9 forums (stuff for encoders) a lot. . . . Then I gradually branched out. Timing, then [typesetting], then edit and qc."

As they become more expert and established in the scene, fansubbers take on the role of experts and are motivated to help and teach others. The geek culture of expertise and learning norms that center on self-motivation and self-direction dictate, however, that fansubbers expect newcomers to do their initial homework on their own and not ask basic questions. Zalas participates actively on forums and will often help with technical questions people have, as long as they are intellectually challenging ones. "If it's something really trivial, I don't really feel bothered to actually go help them, but sometimes if it's something relatively advanced, it's kind of interesting to sort of walk people through it." Fansubbers enjoy knowledge exchange with respected peers, but they look down upon the mass of leechers and newbies who have yet to prove their self-worth. Akira sums up this attitude: "Fansubbing is half filled with people who don't know what they are talking about and the fans 99.9% of them don't know what they're talking about."

Status and Social Belonging

In addition to the sense of mission that fansubbers bring to their work, and their personal motivations around learning and accomplishment, fansubbers are also motivated by social belonging and reputation. When I ask razz what keeps him going in the two groups he is involved in, he says, "The people in the group are fun to work with. Both groups have really cool members." This team spirit and expectations drive a strong sense of commitment to the work. "Because [my group] was really struggling I felt personally obligated to do everything I could to help keep it alive," explains Sai. The tight-knit nature of the work team, and the immediate communication and feedback with both her team and her audience, drove her to become one of the most prolific translators in the scene. Of her peak years of fansubbing during college, she says, "The compulsion was unbelievable. . . . The feedback is immediate. It's IRC. . . . You'd have people jubilating because you're doing something at the time. I'm like, I'm translating [x series] and they're like, 'Oh, my God. That's awesome. Thank you.' You don't get that kind of feedback."

The large audiences for digisubbing mean that successful fansubbers can gain large followings. Akira sees one of the primary motivations of fansubbing as "instant reputation. Just saying you worked on a series gets you respect." The politics of how groups and individual subbers gain reputation in the scene often can be fraught. Kurechan describes "ego subbers" who gravitate toward the most popular shows as the quickest means to get a reputation and download numbers. His respect is reserved for fansubbers who achieve their status through high-quality and sustained work. For example, he argues that Sai had to translate 900 episodes before "she was recognized as a good tl [translator] by the masses" because she did not choose to translate popular shows. Fansubbers I spoke to all agreed that download numbers were not a proxy for quality and that motivations driven purely by leecher popularity were suspect. At the same time, all fansubbers also admitted that the numbers did matter to them. Lantis says, somewhat sheepishly, that "I'd be lying if I didn't check [the download counts] out of curiosity ^^;; but it's not like I decide what to sub because I think I'll get more downloads that way." The quest for download counts also drives the quest for speed. "Usually the group that releases first, assuming equal quality, gets the most downloads," razz explains. "You can hear people talking about group reputations and what not, but the fact of the matter is that the average person will get [the episodes of] the group that releases first. . . . Deep down inside, every fansubber wants to have their work watched and a high amount of viewers causes them some kind of joy whether or not they express it."

In summary, all fansubbers bring to their work multiple motivations that are altruistic, personal, and social in nature. Zalas offers a concise summary. "Some people do it for fun because it's kind of neat to play around with this stuff. Some people do it because they want to be popular. . . . There's groups out there who just want to get as many downloads as possible because they'll be like, 'Oh. Wow. I'm so cool. I rule over a channel of 300 people.'" I ask about his own motivations. "Well, a lot of it is just socialization. I get to talk to people about things I like. Sometimes it's just I want to give back to the fansubbing community." Fansubbing has sustained itself as a noncommercial, voluntary, and participatory practice because it supports this entire constellation of motivations and ways of participating.

LEECHERS

Although fansubbers clearly differentiate between those who are contributors and those who are leechers, the two groups are codependent, just as fans are codependent with the industry. Leechers have their own modes of participation in the fansub scene that are also guided by ethics and norms for participation, though of a different nature from those of contributors. Leechers are either casual fans or fans who are deeply involved in other dimensions of the fandom, such as convention organizing, cosplay, AMVs, or fan fiction. As such, they do not take as exacting an interest as contributors do in the minute differences in quality between different fansubs, and their interest is in getting the most expedient access to the episodes that they desire. When asked if there were particular groups that they followed, most leechers could name at most two or three of the most prominent groups. The majority simply watch episodes that they can access most expediently without noticing which group fansubbed it.

It is important to recognize that although as a whole they are not as specialized in their fansub knowledge as contributors, even the most casual leecher is a more sophisticated media consumer than the average television viewer. Although fansubs now circulate on YouTube and other consumer sites, leechers must still go directly to fansub sites and IRC channels to access most fansubbed episodes. As such, they come into contact with the chatter on fansub forums and channels, and they develop knowledge about fansub groups, differences in approach and quality, and fansub ethics. For example, although she couldn't remember the names of the groups, one leecher noted that one group "translates better and has better quality," but another group "produces faster," indicating the established distinction between quality and speed groups that contributors cite (interview by Rachel Cody).

Fansubber efforts at going the extra mile in pursuing quality did not go unnoticed. For example, one fan noted with appreciation that "the fansub versions get more of the context of the language. You don't have some editor that comes in and changes it around so that it will make sense to a Western audience. These people say exactly what it is, and if there's something that seems to be a little weird to understand, they'll put little gloss notes in there" (interview by Annie Manion). Another fan I interviewed is even more emphatic. "I've become so, I guess, elitist, like I can't even watch the American dubbing any more. Like it's just so terribly done and they've dumbed down the plots, and they just edit things poorly. And it just drives me crazy. . . . They just really really need to allow the fansubbers, which are better than the actual professional-done subbing, to sub anime on TV." Other leechers, by contrast, complain about the poor quality of fansubs compared with the video quality they can expect on DVD. The overwhelming majority of leechers acknowledge, however, that the quality of typesetting and translation of high-quality fansubs exceeds professional standards. At the same time, some fans disputed this as a reason for not viewing commercial releases. "A lot of people complain about oh the dubs are terrible and oh Americans don't do a good job. But . . . I'm not bothered by what I can get here. I feel like we need to patronize the people who are trying to bring stuff here."

These questions about the ethics of leeching are highly controversial in the fandom. Although only two of the fans I interviewed were not leechers, even among leechers there was a high degree of variability in how much they felt an ethical obligation to "give back to the industry." Some leechers, emphasizing this ethic, will download only anime that has not been licensed in English, and they condemn fansub groups that continue to sub after licensing. "When I know the anime is not licensed by any company or I know it has no chance of coming to the US, then I download it." These fans also emphasized their efforts to buy DVDs. XStylus, for example, has a rule that "if you watch a [fansubbed] show, you should buy the DVD for every 4 episodes." More typical of an "ethical" approach to leeching are fans who say that they will watch fansubs until they are licensed, and then they buy or rent the DVD to finish off the series.

Many leechers felt an ethical obligation to contribute financially to the anime industry but failed to do so for one reason or another. Leechers in Australia and the United Kingdom often believe they have a legitimate reason to demand fansubbed versions even when series are licensed in the United States. Some fans who generally did not leech licensed anime would make exceptions for long-running series for which they knew they would have to wait many years until the industry subtitling could catch up. Other leechers say they wish they could buy but do not have the financial means. One leecher I spoke to said that she started buying after she got a job to build her collection as well as to fulfill her ethical obligation. "I'm slowly trying to buy everything I watched and really loved."

Other fans think that fansubs are justified because they test the market for new releases, and they allow viewers to preview before buying a DVD. "I never buy a DVD to an anime that I haven't seen. I always look for a fansub first, then watch it. If I like it, I buy the DVDs (If I can find them; but I do look hard since I *want* to buy them)." Many leechers I spoke to echoed this sentiment. A few leechers thought that the industry was charging too much for DVDs, so they felt justified for not buying. Only two fans I spoke to, however, felt no need to justify their leeching activity in any way. Overall, leechers exhibited a strong desire to support the anime industry, but many justified their leeching because of the ineffectiveness of professional localization efforts, or because of their lack of financial and other forms of access to the episodes that they wanted to view.

TOWARD A HYBRID PUBLIC CULTURE

By describing the practices, norms, and ethics involved in fansubbing and leeching, I have indicated the diversity of motivations that people bring to the scene. Although fansubbers and leechers subscribe to diverse norms and motivations, a commitment to building a sustainable, expanding, and high-quality public culture of anime content and communication is shared across all these groups. In this sense, the interests of fans are in close alignment with the interests of anime producers. The ethical norms to "give back to the industry" so it can continue to produce anime, and the intense efforts to achieve high-fidelity translations and video, are all motivated by fans' commitment to the medium that they love and the fandom surrounding it. Fansubbers are motivated to contribute enormous amounts of voluntary labor and expertise in the service of this broader sense of mission; they also contribute out of a sense of efficacy and for the recognition they achieve by successfully filling an unmet need for high-quality anime localized for different languages.

Contrary to some models of motivation, the presence of commercial actors does not necessarily crowd out the motivations of noncommercial participants. Many subbers I spoke to said they would be willing to sub for free for the industry and do not see fansubbing as part of their professional career trajectory. The key to effective enlistment of noncommercial players is the presence of compelling noncommercial motivations and incentives, including shared purpose and values as well as personal motivations for learning and recognition. Commercial motives and interests will not always corrupt the commons or the public domain; collective values and interests might at times best be served by an integration of commercial and noncommercial motives. The case of fansubbing also demonstrates how crucial it is to differentiate the motivations for participation between consumers and contributors to a shared public culture. The motivations of contributing and leeching are fundamentally different, though many fans engage in both. Contributors need to be recognized and rewarded for their exacting commitment to standards of work and quality, while leechers must be offered accessible and high-quality content that motivates them to provide financial and attentional contributions.

Despite alignment of many broad goals and interests, however, industry-fansubber relations are fraught with tension and controversy. In recent years, the DVD market has been collapsing, and prominent companies that had been distributing anime overseas, such as ADV and Central Park Media, have folded. These developments have contributed to the polarization of the debate about the legitimacy of fansubbing in supporting the anime industry and the fandom. Although earlier generations of fansubbers could justify their practices as opening new and untapped markets, today's English-language audiences for anime are now well established, and fansub distribution often goes head-to-head with its commercial counterpart. Both fansubbers and leechers try to bring their practices into alignment with industry interests, but they often express frustration at the lack of what they see as viable alternatives that still meet the needs of fans for speedy and high-quality access to titles.

Some new experiments in digital distribution are suggesting a model of a hybrid public culture in anime that resolves some of these tensions while meeting the broader goals that unite the fandom and the industry. In 2008, Crunchyroll, a site initially dedicated to streaming fansub content, received venture funding and began developing a model for legal, licensed online distribution of subtitled anime that is simultaneous with release in Japan. Crunchyroll has secured distribution deals for many popular series, and now it streams only content that is licensed and is subtitled by the commercial localization companies. Crunchyroll secured the licensing deal for *Naruto Shippuden*, one of the most popular of the current anime series. This prompted Dattebayo (the group that made its name subbing *Naruto*) to drop the series, although it had continued subbing the series for many years after it had started airing in the United States. More recently, Crunchyroll has been trying to license another major series that Dattebayo subs, *Bleach*. In an online press release, Dattebayo announced that it is dropping *Bleach* because of Crunchyroll's plans, and it is lobbying the site to allow the group to provide the subs for the series.[4] Within the press release is also an acknowledgment of the changing landscape of fansubbing. "DB came along at just the right moment in fansubbing. It has existed through the moments I feel were fansubbing's zenith. Now fansubbing is clearly in its decline, as it has been for two years now, replaced by legal alternatives."

Fansubbing arose to meet a compelling need of overseas fans that was not met by commercial alternatives. As the anime industry adapts to take advantage of the opportunities of online distribution, fansubbing's mission to distribute anime overseas will decline in importance. At the same time, as acknowledged in the Dattebayo press release, fansubbing still provides a unique value that is very difficult for commercial industries to compete with, which is high-quality "crowdsourced" (Howe 2009) subtitling. As other volunteer subtitling sites such as dotsub have demonstrated, translation is an activity that is uniquely well suited to peer production because tasks can be decomposed and people can contribute in a distributed fashion to translation, editing, and QC. Viikii.net is a commercial site that licenses and distributes Taiwanese and Korean dramas in multiple languages. It relies on crowdsourced fansubbing for its subtitles.

These new experiments in online distribution suggest that there are viable hybrid models that integrate noncommercial peer production with professional media production, localization, and distribution. Just as the earlier generation of fansubbers opened a new market for anime industries overseas, today's digisubbers and leechers would see their interests served by new legal and revenue-generating forms of online distribution, if they would allow for fans to contribute to higher standards for localization and subtitling. Shifting the view from the question of who extracts value, to a vision of who is allowed to add value, changes the view of how a hybrid economy can work. Rather than assume that incorporation of volunteer labor for commercial gain is a form of digital sharecropping (Carr 2006; Terranova 2000), we should consider how the ability to contribute to a collectively meaningful endeavor can be itself a source of value and efficacy that often requires no other rewards. Individual motivations are tightly tied to collective public recognition and value creation. The fansubbing case demonstrates how economic models of individual value extraction and maximization provide an inadequate view into the motivations for contribution.

In this chapter, I have argued for attention to the underlying social patterns and meaningful values that motivate people's participation in and contributions to a shared and networked public culture. One of the key lessons of the networked age has been that the days of proprietary locked-down culture and winner-take-all scenarios are definitively over. Conversely, we cannot rely on a narrow vision of the commons or the public domain that is free of commercial interests and financial incentives. A notion of public culture has from the start been about collectives that include both commercial and noncommercial incentives for participation. Arguing for a hybrid public culture is not an act of capitulating to a capitalist imperative that reduces the pool of common culture, but rather it is a way of arguing for an enriching public life that values diverse forms of contribution.

ACKNOWLEDGMENTS

This research would not have been possible without the generosity of the fansubbers and fans who decoded the world of subbing and file sharing for me and my research team. I would particularly like to thank Zalas and Kinovas, who opened the doors to the fansub world for me. This work was supported by a grant from the John D. and Catherine T. MacArthur Foundation and by the Annenberg Center for Communication at the University of Southern California. My research assistants on this project included Rachel Cody, Renee Saito, Annie Manion, Brendan Callum, and Judy Suwatanapongched. Without them my knowledge of the anime fandom would have been much more impoverished, and cons would have been much less enjoyable. This work has also benefited from an ongoing collaboration and conversations with Jennifer Urban.

Notes

1. I was the lead researcher of a team that included several graduate and undergraduate students, including Rachel Cody, Annie Manion, Renee Saito, Brendan Callum, and Judy Suwatanapongched. Jennifer Urban, a collaborator on this work, also participated in the fieldwork. When the observation or interview was conducted by somebody other than me, this is noted in the text. I offered all fans the option of having their real names, fan names, or pseudonyms used in publications that resulted from the research. Most involved in fansubbing chose a pseudonym, and I have noted in a footnote only those instances when I have used a "real" fan name. In the case of leechers, to protect their identities, I have not mentioned their names or assigned pseudonyms, as their quotes were illustrative of generalized practices rather than individual life histories.

2. This history of fansubbing is derived from a more detailed history of fansubbing from 1979 to 1993 compiled by Sean Leonard (2005), Eng's history of the U.S. fandom in Chapter 7, and my own interviews with fans.

3. This is a real fan name.

4. www.dattebayo.com/pr/134

References

Appadurai, Arjun, and Carol Breckenridge. 1988. Why public culture. *Public Culture Bulletin* 1 (1): 5–9.

Benkler, Yochai. 2006. *The wealth of networks: How social production transforms markets and freedom.* New Haven, CT: Yale University Press.

Carr, Nicholas. 2006. Sharecropping the long tail. *Rough type*, www.roughtype.com/archives/2006/12/sharecropping_t.php (retrieved January 13, 2011).

Condry, Ian. 2010. Dark energy: What fansubs reveal about the copyright wars. In *Mechademia 5: Fanthropologies*, ed. Frenchy Lunning, 232–251. Minneapolis: University of Minnesota Press.

Feller, Joseph, Brian Fitzgerald, Scott A. Hissam, and Karim R. Lakhani, eds. 2005. *Perspectives on free and open source software.* Cambridge, MA: MIT Press.

Giles, Jim. 2005. Special report: Internet encyclopedias go head to head. *Nature* 438: 900–901.

Hatcher, Jordan S. 2005. Of otakus and fansubs: A critical look at anime online in light of current issues in copyright law. *SCRIPTed* 2 (4): 514–542, www.law.ed.ac.uk/ahrc/script-ed/vol2-4/hatcher.asp (retrieved January 13, 2011).

Hippel, Eric Von. 2005. *Democratizing innovation.* Cambridge, MA: MIT Press.

Howe, Jeff. 2009. *Crowdsourcing: Why the power of the crowd is driving the future of business.* New York: Three Rivers Press.

Ito, Mizuko, Sonja Baumer, Matteo Bittanti, danah boyd, Rachel Cody, Becky Herr-Stephenson, Heather Horst, Katynka Z. Martínez, C. J. Pascoe, Dan Perkel, Laura Robinson, Christo Sims, and Lisa Tripp. 2009. *Hanging out, messing around, and geeking out: Kids living and learning with new media.* The John D. and Catherine T. MacArthur Foundation Series on Digital Media and Learning. Cambridge, MA: MIT Press.

Jenkins, Henry. 2006. *Convergence culture: Where old and new media collide.* New York: New York University Press.

Kow, Yong Ming, and Bonnie Nardi. 2010. Who owns the mods? *First Monday* 15 (5), http://firstmonday.org/htbin/cgiwrap/bin/ojs/index.php/fm/article/view/2971/2529 (retrieved January 13, 2011).

Lakhani, Karim R., and Robert G. Wolf. 2005. Why hackers do what they do: Understanding motivation and effort in free/open source software project. In *Perspectives on free and open software*, ed. J. Feller, B. Fitzgerald, S. Hissam, and K. R. Lakhani, 3–22. Cambridge, MA: MIT Press.

Leadbeater, Charles. 2004. *The pro-am revolution: How enthusiasts are changing our economy and society.* London: Demos.

Leonard, Sean. 2005. Celebrating two decades of unlawful progress: Fan distribution, proselytization commons, and the explosive growth of Japanese animation. *UCLA*

Entertainment Law Review (Spring 2005), http://papers.ssrn.com/sol3/papers.cfm ?abstract_id=696402#PaperDownload (retrieved January 13, 2011).

Lessig, Lawrence. 2008. *Remix: Making art and commerce thrive in the hybrid economy.* New York: Penguin Press.

Postigo, Hector. 2010. Modding to the big leagues: Exploring the space between modders and the game industry. *First Monday* 15 (5), http://firstmonday.org/htbin/cgiwrap/bin/ojs/index.php/fm/article/view/2972/2530 (retrieved January 13, 2011).

Russell, Adrienne, Mizuko Ito, Todd Richmond, and Marc Tuters. 2008. Culture: Media convergence and networked participation. In *Networked publics*, ed. K. Varnelis, 43–76. Cambridge, MA: MIT Press.

Scacchi, Walt. 2010. Computer game mods, modders, modding, and the mod scene. *First Monday* 15 (5), http://firstmonday.org/htbin/cgiwrap/bin/ojs/index.php/fm/article/view/2965/2526 (retrieved January 13, 2011).

Shirky, Clay. 2010. *Cognitive surplus: Creativity and generosity in a connected age.* New York: Penguin Press.

Sotamaa, Ollii. 2007. On modder labour, commodification of play, and mod competitions. *First Monday* 12 (9), http://131.193.153.231/www/issues/issue12_9/sotamaa (retrieved January 13, 2011).

Swartz, Aaron. 2006. Who writes Wikipedia? In *Raw thought*, www.aaronsw.com/weblog/whowriteswikipedia (retrieved January 13, 2011).

Terranova, Tiziana. 2000. Free labor: Producing culture for the digital economy. *Social Text* 18 (2): 33–58.

Varnelis, Kazys, ed. 2008. *Networked publics.* Cambridge, MA: MIT Press.

Weber, Steven. 2004. *The success of open source.* Cambridge, MA: Harvard University Press.

III
COMMUNITY AND IDENTITY

9

Making *Fujoshi* Identity Visible and Invisible

DAISUKE OKABE AND KIMI ISHIDA

INTRODUCTION

In this chapter, we analyze the identity construction of female otaku. More specifically, we examine the practices of otaku whose interests center on anime and manga and who create *doujinshi* (fan-created manga). More females than males are otaku of this type. These women refer to themselves by the playfully self-critical term *fujoshi*. The term literally means "rotten women" and is a pun playing on the homonym with different Chinese characters that means "respectable women." Broadly speaking, "fujoshi" describes all female otaku, but the term often refers more specifically to female otaku who are fans of *yaoi* and "boys' love" (BL) manga and anime that portray gay relationships between men. Yaoi doujin and BL novels are considered deviant works in opposition to mainstream commercial manga and novels. The stigma attached to this subcultural identity means that fujoshi manage the expression and concealment of their identity in unique ways. This chapter focuses on these characteristics of fujoshi identity construction.

Fujoshi identity is constructed through a relational process and ongoing social interaction. Goffman (1963) argued that, rather than being an exclusive property of the individual, the self is made visible by circumstance and interpersonal relationships. Work in cultural studies has described how these processes play out as different social groups define themselves in opposition to one another (for example, Eckert 1990; Miyazaki 1993; Willis 1977). For example, Willis (1977) analyzed the identity construction of disaffected male students in an ethnographic study of a high school in a working-class town in Britain. He found that these students derided instructors and exemplary students who behaved according to middle-class norms. Through such episodic opposition to the structured, regulated community of the school, the students constructed a situated identity that ran counter to that of the model student. Eckert (1990) similarly focused on the relationship between the different kinds of knowledge and identity construction between two groups of students: the burnouts, who primarily shared knowledge with each other outside of the school environment, and the jocks, who sought to gain knowledge in domains such as science and math from their instructors. Members of each group of students expressed their identity by communicating with other group members via their own in-group knowledge and cultural forms. Although the two groups resisted one another, their identities were interactively co-constructed.

A similar perspective on the construction of self as a relationship of the individual to his society has also been posited in social constructivist approaches in sociology (for example, Gergen 1999; Milner 2004; Ueno 2005). Studies in this vein have indicated a strong link between the expression of identity and everyday discourse, as well as the highly dynamic aspects of identity. A classic ethnographic study by Becker (1963) of mainstream musicians and dance musicians explains how countercultural identities are defined in relation to dominant ones. According to Becker, dance musicians called the more mainstream musicians "square (serious and old-fashioned)" and differentiated themselves from such groups. Everyday discourse is a means of making identity visible and reifying intercommunity boundaries.

Bucholtz's ethnographic study (1999) of a female high school "nerd" community offers another example of how subcultural identity is constructed. Nerds are exemplary students who are studious and fond of relatively esoteric topics and hobbies instead of sports and popular trends. Bucholtz focused in particular on how the use of language in the nerd community set it apart from the other student communities, citing the sharing of scientific knowledge as these students went about their everyday lives as a strategy to make their identity visible. Similarly, in their 2005 study of the fujoshi community, Ishida and Miyamoto describe how the community's distinctive use of language and means of expression enabled members to communicate with each other. These studies are examples of how multiple and subcultural gender identities are constructed through ongoing discursive practices.

Drawing from these works, we consider fujoshi self and identity as a situational achievement made visible through moment-by-moment interactions. "Otaku" has generally been a highly derogatory term, used to point out people with a deviant culture or psychology. The fujoshi community faces a similar cultural context, in which non-members perceive fujoshi in a negative light. This has contributed to the unique construction of fujoshi identity as a combination of making one's identity both visible and invisible. In this chapter, we argue that fujoshi identity construction represents an example of a subcultural and oppositional feminine identity constructed in a self-deprecating and "undercover" mode. While fujoshi develop their identities in opposition to the mainstream like many other subcultures do, they do as much work to erase, or make invisible, their fujoshi identity as they do in making it selectively visible. These processes of visualization and erasure work in tandem to create a unique subcultural identity.

In the next section, we discuss the various strategies involved in the unique identity construction of fujoshi: (1) the visualization and devisualization of fujoshi identity, and (2) the irony inherent in identity construction through identity devisualization. We begin with an overview of how female otaku and their activities have been depicted in the past, followed by a description of the methodology of the study that this chapter is based on and an analysis of the interview and fieldwork data.[1]

FUJOSHI AND TEXTUAL POACHING

According to the Nomura Research Institute (2005), in 2004 otaku consumers in Japan represented a market size of 350,000 people and 8.3 billion yen (approximately US$83 million) for manga and 110,000 people and 2 billion yen (approximately US$20 million) for anime. Comic Market (known as Comiket; see Chapter 5), a convention dedicated to the buying and selling of doujin, draws 400,000 visitors twice a year. According to Nagayama (2006), manga and anime otaku derive pleasure from deconstructing commercial works and creating derivative works in different media formats. In addition to manga and anime, otaku also create derivative works based on novels, movies, and TV dramas. Kobayashi (1999) describes how manga and anime otaku evaluate, interpret, explain, and adapt existing texts to create and consume doujin that are collages, pastiches, and parodies of these texts. While manga is the dominant form of doujin creations, the format of these derivative works can be highly diverse, varying from brochures and music to game CDs and figurines.

Male and female otaku diverge in how they create doujin. Many doujin targeting male otaku feature heterosexual sex, whereas doujin targeting female otaku tend to feature romantic relationships between male characters that never existed in the original work. The latter is the outcome of "yaoi read-in," in which homosexual relationships are "read" into an existing cast of male characters and given shape through expression in doujin. These homosexual relationships encompass the entire spectrum of love, from pure romance to passionate love, and the characters' emotions are expressed in minute detail and with meticulous care. These characteristics of yaoi and BL culture in Japan share many parallels with U.S. female "slash" fandoms (Bacon-Smith 1991; Jenkins 1992; Penley 1997).

In the past, otaku have often been described as a passive audience, merely following works aired on TV. The nature of otaku activity is increasingly the subject of debate as the image of television viewers as passive has been challenged (for example, Okabe and Fukuda 2006; Penley 1997). Jenkins (1992) characterized fans who appropriate texts to create derivative works as "textual poachers." He described fans as actively creating their own meanings by drawing on the original text, making episodes that did not exist in the original narrative, and forging links with other texts. Fujoshi in many ways exemplify these active and productive dimensions of television fandom, in that they read texts from vantage points that differ substantially from mainstream ones and produce a wide variety of derivative works based on these alternative readings.

METHODOLOGY

For this study, Okabe interviewed twelve single women in their twenties and conducted field observations.[2] Participants all lived in the Kanto region and were either creators and/or consumers of doujin. Given the focus on identity construction, ethnographic methods were the most appropriate way of gathering detailed and contextualized information about how fujoshi negotiated knowledge and social relationships with their community and with outsiders. We employed a mix of interview-based and observational approaches to get at both the discourse of fujoshi and how they construct their identity in their everyday practice.

Our informants are listed in Table 9.1. They include working adults and students, and they represent a range of ages as to when they first created doujin. While some started in a middle school or high school club, others became part of the doujin scene after high school as part of a doujin convention.

We recruited informants via snowball sampling, with informants info.5 and info.9 serving as initial contacts. The two subjects were not acquainted with each other before the study. We chose this sampling method because of the importance of building rapport for interviews and field observations. We asked our two initial contacts to introduce Okabe to their friends in the fujoshi community and to sit in on initial interviews with additional informants whenever possible. Informants were limited to women in their twenties partly because of the chosen sampling method but also because this age group is best equipped with the resources necessary for engaging in otaku activities such as the creation and purchase of doujin: high disposable income and correspondingly high participation in the consumption and production of doujin goods. The informants were all aware that they were being interviewed because they were fujoshi, and they did not exhibit any particular resistance to that categorization.

The study was conducted between August 2004 and December 2006. Fieldwork observations at doujin wholesale events and after-event parties were recorded in audio and video formats with permission. Interview protocols were developed after preliminary fieldwork, following a semistructured format, and interviews ranged from one and a half hours to three hours. Interview questions sought to elucidate the timeline of the informants' participation in the fujoshi community via doujin conventions and other related events. The sequence of questions usually began by Okabe's asking informants about their induction into the community and ended with their present modes of participation. If the informant chose to digress or revisit previously discussed topics, no particular effort was made to correct the flow of

Table 9.1 Informants interviewed

ID	Age at time of interview	Age at time of first purchase of doujin	Age at time of first creation of doujin
info.1	25	10	13
info.2	22	11	15
info.3	27	15–16	16
info.4	26	11	24
info.5	24	11–12	n/a
info.6	24	13	n/a
info.7	28	15–16	20
info.8	25	14–15	23
info.9	24	19	22
info.10	24	unknown	unknown
info.11	28	16	19
info.12	23	unknown	n/a

the interview. Okabe's goal was to make the informant feel at ease throughout the interview.

Our analysis in this chapter draws from interviews with informants info.1, info.2, info.4, info.5, info.6, info.9, and info.10. These seven informants were all interviewed in groups of three or more, which facilitated conversations that were more typical of gatherings between fujoshi than the one-on-one context. While informants info.11 and info.12 were also interviewed in group settings, they did not give permission to quote from their interviews, so their interview data were used only for comparison in the analysis.

DISCUSSION AND ANALYSIS

Making Fujoshi Identity Visible and Invisible

Fujoshi engage in cultural activities that are stigmatized by the mainstream. In addition to being identified as otaku, they also favor doujin that depict gay male relationships, often in sexually explicit ways. This marginalization and stigmatization means that they generally conceal their fujoshi identity except when they are with fellow fujoshi. Within their fan community, fujoshi employ particular strategies to make their identity as fujoshi visible, but they act in accordance with mainstream norms in situations in which fujoshi culture would be inappropriate. Fujoshi do not make these decisions about making their otaku identity visible in a spontaneous and situational way; rather, these decisions are the outcomes of ongoing and serious reflection about their self-presentation in different social contexts. In their interviews, informants tell stories about how they managed to avoid exposing themselves as fujoshi and describe how they hide their fujoshi identity in their everyday lives. The practices of concealing identity have special meaning in the fujoshi community and are part of the building of a sense of community and shared identity. Hiding fujoshi identity is both a means of selectively managing self-presentation and of making visible one's identity as a fujoshi. In this sense, fujoshi identity involves the paradoxical practice of rendering identity visible by making it invisible.

We turn now to specific examples of this practice of controlling the visibility of one's identity as a fujoshi or a woman and how these practices collectively comprise the fujoshi identity.

MAKING FUJOSHI IDENTITY VISIBLE   We made a special effort to include more than one informant per interview session in order to investigate how fujoshi structure conversations with their peers. In these interviews, and in social gatherings that we observed in the field, the majority of conversation topics involve what fujoshi call *moe-gatari*, or discussions about works and characters that fujoshi find particularly appealing (see Chapter 2 for an explication of *moe*). Like nerds discussing science or geeks discussing technology, moe-gatari involve social interaction around a topic of deep and often esoteric interest. Below is an example of moe-gatari involving a series written by author Natsuhiko Kyogoku with informants info.9 and info.10:

EXAMPLE 1

info9: This [novel by Natsuhiko Kyogoku] is very light stuff compared
     to the main story line. And, well, right?

info10: He's so cute.

info9: He is.

Interviewer: Uh, who is?

info9: Enokizu. Oh, Chuzenji is, too. It depends on who you ask, so I
     can't really say.

info10: Yeah, you can't. Some people find Sekiguchi cute. . . . Well, not many do.

info9: [Pointing at info.10] Here's one right here.

info10: Yeah.

info9: So that's the most common. . . . I like the *Enokizu x Sekiguchi* pairing. It's more popular. *Sekiguchi-uke* is the most common.

Note: Terms in italics denote genres or couplings.

In this example, informants employ common yaoi protocols to refer to genres and couplings, some of the most important concepts in fujoshi culture. Genres are units of classification generally used to refer to the original work that forms the basis of derivative works. Couplings are character pairings employed in yaoi works depicting male homosexual relationships. Couplings use the symbolic notation "x"; the character to the left of the letter "x" is called "seme" (literally "attacker") and takes the dominant role in the relationship, both sexually and romantically. The character to the right of the letter "x" is called "uke" ("defender" or "receiver") and is the more submissive of the pair. Fans have particular preferences and attach great significance to whether a particular character is in the seme or uke role. Discussions of coupling decisions are prominent in fujoshi conversations. In a sense, these genres and couplings are a sort of cultural device that allows fujoshi to express their inclinations and interests to one other.

In the example below, informants info.1 and info.4 discuss which genres piqued their initial interests in yaoi and BL and then discuss how they share an interest in the same genre now:

EXAMPLE 2

info.4: After *Slamdunk* [a manga series serialized in *Weekly Shonen Jump*] ended, I got into *KOF* [*King of Fighters*, a fighting game] and graduated [from *Jump*].

info.1: *KOF . . . KOF?*

Interviewer: Why the pause, or actually, why did you repeat the title?

info.1: Well, it's just different with people who liked the same genres as you. Even though people may like *Full Metal Alchemist* [a manga series serialized in *Monthly Shonen Gangan*], people who came in from a *Jump* series and people who came in from fighting games are different.

Interviewer: Oh, so you're commenting on their history—where they came from before finding *Full Metal Alchemist*.

info.1: Right. So we can assume that there's a common ground somewhere. But I also have a bit of a bias that there I'll have some incompatibilities with people coming in from *Jump*.

Here, info.1, by reinforcing info.4's narrative, also indicates that she was a fan of the *KOF* genre before moving to the *Full Metal Alchemist* genre. The two informants were already close acquaintances at the time of the interview, but upon discovering that info.4 has a similar "history," info.1 reacknowledges their relationship as having a common ground. What is notable in this exchange is that genres are a common cultural device that fujoshi employ to make their own identity visible and to assess and negotiate their relationships with other fujoshi. Info.4 makes her fujoshi identity visible by linking to various genres. Okabe observed the same processes at play with couplings. How fujoshi choose to categorize characters from the original work can energize or ruin their communication with one another. Thus, genres and couplings function as tools of negotiation that express fujoshi interests and history, employed in their distinctive modes of storytelling to make their identity visible.

MAKING FUJOSHI IDENTITY INVISIBLE   For fujoshi, the practice of identity construction does not solely consist of making their identity visible, however. Paradoxically, making their identity invisible also contributes to their identity construction.

Fujoshi call the act of hiding their identity and covering up fujoshi-like behavior "concealment." The gendered dimensions of otaku identity are a major factor in this concealment, as evident in the exchange below:

EXAMPLE 3

info.6: Guys tend not to consider otaku dating material. A lot of people misunderstand, so I don't want to tell anyone unless I know them. Even though there are many types of yaoi, people tend to think of you as a pervert who only reads hard-core stuff, so I don't want to tell them. . . . I was once reading a doujin at school when a guy sitting next to me

found out and thought I was reading something freaky, so he
treated me like a girl who read really gross stuff.

Like info.6, the majority of the informants in this study held the
view that fujoshi are perceived negatively by others. Consequently,
fujoshi are always sensitive about any behavior that may reveal their
identity. For instance, info.9 stated that "on mixi [a social network
site], I present myself as a nice OL [office lady] and hide my otaku hobbies." Fujoshi generally try to minimize disclosure of their otaku identity.

Okabe also encountered concealment activities when he initially
contacted the informants. For example, he made contact with info.9
through a different line of research. Whenever he made small talk about
manga, info.9 never showed overt interest in the topic. However, once
he disclosed that he was doing research on otaku culture, had gone to
Comiket several times, and liked reading manga and doujin, info.9
mentioned that she was writing a novel. She eventually disclosed that
it was a doujin novel and agreed to provide information about her activities for this study.

He observed similar caution when setting up interview locations
with informants. In particular, informants info.2, info.4, and info.6
preferred private rooms or franchises of *izakaya* (Japanese pubs) that
they knew had private dining rooms or had dividers between tables.
Such locations allow fujoshi to speak freely without worrying about
adjoining tables, so informants said that such places were often chosen
for after-event parties after doujin conventions. Informants info.11
and info.12 were interviewed in cafés. Whenever they noticed a server
approaching their table, they would casually hide magazines and other
materials that they had laid out on the table. Okabe's informants all
thought that concealing their cultural practices from those outside of
their community was a prerequisite for being considered a model fujoshi.

MAKING FUJOSHI IDENTITY VISIBLE THROUGH CONCEALMENT   In addition to the processes of concealment that are central to fujoshi identity,
fujoshi also engage in self-conscious strategies for displaying normalcy.
For the informants, discussion of how they behave like normal women
constitutes a certain conversation topic. An excerpt from an interview

with info.2 serves as an example. Info.2 had been buying doujin from the time she was an elementary school student, and at the time of the interview, she was an assistant for a famous doujin manga artist. The informant also admitted that she regularly reads *Weekly Shonen Jump* but hides the fact from her peers.

EXAMPLE 4

info.2: I tell my boyfriend that I've never read *Jump*. I still buy it every week and read it, though. But in front of my boyfriend, I act like I know nothing about it.

Interviewer: Doesn't it get frustrating when your boyfriend tries to explain *Jump* series?

info.2: I just smile and go, "Oh, really?" while thinking that I know more than he does.

. . .

Interviewer: What kind of people did you hang out with in high school?

info.2: Well, some of my friends read *non-no*; the more mature ones read *CanCam* [both are fashion magazines popular among teens and tweens, especially college students and older]. We'd talk about guys.

info.5: So basically a girly group. A normal girly group.

info.2: We'd talk about boyfriends and clothes. . . . . But sometimes I'd let something slip, and I'd get stressed. Going to Comiket twice a year was my way of reducing stress.

Weekly Shonen Jump is a manga magazine targeting adolescent boys. However, the series featured in *Jump* are extremely popular source material for doujin. Fujoshi are aware of what it means to be noticed as a woman who is a dedicated reader of manga serials for adolescent boys. Because they are fujoshi, they conceal the fact that they read these serials to avoid the possibility of being identified as fujoshi. However, as seen in the above excerpt, info.2 and many other informants display the fact that they are avid consumers of fashion magazines and clothes. They conceal their fujoshi identity while also presenting the socially expected image of normal women.

What is noteworthy in the case of fujoshi is that their practices of concealment are well-established conversation topics among their otaku community. Not only are they concealing their identity from others, but they are also making this practice visible to members in their community and using it as an opportunity for self-deprecating humor. Informants talked about identity concealment as a conversation topic multiple times during their interviews, indicating how these practices have special meaning for fujoshi. Paradoxically, continuing to engage in and share these practices with other fujoshi renders concealment visible and legitimizes the practices within the fujoshi community.

Given these dynamics, fujoshi identity construction is more complex than simply making identity visible in a situationally responsive way. In accounts of subculture such as that by Hebdige (1979), the emphasis has been overwhelmingly on the side of displaying identity. In fujoshi culture, the practice of identity concealment is also central to identity construction. Rendering identity invisible is a unique concealment strategy in that it refers not only to the situational concealment of one's identity but also to the visualization of identity through concealment. In this way, fujoshi is a category constructed through a complex set of practices of visibility and invisibility.

Ironic Identity Construction

As discussed in previous sections, fujoshi conceal their identity to resist stigmatization by the general public. Disclosure can have social consequences, such as rendering a woman undesirable to men, as described in Example 3.

The general public does not understand the cultural practices of fujoshi and simply labels them as unintelligible. In turn, fujoshi conceal their identity to avoid stigmatization. However, as info.2 mentioned in Example 4, concealment can be stressful, and fujoshi need an outlet for their stress. Telling each other about concealment practices is a communication strategy in which fujoshi express their behavior as fujoshi to their peers in an ironic and playful way.

For example, consider the reference to "a normal girly group" by info.2 and info.5 in Example 4. They position this group as being separate from the fujoshi community. Furthermore, they are not simply discussing the practices of such normal girls but also making visible the boundaries and hierarchies between normal girls and the fujoshi community. Fujoshi emphasize that their community is deviant and subordinate to the "normal" community and deride their own practices as fujoshi. Similar forms of self-deprecating humor are evident in the following two examples.

EXAMPLE 5

info.1: I didn't want to dress like otaku girls [who have no fashion sense]. So I'd try to dress like an adult when I'd go to Comiket, wearing earrings and so on. Well, not that the outfit was great—I'd pair a beret with my clothes. It was off base by one accessory.

EXAMPLE 6

info.5: I think doujin are a great culture, but in the end, we're just drooling over gay guys. I may rave about it, but I hide my [doujin] in a cardboard box that has my [fujoshi] friend's address so I'm prepared in case I die suddenly.
Interviewer: So if you were to die, the box will be automatically delivered to a fujoshi friend?
info.5: That's right. That way, my parents won't have to cry when they go through my things.

In the case of dance musicians studied by Becker (1963), artists derided other communities and established their own community's legitimacy. However, in the case of the fujoshi community, fujoshi position their practices, themselves, and their community as subordinate to other communities. In these quotes, fujoshi display an ironic form of identity construction, making fun of their own otaku fashion sense and of their imagination of how dismayed their parents would be if the parents discovered after their daughter's death that she read doujin. According to Utsumi (1997), Tsuji (1997), and others, irony is a rhetorical device that constructs an implicit disparity between the spoken word and the actual context and circumstance. The nature of irony depends upon the deliberate exposure of this incongruity, resulting in derisive humor. The irony in fujoshi conversations consists of self-punishing self-degradation. Subordinating their practices to those of other communities, they communicate with each other by construing their practices as targets of derision.

Fujoshi create frequent opportunities to talk about their activities and laugh at themselves. In one interview, info.10 commented that they are always looking for such opportunities. When a recorder mal-functioned in another interview, the informants attributed the mal-function to their "rotten energy," taking an opportunity to make fun of themselves.[3] Indeed, maintaining self-derisive discussions about be-ing fujoshi seemed to be a goal in itself, a reason for them to gather and bond with fellow fujoshi.

Their use of irony to discuss their own practice is important in fujoshi identity construction. Since it is rare for fujoshi to discuss their practices with outsiders, it is also rare for fujoshi to experience direct criticism. However, informants are aware of the possibility for critique and derision by outsiders because the general mass media have taken up fujoshi culture and portrayed it to the public. Aware that their ac-tivities are stigmatized, fujoshi cope by proactively discussing and de-riding practices that are potentially subject to outside critique.

Sacks, Shegloff, and Jefferson's construct of adjacency pairs (1974) provides an analytical framework for this understanding of irony. Answer-response and proposal-uptake are examples of adjacency pairs in which the first member of a pair initiates and the second member completes one cycle in verbal communication. Applied to fujoshi conver-sations, ironic statements and commentary on these statements com-prise an adjacency pair. For instance, if an individual makes an error, he can point out and evaluate that error before someone else does (for example, disparaging himself by saying, "I'm such a klutz."). By doing so, the speaker can initiate and complete the cycle and thereby prevent the occurrence of derision and denigration by other participants in subsequent conversation cycles.

In this sense, the ironic self-punishing practices of fujoshi are a means of self-evaluating their behavior in self-contained discursive adjacency pairs that have the effect of supporting their behavior. Fu-joshi fully understand the negative social consequences of engaging in their community of practice, yet they still choose to do so. Then they laugh at the shared irony of their self-destructive choice among them-selves. This ironic self-contained conversation is yet another commu-nication strategy unique to the fujoshi community.

Such strategies are evidence that fujoshi grasp how outsiders view and talk about their activities and identity. As seen in the example below, when their practices are criticized, their strategy is to respond by indi-cating that they are fully aware of what their actions mean to outsiders.

EXAMPLE 7

> info.9: There was this huge fight between fujoshi and *tetsu-ota* [train otaku; see Chapter 1] on 2ch [a massive online forum; see Chapter 3]. The tetsu-ota would make all these posts about how fujoshi are creepy and gross, but the fujoshi wouldn't get angry and instead would just accept the comments. They would go like, "Yeah, yeah. And?" In the end, they smothered the tetsu-ota with that kind of response, and the tetsu-ota shut up. . . . We won the war.

In this way, rather than being defensive about the negative consequences of their behavior, fujoshi respond to and negate external criticism by taking the stance that they are already aware of these consequences. By treating their practices as opportunities for self-derisive humor and conversation, they are accepting the fact that their practices are valid objects of criticism. Although self-deprecating at first glance, this approach allows them to ridicule outsiders who go through the trouble of criticizing practices that they have already criticized themselves.

By declaring their practices as targets for derision, fujoshi objectify their behavior. In addition, they seek to nullify criticism by indicating that their practices are targets for derision and by swiftly pointing out "mistakes" in their practice and completing the cycle of portraying and commenting on behavior. In this way, the self-punishing, ironic conversations of fujoshi function as a unique communication strategy.

CONCLUSION

This study sought to elucidate the processes underlying the identity construction of fujoshi by conducting interviews and group discussions with women engaging in creative activities such as doujin and cosplay. Because fujoshi practices vary by interests and region, the practices discussed here do not encompass the entire range of practices. However, we believe that the practices we have described provide insights into fujoshi identity.

Belonging to a subculture both unfamiliar to and stigmatized by mainstream culture, fujoshi reject dominant feminine cultures that center on fashion and heteronormative romance. Japan has tended toward a relatively fluid set of norms around gender identity and a tolerant view of homosexuality compared with Euro-American contexts (McLelland 2000), but it still has strong values surrounding appropriate feminine culture and behavior. As is typical of teen cultures in consumer societies (Milner 2004; Pascoe 2007), young Japanese women feel pressures to conform to a set of heteronormative standards that dictate interests in boys, romance, consumerism, fashion, and peer status (Skov and Moeran 1995).

In her study of female fandoms in the United States, Bacon-Smith describes slash fandoms as a form of subversion and civil disobedience against norms of copyright as well as against gender expectations (Bacon-Smith 1991). Fujoshi also see themselves as non-mainstream, and they are highly cognizant and self-reflective about how they depart from a mainstream feminine identity. Unlike members of other "bad girl" subcultures who might flaunt extreme fashions or makeup in highly visible street cultures, however, fujoshi avoid making their identities visible in public and mainstream contexts.[4] In order to manage their stigmatized identity, fujoshi engage in strategies of identity concealment from their mainstream friends and families, making their subcultural identity visible only to their fujoshi peers in a humorously self-deprecating approach to identity construction. Their practices of shared self-derision become a vehicle for subcultural bonding, in which they ironically view their own subculture through the unflattering lens of the mainstream and take pleasure in a secretly subversive identity.

As an example of a uniquely oppositional but self-denigrating feminine subculture, fujoshi underscore the multiplicity of forms of female gender identity, and how they are constructed relationally and through interaction within and between genders. In this way, this work is another illustration of the performative and situational nature of gender (Butler 1990; Garfinkel 1967; Thorne 1993), expanding on existing accounts of multiple masculinities and femininities available to young women and men (Bucholtz 1999; Miller and Bardsley 2005; Pascoe 2007; Thorne 1993; Yochim 2010). Otaku culture and fujoshi culture involve not only the creative reshaping of mainstream fantasy narratives and sexuality but also the playfully undercover subversion of gender expectations.

Notes

1. Portions of this chapter were previously published in Japanese in Daisuke Okabe (2008). Making "fujoshi" identity visible/invisible. *Cognitive Studies* 15: 671–681.

2. Both authors conducted fieldwork, recruitment, and analysis, and Okabe conducted the interviews.

3. This was a pun replacing the character *fu* (meaning negative) in negative energy with *fu* (literally meaning rotten) in *fujoshi*.

4. Some examples of girls' subcultures that have been taken up extensively by both the U.S. and Japanese press include biker girls, *kogyaru* high school girls' street culture, and gothic-lolita (see Miller and Bardsley 2005).

References

Bacon-Smith, Camille. 1991. *Enterprising women: Television fandom and the creation of popular myth.* Philadelphia: University of Pennsylvania Press.

Becker, S. Howard. 1963. *Outsiders.* New York: The Free Press.

Bucholtz, Mary. 1999. Why be normal? Language and identity practices in a community of nerd girls. *Language in Society* 28 (2): 203–224.

Butler, Judith. 1990. *Gender trouble: Feminism and the subversion of identity.* New York: Routledge.

Eckert, Penelope. 1990. Adolescent social categories, information and science learning. In *Toward a scientific practice of science education*, ed. Marjorie Gardner, James G. Greeno, Frederick Reif, and Alan H. Schoenfeld, 203–217. Hillsdale, NJ: Lawrence Erlbaum.

Garfinkel, Harold. 1967. Passing and the managed achievement of sex status in an "intersexed" person, part 1. In *Studies in ethnomethodology*, 116–185. Englewood Cliffs, NJ: Prentice-Hall.

Gergen, Kenneth J. 1999. *An invitation to social construction.* Thousand Oaks, CA: Sage.

Goffman, Erving. 1963. *Stigma: Notes on the management of spoiled identity.* Upper Saddle River, NJ: Prentice-Hall.

Hebdige, Dick. 1979. *Subculture: The meaning of style.* London: Methuen.

Ishida, Kimi, and Chihiro Miyamoto. 2005. Community henno sanka niyoru genjitu no henyo. *Japan Cognitive Science, Design of Educational Environment* 12 (1): 6–18.

Jenkins, Henry. 1992. *Textual poachers: Television fans and participatory culture: Studies in culture and communication.* New York: Routledge.

Kobayashi, Yoshinori. 1999. TV, anime no media fandom: Majoko anime nosekai. In *Television polyphony: Bangumi, shichosya bunseki no kokoromi*, ed. Mamoru Ito and Masafumi Fujita, 68–84. Tokyo: Sekaishisosya.

McLelland, Mark. 2000. *Male homosexuality in modern Japan: Cultural myths and social realities.* New York: Routledge.

Miller, Laura, and Jan Bardsley, eds. 2005. *Bad girls of Japan.* New York: Palgrave Macmillan.

Milner, Murray. 2004. *Freaks, geeks, and cool kids: American teenagers, schools, and the culture of consumption.* New York: Routledge.

Miyazaki, Ayumi. 1993. Gender, subculture no dynamics: Joshiko ni okeru ethnography wo motoni. *Journal of Educational Sociology* 52: 157–177.

Nagayama, Kaoru. 2006. *Eromanga studies: Kairakusochi to shiteno manga nyumon.* Tokyo: East Press.

Nomura Research Institute. 2005. *Otaku shijo nokenkyu.* Tokyo: Toyo keizai shinpousha.

Okabe, Daisuke, and Megumi Fukuda. 2006. Audience no kouchiku ni miru eizou contents no design. In *Kagaku gijutsu jisen no fieldwork: Hybrid no design*, ed. Ueno Naoki and Dobashi Shingo, 90–109. Tokyo: Serikashobo.

Pascoe, C. J. 2007. *Dude, you're a fag: Masculinity and sexuality in high school.* Berkeley, CA: University of California Press.

Penley, Constance. 1997. *Nasa/Trek: Popular science and sex in America.* London: Verso Books.

Sacks, Harvey, Emanuel A. Shegloff, and Gail Jefferson. 1974. A simplest systematics for the organization of turn-taking for conversation. *Language* 50 (4): 696–735.

Skov, Lise, and Brian Moeran. 1995. Introduction: Hiding in the light: From Oshin to Yoshimoto Banana. In *Women, media and consumption in Japan*, ed. Lise Skove and Brian Moeran, 1–74. Honolulu: University of Hawaii Press.

Thorne, Barrie. 1993. *Gender play: Girls and boys in school.* New Brunswick, NJ: Rutgers University Press.

Tsuji, Daisuke. 1997. Irony no communication ron. *Bulletin of the Institute of Socio-Information and Communication Studies* 55: 91–127.

Willis, Paul. E. 1977. *Learning to labor: How working class kids get working class jobs.* New York: Columbia University Press.

Ueno, Chizuko. 2005. Datsu identity no riron. In *Datsu identity*, ed. Chizuko Ueno, 1–41. Tokyo: Keisoshobo.

Utsumi, Akira. 1997. Irony to ha nani ka? Irony no anmokuteki teiji riron. *Cognitive Science* 4 (4): 99–112.

Yochim, Emily Chivers. 2010. *Skate life: Re-imagining white masculinity.* Ann Arbor: University of Michigan Press.

10

Cosplay, Learning, and Cultural Practice

. . . .

DAISUKE OKABE

INTRODUCTION

My first encounter with cosplay culture occurred in the summer of 2003 when one of my students proposed cosplay as her thesis topic. My guide-to-be was a cosplayer herself. Once I set foot in a cosplay event hall, I was completely taken by the faithful reproductions of characters from a myriad of series such as *Naruto* and *Mobile Suit Gundam*. I found it particularly exciting to witness *awase*, group photo shoots of characters from the same series (see Figure 10.1). Upon talking to some of the cosplayers, I was surprised to learn that many of them buy the necessary materials from craft stores and make their own costumes. Given the unique nature of costumes donned by anime and game characters, they have no alternative but to take a do-it-yourself (DIY) approach, and cosplayers also value keeping costs down by buying materials at the lowest price possible. Still, the attention spent on every detail, from the wigs duplicating the characters' hairstyles to the characters' accessories, was well beyond what I had expected from an amateur costuming hobby.

"Cosplay" is an abbreviated term for costume play. The term originally referred to period dramas and historical plays and rehearsals that required costumes appropriate to the period. The term has gained currency in Japan since the 1970s to describe the practice of dressing up as characters from anime, manga, and games.

The majority of cosplayers in Japan are women, mostly college students and people in their twenties, who otherwise lead conventional adult lives. For them, cosplay is a hobby, and they do not devote all of their time to its pursuit. However, before an upcoming event, cosplayers can become so engrossed in finishing their outfits that they lose

Figure 10.1. *Awase* of *Gintama* characters at the 2008 World Cosplay Summit. Credit: Photo by Daisuke Okabe.

track of time. Depending on the outfit's complexity, they have to make do without any sewing patterns or how-to manuals and rely on their own ingenuity. Making one's own outfit instead of buying or commissioning a costume has high value within the cosplay community. Cosplay events are a valuable venue for exchanging information and learning from each other about costume making, as well as for evaluating each other's work. Cosplayers also devalue certain approaches to cosplay, such as costumes designed to attract attention to the cosplayer rather than being focused on fidelity to the fantasy character. Cosplay comprises an assortment of cultural practices that have unique significance and value for its participants.[1] These practices can be both collaborative and competitive—fans often work together in groups, but there can also be tensions and conflicts within and between groups. In this way, cosplayers form a distinct community with shared values and boundaries. The cultural practice of cosplay has significance only within this community, and the community exists only through its members' active participation in these shared practices.

In this chapter, I discuss various cultural practices characterizing the cosplay community. My observations are based on interviews with female cosplayers and fieldwork, carried out at several event sites. The discourse of cosplayers not only represents individual feelings and opinions, but it is also an expression of the history of the cosplay community and its relationship with the outside world. Veteran cosplayers spoke about their experiences, criticized the media's portrayal of otaku and cosplayers, and explained the connections between the industry and the characters and people being portrayed in cosplay.[2] In effect, these individual narratives and practices are inseparable from the relationships both internal and external to the community that give the community its shape.

In sum, the cosplay fandom is shaped by the cosplayers' cultural practices, and their community is a space in which harmony and discord coexist through ongoing negotiations. In this chapter, I first give a broad overview of the history of the cosplay community and cosplay in Japan, introduce the theoretical background and methodologies I employ, and then discuss in detail the following aspects of the cosplay community: (1) DIY culture, (2) peer review, and (3) reciprocal learning.

THE COSPLAY SCENE

Japan is home to numerous amateur cosplay events. Some are events where cosplay is an optional activity, including large *doujin* (fan-created manga) events such as Comic Market (known as Comiket; see Chapter 5), smaller doujin events centered on a particular series or genre, and conventions for DIY figure and model creation such as Wonder Festival. In addition, some events have cosplay as the main attraction. These events are highly diverse. Many are held in convention halls such as Tokyo Fashion Town and theme parks such as Toshimaen, with occasional large-scale events such as the World Cosplay Summit, in which cosplayers parade through a shopping district, and more frequent smaller events in clubs in which cosplayers dance to anime songs.

Cosplay events are often managed by cosplay event clubs, in which most members are also cosplayers. Participation can be free, but some events charge registration fees and additional fees for use of changing rooms that range from several hundred to several thousand yen (approximately several U.S. dollars to tens of U.S. dollars). If we include small-scale photo-shoot events in the mix, at least one cosplay event is held in Japan every week. Official reports released by Comic Market, Japan's largest doujin event, state that in the summer of 2006, of the 430,000 who came to the event over a three-day period, 10,280 were female cosplayers and 2,170 were male cosplayers (Comic Market Junbikai 2006). These numbers refer only to cosplayers who used the changing rooms provided by the Comic Market Preparations Committee, so the actual number of participants is greater.

My cosplayer informants were all authors or consumers of doujin. While women who are fans of *yaoi doujin* (fan-created manga depicting gay male relationships) call themselves *fujoshi* (Okabe 2008; see Chapter 9), my cosplay informants would alternately refer to themselves as fujoshi, otaku, and *layers* (cosplayers). In other words, they consider cosplayers a subcategory of fujoshi, and their practices are tightly entwined with the doujin scene.

In addition to conventions, cosplayers also use a variety of media to communicate and organize. Information about events is transmitted via websites and flyers. The majority of cosplayers upload photos of themselves in costume online for public viewing. Some of them have their own sites; others set up user accounts at cosplay community

sites such as Cure (http://ja.curecos.com) and Cosplayers (www.cosp
.jp) and display their photos there. Many have described how otaku
have a high affinity with new media (see the Introduction and Chapters 1, 4, and 7), and cosplayers also exhibit this tendency. Many female cosplayers incorporate new media and technologies into their
daily lives, toting digital single-lens reflex cameras, modifying their
photos using image-editing software such as Photoshop and Illustra-
tor, and studying HTML on their own to create websites. Cosplay
has additional outlets in various media such as *Cosmode*, a magazine
specializing in cosplay, and TV shows with cosplaying TV personalities. Cosplayers also have employment opportunities in maid cafés
(where waitresses dress up as fantasy maids), cosplay costume specialty stores, and secondhand manga stores. Some of the informants
had interviewed for jobs at maid cafés. However, many cosplayers
want to keep cosplay strictly a hobby and consider cosplay for pay in
an entirely different light.

HISTORY OF COSPLAY IN JAPAN

Cosplay in Japan has a history spanning three decades. Cosplay
became a fixture at doujin and science fiction events from about 1975.
Japanese fans gave momentum to the movement when they began to
borrow the practice of masquerades from U.S. science fiction conventions, where fans don costumes and reenact scenes from popular shows.
With the introduction of hit series such as *Mobile Suit Gundam* in 1979
and *Urusei Yatsura* in 1980, cosplay took off. Before this period, events
did not have clear policies on dress codes and locations for cosplay.
With the appearance of scantily clad characters in works such as *Urusei Yatsura*, residents who lived near cosplay event locations began to
complain about indecent outfits. As a result, as early as the 1983 Comic
Market, event organizers began to limit cosplay to the boundaries of
the convention hall. These restrictions were initiated by requests from
the police, but they also involved defensive self-policing by members
of the cosplay community in an effort to protect their culture from
negative attention from outsiders. The cosplay community enjoyed
further growth when *Captain Tsubasa*, a series about a soccer team,
became popular in 1984, and new fans were attracted by the ease of
cosplaying soccer uniforms (Shinomiya 1998).

In the 1990s, cosplay themes expanded beyond anime, manga, and games to include members of *visual-kei* bands and male idols.[3] In the early 1990s, most visual-kei cosplayers were female rock band fans, but they were linked with the broader cosplay community in the late 1990s (Koizumi 2003; Ushiyama 2005).

As the cosplay fan base expanded, media coverage increased, as did problems with cosplayer conduct at doujin conventions. According to Shinomiya (1998), the 1990s were a difficult period for cosplayers. Organizers started prohibiting handmade swords at Comic Market after an incident, and they established dress codes preventing indecent costumes after a crackdown on *bishojo-kei* doujin in 1991.[4] More regulations followed. Some doujin fans were also the source of these complaints. Doujin and cosplay fandoms do not necessarily conflict with each other, since there are many fans belonging to both communities. In the 1990s, however, members of the doujin community began criticizing cosplayers for their behavior at events. These events shaped the mindset evident in current cosplay guidelines. Below is an excerpt from a cosplay guidelines handout for a cosplay event in 2006. By following these kinds of rules and codes of conduct, cosplayers participate in a shared body of cultural practices.

COSPLAY GUIDELINES (EXCERPT)

- Do not wear your costume to the event or on your way home. Cosplaying outside event locations is strictly forbidden. Use of the changing rooms provided is required.
- Do not photograph cosplayers except in designated areas. . . . Loitering and taking photographs on sidewalks and in other public areas are not permitted. While you may be asked for permission on your way to designated areas, please turn down photography requests. Photography is permitted in designated areas. It is unfortunate that all these restrictions are necessary, but if there are too many infractions, cosplay will no longer be permitted at this location. We ask for your understanding and cooperation.

CONCEPTUAL FRAMEWORK

Fans are not merely consumers of content but also creators of content that is of special significance to them (Jenkins 1992; Penley 1997).

Part of what Jenkins (1992, 2006) has described as a participatory media culture, fans are an audience that actively and proactively creates meaning. Cosplayers fit this description, effectively consuming anime and manga characters while recreating them through unique acts of creation and performance.

Cosplayers' meaning creation is not a solitary or temporary activity. Through the continued participation and activity of a multitude, cosplay becomes a cultural practice. It is rare for cosplayers to attend events alone. Many decide which characters to cosplay as a group with friends and go to events together. Cosplay is an extremely collaborative activity and is, by necessity, a social activity. In this way, cosplayers inhabit what Lave and Wenger have described as a community of practice (Lave and Wenger 1991; Wenger 1998), social groups that are defined by a shared set of practices, norms, and roles.[5] Work on communities of practice and ethnographic studies of youth subcultures (Eckert 1990; Willis 1997) have documented how values and identities emerge not simply from individual properties but from shared practices and social relationships.

In turn, each member's individual characteristics and practices are constructed via relationships within the community (Dreier 1999; Ueno 1999; Wieder 1974). A member's unique identity within a community is constructed from conflicts and differentiation among community members. When members assert their membership in a particular community, they also assert their nonmembership in other communities. By rejecting the value system of a particular community, they make their own community's characteristics visible. For example, in her study of a U.S. high school, Eckert (1990) examined how two different communities—jocks and burnouts—accessed different sources of knowledge in constructing their identities. Jocks are students who are motivated to acquire traditional academic knowledge from teachers, while burnouts are students who were primarily identified with knowledge shared among peers outside of school. Members express their identity by drawing on community-specific knowledge in a context-dependent manner. Each group rejects the other, but they are co-constructed and maintained through these kinds of hostile interactions.

Analyzing the characteristics and practices of cosplayers similarly requires consideration of the multilayered interactions internal to the community. The cosplay community is not a homogenous entity but a place of negotiated meaning. Cosplayers also navigate multiple identities, belonging to communities outside the fandom as university students and young working adults. They are well aware of how the media and the general public view them, and they reference this viewpoint when talking about cosplay. This chapter discusses the individual characteristics and practices of cosplayers as representing conflicts and differentiation both within the community and in relation to outsiders.

INVESTIGATING THE COSPLAY COMMUNITY

The data introduced in this section were collected using ethnographic methods, a combination of interviews and field observations. Ten informants, all female, were interviewed (see Table 10.1). Because the majority of cosplayers in Japan are female, I focused my research on female cosplayers. The informants' preferred cosplay genres were either listed on their websites or deduced through interviews.

The study was conducted between August 2006 and December 2007. Informants included students and employees. They were restricted to cosplayers in their twenties since most active cosplayers are teens and young adults.[6] Banri was my initial contact, and I used snowball sampling to recruit the other informants and to maximize rapport during interviews and field observations. Banri was asked to sit in on initial interviews whenever possible. Informants had met each other through varied circumstances, not all related to cosplay. Two had met each other as classmates at a voice-acting school. Others had been assistants in the same doujin group or had struck up a conversation when one was cosplaying the other's favorite character. Cosplayers tend not to cosplay the same character for extended periods, so a chance encounter through shared interest in a character does not necessarily guarantee a sustained social connection.

The informants all were attentive to their appearances, which puts them at odds with the stereotypical portrayal of female otaku as unpopular and unattractive. Five out of ten of them had boyfriends at the time of their interview. However, eight of the informants were hesitant about telling their friends and coworkers about the fact that they were cosplayers, citing the risk of being stigmatized with the negative image associated with cosplayers or, more generally, otaku and fujoshi

Table 10.1 Informants and their affiliations

Cos name	Age	Affiliation	Cosplay experience	Preferred cosplay genres
Banri	23	Grad student	4 years	Emo and angst, naughty boys
Tsubasa	22	College student	>3 years	Sexy live action superheroes
Haru	26	Employed	>5 years	Characters from *Full Metal Alchemist, King of Fighters*, etc.
Ricky	27	Employed	>10 years	Masculine men
Sakura	20s	Employed	Unknown	Characters from *Ouran High School Host Club*
Naka	28	Employed	1 month	Male TV personalities
Tomomi	20s	Student	Several months	Male TV personalities
Mami	25	Employed	5 years	School and military uniforms
Usami	20s	Unknown	Unknown	Chain smokers
Nana	21	College student	3 years	Men with weapons, men with ponytails

(see Chapter 9). I have previously argued that hiding one's identity as fujoshi is a cultural practice of fujoshi who are fans of doujin (Okabe 2008). I saw cosplayers engaging in the same practices of concealing their otaku identity. Like doujin fans, cosplayers take measures to avoid stigmatization by outsiders.

During field observations at cosplay events, I used digital cameras, camcorders, digital voice recorders, and field notes to record the flow of events; however, as camcorders are often forbidden at cosplay events there were times I was unable to make recordings. After-event parties are also common, so I recorded conversations that took place at after-event parties when possible. Finally, since many cosplayers would attend events with cosplayers they had met online or at earlier events, I often conducted interviews in groups rather than one-on-one.

The interviews focused on the informant's experiences from the time she first became a participating member in the cosplay community up to the time of the interview. Although I prepared a set of questions to be asked in sequence to follow a rough time line based on the informant's experience, I focused on facilitating the informant's narrative and did not correct digressions when and if they occurred. Representative topics in the interview are as follows:

- Factors that led to the informant's involvement in cosplay
- Anecdotes about her first cosplay event
- Perceived changes in herself as she gained cosplay experience
- Methods employed in creating or buying costumes and in obtaining the necessary information to do so
- Opinions regarding what constitutes taboo behavior at cosplay events
- Characteristics of a cosplayer who is popular within the community

AN OVERVIEW OF THE COSPLAY COMMUNITY

Based on interviews and field observations, this section discusses DIY culture, peer review, and reciprocal learning.

DIY Culture

HANDMADE COSTUMES Cosplayers can buy outfits of popular anime characters in stores specializing in cosplay outfits and through online stores and auction sites. However, the costumes for most characters are not available in commercially made form. Although some companies and individuals make outfits to order, these are costly. For these reasons, many cosplayers make their own outfits. Informants made the following comments on the significance of DIY outfits in the cosplay community:

> Of course your outfit will be better if you spend more money on it. The point is to make a good one with good cost performance. (Banri)
> You have to make your own . . . the fun is in making them with friends. You start off by going to Yuzawaya (a craft store) with friends. It's fun to go through fabric and figure out which one's cheapest. (Naka)

These comments indicate how cosplay involves more than simply wearing an outfit and posing in front of the camera. Having the where-withal to make one's own outfit is a central practice in cosplay. The DIY spirit embodied by this practice has become a standard of sorts in the cosplay community. Failing to make one's own costume can be seen as a rejection of the community's values and standards. Cosplayers attending events wearing premade outfits apologize to other cosplayers:

> Sorry, I got mine from Yahoo! Auction this time. Making school uni-forms can be hit or miss, so I thought it'd be safer to buy it. (Mami)

At this particular event, Mami and several other cosplayers had chosen to cosplay characters from an anime series set in a school. After they changed into their outfits and chatted among themselves, one cosplayer asked Mami if she had made her outfit, to which Mami gave the above response. With more than five years of cosplay experience, Mami would be considered a veteran within the community. Yet she still apologized for having bought the outfit on an auction site and had excuses as to why she had done so. Her remark indicates an underlying reason for apology and explanation when deviating from the DIY cos-tuming standard of the community. Mami not only expresses regret, but she also demonstrates her awareness of the DIY standard. Some of my informants were actually veteran cosplayers who were not very skilled at sewing and either wore premade outfits or asked their friends to make outfits for them. Still, making one's own outfit is a shared cultural practice that serves as a basic indication of one's identity as a cosplayer. Even though Mami attended an event with a premade cos-tume, she was able to partake in the DIY cultural practice of the cos-play community by apologizing and displaying her understanding of the community's standards.

SHARED RULES AND CODES OF CONDUCT   Cosplayers make more than their own outfits. Cosplayers share rules and codes of conduct that are constructed and maintained through their everyday practice.[7] In this sense, community rules and codes of conduct are also created by the amateur community rather than an external authority or pro-fessional standards.

As described in the overview of cosplay history, cosplayers and event organizers have constructed a body of rules and codes of conduct. For example, organizers explicitly prohibit cosplayers from leaving the event without having changed out of their costumes, and they police any behavior that could cause trouble. Informants frequently commented on rules and codes of conduct during their interviews. Cosplayers describe how these rules are part of an effort to avoid negative stereotyping by outsiders. Their comments can be interpreted as the result of cultural appropriation (Wertsch 1998). Value creation by community members is indivisible from the community's history (Cole 1996; Vygotsky 1987).

> Now that anyone can cosplay, there are more young cosplayers with bad manners, and it's a problem. They just rush in and out to take photos, walk around town in their outfits, things like that. I really wish they'd stop doing that. (Haru)
>
> The governor [of Tokyo] doesn't like otaku.[8] So if cosplayers don't behave, we won't be able to rent places [like Tokyo Big Site] for events next year. (Banri)

Cosplayers are polite in both speech and action at events. They often call each other by attaching the polite –*san* suffix to their "cos names" (aliases used during cosplay). If they are referring to cosplayers they do not know, they use the –*san* suffix with the cosplayed character's name. When cosplayers take photos together, they exchange name cards (see Figure 10.2) and ask for permission to post photos online. This politeness is not necessarily an indication of social distancing, however. Cosplayers who cosplay characters belonging to the same genre use their costumes as a tool for expanding their social network. Name cards display contact information such as their cos names, website URLs, social network site IDs, and e-mail addresses.

DIY subcultures of amateur production all develop norms and cultural practices that are unique to their styles and commitments. For instance, remixing in hip-hop music is one example of a long-standing DIY culture that defined a set of practices and genres. Similarly, punk rock is another influential music genre operating outside mainstream music culture, creating its own market and distribution networks (Hebdige 1979). Punk culture was created by members who resisted traditional consumerism and copyrighting, pushed back against normative value systems, and presented an alternative lifestyle. Cosplayers also create their culture through participation in activities varying from costume making to those that build knowledge, values, and order

Figure 10.2. Sample name cards of cosplayers. Credit: Reproduced with permission from Banri.

in the community. These modes of producing amateur knowledge and culture are peer based and bottom up, in contrast to professional production and communities. The community's unique DIY cultures support this ongoing creation and recreation of meaning.

Peer Review

CROSS-DRESSING AND RADICAL COSPLAY   To become a member of a community means acquiring skills to engage in the community's cultural practices. This includes conforming to the community's specific standards: behavior, speech, and knowledge of what other members value, evaluate, and dislike (Arimoto and Okabe 2008). Cosplayers exist within the community's framework of standards and values. Regardless of whether the community is about punk rock, soccer, or psychological research, members of the community practice methods of evaluation that can be carried out only by members of the same community. A cosplayer's assessment of her own costume is meaningless on its own. The standards that define the quality of cosplay are not based on individual assessment, nor are they based on assessments accessible to the general public. It is considered more meaningful to create an outfit that garners acclaim from a few community members than from the general public. Whether a cosplay outfit is "good" or "bad" is meaningless if taken out of the context of a peer review by members of the subcultural community. Bucholtz (1999) noted similar proclivities in her ethnographic study of female nerds in high school. Nerds are generally seen as people who prefer relatively esoteric and intellectual activities over more mainstream, popular pursuits such as sports. Like cosplayers, nerds gain stature in their community by acquiring knowledge that is valued within the community (for example, knowledge about science), and they enjoy sharing this knowledge with community members.

For cosplayers, it is more important to be valued by high-status insiders who understand cosplay culture than by some external metric. Cosplayers receive high praise when they choose characters that suit them and recreate the character's appearance with attention to detail. Even as an outside observer, I was able to grasp this rubric for evaluation. During interviews and through the course of fieldwork, cosplayers also mentioned how they particularly appreciated beautiful cross-dressing and cosplay that recreated a character's appearance down to even subtle details.

Cross-dressing is a case worth exploring further. Many female cosplayers portray male characters. Manga serials that are popular with female cosplayers such as *Weekly Shonen Jump* feature works with a mostly male cast of characters. Consequently, many cosplayers, my informants included, have experience cross-dressing. Cosplayers who look good as men are highly rated by the community. These cosplayers are not trying to replicate masculinity in a realistic sense, however. As Banri and Tsubasa's comments below indicate, cross-dressing requires the cosplayer to be beautiful while also portraying the male character in question:

People were cross-dressing as Naruhodou-kun [male character featured in the game *Phoenix Wright: Ace Attorney*], and they were stunning. I've seen a lot since I became a cosplayer and I have pretty high standards now, but I got really excited because I'd never seen such wonderful cos-players. (Banri)

> I've tried cross-dressing, but I don't look good doing it. . . . I mean, there are people like Usami-san. It's impossible. I tried putting on a costume of a boy-type character with beautiful people like her around, but I felt like my ribs were going to snap from the wrappings I put over my chest to flatten them. There's more to cross-dressing than meets the eye. (Tsubasa)

Female cosplayers who cross-dress seek to convey masculinity in the fictional or parodied sense and not in the conventional mainstream sense. To borrow the words of Butler (1990) and Meito (2007), the masculinity mimicked by cosplayers is a copy without an original. The men modeled by cross-dressing cosplayers do not exist in reality. Rather, cosplayers are referencing the cross-dressing model constructed by the cosplay community, and they express the idealized masculinity that the community has created. Cosplayers adore and respect cosplayers who succeed in cross-dressing according to these community standards.

Banri uses honorifics and polite Japanese in her description of cross-dressing cosplayers. Although cosplayers are generally polite in their conversations with one another, the way she uses honorifics to describe beautiful cross-dressing cosplayers is unusually respectful. By using respectful language, Banri takes a humble stance in relation to high-status cosplayers, indicating the hierarchies within the community. Cosplayers produce distinctions and hierarchies through their ongoing practices of deference to highly attractive and successful cosplayers.

Highly rated cosplayers are attentive not only to the quality of the outfit but also to how closely they approximate the physical characteristics of the character, which locations they choose for photo shoots, and whether they reproduce the character's accessories:

> When I cosplayed Havoc [a male character] from *Full Metal Alchemist*, it was so popular that people lined up for one and a half hours to take my photo. Havoc has huge biceps, so I spent a month doing push-ups. I'm probably the only person in the world who went that far to portray the character. (Ricky)

> Banri has cosplayed Misa from *Death Note*, but she's the only one I know of who ever recreated the captivity scene [the character was held captive for a time in *Death Note*]. I was really surprised when I first saw [the photo]. (Sakura)

These quotes are examples of cosplayers making extraordinary efforts to portray their characters. Ricky did push-ups for a month to develop her biceps to portray Havoc, a muscular male character. Other cosplayers seek locations where they can adequately recreate scenes from anime series set in a desolate urban environment, or they even go so far as to make a costume for the sole purpose of capturing a specific pose, such as in Banri's captivity scene (see Figure 10.3). One of my informants even planned a graduation trip to Egypt to cosplay a scene from a historical romance manga. In describing the captivity scene she recreated, Banri stated that she wanted the photo to be highly regarded by other cosplayers such as Sakura, but she is not concerned about what non-cosplayers might think of it.

REJECTING COMMERCIAL AND MAINSTREAM COSPLAY   Ricky and Sakura's narratives are the cosplay versions of heroic tales. Ricky's cosplay friends talk about her Havoc cosplay as a heroic feat. Cosplayers are evaluated strictly by other cosplayers; their narratives are distributed,

Figure 10.3. Recreation of a captivity scene involving a character from the *Death Note* manga. Credit: Reproduced with permission from Banri.

exchanged, and used as representations of shared knowledge within the cosplay community. Conversely, cosplay that is looked upon favorably by outsiders loses value. My informants did not have favorable opinions of cosplay that was popular with the industry, men, and the media. As amateurs, praise from their peers in the community is what confers status, not appreciation by outsiders.

> *Torareta* are losers. There are people like that who dress up just to get attention. (Hara)
>
> If you show enough skin, it's obvious that you'll attract *kameko*. TV shows only take up the obvious examples, like ones showing too much skin. Then cosplay gets a bad rep for being erotic. (Banri)

The term "torareta" is an abbreviation of *toraretai* (I want to be photographed) and refers to attention seekers who want their photographs taken. A "kameko" is an abbreviation of *kamera kozou* (camera kid), and it refers to men who show up at events with professional-quality cameras to photograph cosplayers and women working the booths at industry events. Several of my informants referred disparagingly to cosplayers who choose revealing outfits or are popular with kameko as torareta. If a cosplayer chooses to portray a character who really does wear revealing clothing, and she exhibits a deep understanding of the character, she is not classified as torareta. However, if other cosplayers think her intent is simply to get attention, she is looked down upon and labeled as a torareta. Contrary to the values internal to the cosplay community, kameko and the media are looking for cosplayers based on mainstream standards of cuteness or feminine sexuality. Aiming to embody and objectify the characters of the media they love in a vision unique to the female fandom, cosplayers see their audience as other women fans and not the heterosexual male gaze.

During field observations, my informants would point out torareta cosplayers, who would invariably be surrounded by kameko. We had no way of determining whether these cosplayers really were torareta who were intentionally seeking male attention. The key issue is not whether these cosplayers are actually torareta, but rather it is the ways in which cosplayers classify each other as torareta as a way of constructing boundaries and standards for their community. By designating a torareta group, the informants are delineating their own way of doing cosplay.

During their interviews, Banri, Tsubasa, and Ricky made comments such as "I want cute girls to cosplay" and "To be honest, I don't want unattractive girls to cosplay," indicating that cute cosplayers are welcome in the community. This point of view is based on the assumption, however, that a cute cosplayer would need to have an understanding of the character to be accepted by the community. Cute girls who use cosplay as an occasion to wear sexy outfits and get attention are at odds with the community's values. Emphasizing value systems that have currency only within the community is a distinct feature of interest-driven communities. Hamano (2008) introduced the concept of "limited objectivity" as a standard that is firmly established and recognized within a particular community but that is not known or recognized by outsiders. According to Hamano, limited objectivity is one characteristic of an information society with diversified value systems. What constitutes "good" cosplay is opaque to outsiders and is clear only to practitioners. Cosplayers subscribe to an amateur and DIY ethic and look askance at commercial motivations and standards for cosplay. Instead, they subscribe to a peer-based model of assessment in which the opinions of high-status members of their community carry the most weight. This amateur, peer-based, and noncommercial ethic is similar to that of other otaku and fan groups that see themselves as fans motivated by love of particular media, rather than by a desire for fame or financial gain (see Chapter 8).

Reciprocal Learning

The value systems and evaluation standards I have discussed have meaning only within the cosplay community. Stories about cross-dressing and heroic cosplay reinforce the values of the community, and discussing the community's relationship with outsiders such as the media and the general public defines the community's boundaries. Fan-based communities such as the cosplay community make visible their processes of community self-definition. The cosplay community is constructed and maintained from the bottom up by its members.

Learning in the cosplay community does not involve guidebooks or top-down teaching. It has no institutionalized hierarchies, no formal assessments, and no applications or official markers of membership. Consequently, the learning environment differs from traditional classrooms and apprenticeships, and it is grounded in the reciprocal nature of learning between members.[9] These peer-based learning dynamics are often shared across different otaku and amateur groups (see Chapters 8 and 12).

SHARING COSPLAY KNOWLEDGE AND INFORMATION   It is rare for cosplayers to attend a convention alone. The vast majority go with friends or people they met at previous events (several informants termed this as getting "picked up"). Events serve as a place for exchanging information. After changing into their outfits in changing rooms, cosplayers exchange information on various topics that vary from costume making (for example, tips and pitfalls and where to buy fabric, costumes, and accessories) to plans (for example, events to attend, characters to cosplay). At after-event parties, cosplayers examine the source material for their cosplayed characters and discuss various portrayal methods. These discussions vary from how to recreate a character's peculiar hairstyle to whether costumes should have lining. The information is shared through these conversations and accumulated as a body of knowledge shared by the cosplay community. Additionally, collaborative problem solving takes place when somebody raises a question or a challenge she is facing.

> I wonder how you can make this drill-like hairstyle. Probably with glue . . . wrapping hair around some mold and making a cone shape. Maybe attach it to a hair band. (Sakura)
>
> The most important thing is for the outfit to look good in photos, so you don't have to worry about comfort. You don't need lining like you would with normal clothes. (Banri)

Opportunities for reciprocal learning also present themselves in conversations between novices and veterans. During an interview, the relatively inexperienced Nakamura asked Banri, who has four years of cosplay experience, a question about costume making. Nakamura primarily cosplays idols, and Banri cosplays anime and game characters, so their preferred cosplay genres differ. Nonetheless, the two of them looked at the idol's photograph and discussed what kind of fabric and pattern to use and how to keep costs down. Although Banri led the discussion, it was collaborative in nature. Cosplayers become experts in their domain because it is a niche activity involving esoteric forms of knowledge. After one participant makes a certain outfit, others trying to make similar outfits can turn to the participant's knowledge and experience. This knowledge is not amassed in one place but is stored in distributed form among community members. Each member therefore represents a learning opportunity to her peers. The peer-based and reciprocal nature of these relationships is another hallmark of fan-based communities.

LEARNING FROM OTHERS   Unlike formal educational institutions, the cosplay community does not have systematic means for transmitting necessary knowledge and skills. Novices refer to media such as magazines and online sources and learn about community practices under the guidance of more senior members. According to our informants, it is difficult for novices to integrate themselves into the community on their own.

> I'd always wanted to try cosplay, but I didn't know how to start. When I mentioned that to Usami-san, she asked, "Which character do you like, X or Y?" When I replied, "X," she said, "Just show up [at event Z]." When I went there, she said, "OK, wear this, we're going to take a picture." Then we took a picture. (Banri)

Banri describes how novices start off by following the more experienced cosplayers' example and posing in front of the camera. This example gives evidence of supporting frameworks and mentorship for learning how to gain access to the cultural practices in cosplay. When learners are forced to participate by external motivations, their learning may just be a façade and lack substance. However, in the cosplay community, participation and learning is interest driven, and more experienced peers in the community initiate newcomers.

Novices are not necessarily excluded from the community or specific practices because of their status as newcomers. They learn the ropes from veterans through guided participation (Rogoff 2003) and through the peculiar reciprocal learning structure of the community that enables everyone to become a knowledge provider. Consequently, as they begin to participate, they will also be contributing to the cosplay community's cultural practices and join other members in maintaining the community. Perhaps what is important in the community is for cosplayers to contribute to the community, and those who fail to do so cannot call themselves members of the cosplay community or the fandom more broadly.[10]

CONCLUSION: OTAKU LEARNING

Members of fan-based or otaku communities such as the cosplay community became participants through their own interests and curiosity. However, their practices within the community are not haphazard expressions of individual interests but follow a certain shared set of specific guidelines.

Cosplayers devote a significant amount of their time and energy in their participation within the community and continue to engage in reciprocal learning. What triggers such loyalty in cosplayers? The possible angles of analysis are multiple, but I will focus on the nature of knowledge and information in the cosplay community. As a subculture, the cosplay community possesses values and standards that are inaccessible and esoteric to outsiders who are aligned with mainstream culture. In such fan-based communities, community knowledge is open to people as long as they are participating members. Fans, or otaku, enjoy drawing on such esoteric knowledge when they engage in conversation and activities within the community. If the knowledge were ubiquitous and accessible to anyone, it would lose its meaning for fans. The value of subcultural knowledge lies in the fact that it is accessible only to the limited few who join the community. Fans also gain pleasure in contributing to that knowledge. In other words, cosplayers and other otaku are motivated by niche knowledge, reciprocal relationships with those who share their niche identity, and positive evaluation by a niche audience (see Chapter 4).

The DIY ethic and practices of peer-based niche knowledge exchange make the cosplay community distinct and a meaningful object of study. For example, some schools are engaged in efforts to design a learning environment that encourages peer-based, reciprocal learning (for example, Johnson et al. 1993). This kind of learning environment goes against the dominance of top-down instruction that has been institutionalized in most schools. The cosplay community, in contrast, has always been based on peer-based, reciprocal learning, with members creating their own rules and codes of conduct. School learning, with its superior/subordinate teacher/learner relationships, has become the norm, and interest-driven learning has become marginalized. That may be why cosplayers and other otaku appear so odd to the mainstream. Rather than marginalize or stigmatize these groups, however, we might look to them as models for designing interest-driven communities and collaborative learning environments.

Notes

1. There are many definitions for "culture" and "cultural practice," but I am referring to those postulated by Saeki (1983). Saeki argued that we have an intrinsic desire to "better" our lives and act on that desire in four ways: (1) explore what it means to be better (value discovery), (2) share beliefs pertaining to (1) with others (value sharing), (3) create representations of our beliefs (value creation), and (4) develop ways to mass-produce and/or disperse these creations (value distribution). Saeki defined "culture" as an end product of these activities and "cultural practice" as the four kinds of activities given above.

2. According to one informant, cosplaying a popular idol can make one a target of negative criticism from the idol's agency and non-cosplayer fans.

3. *Visual-kei* is a movement that features male rock groups dressed in elaborate costumes with heavy makeup, drawing from styles of punk and heavy metal.

4. *Bishojo-kei* refers to manga, anime, and games that depict cute and sexy girls and women, often with sexually explicit content.

5. Lave and Wenger (1991) reexamined the learning process by deliberately choosing learning contexts that were culturally distant from formal learning contexts (for example, schools), such as tailors in Liberia and U.S. Navy quartermasters. In the case of tailors, those new to the trade would first be entrusted with peripheral tasks such as affixing buttons and sleeve cuffs. Central tasks are under the jurisdiction of veterans, but the apprentices have the opportunity to observe the entire production. Furthermore, while the peripheral tasks may seem trivial at first glance, apprentices can discern that the tasks are situated in legitimate practices of production. Lave and Wenger argued that this participation in peripheral but legitimate practices in tailoring was crucial in the construction of identity and cultural learning in new apprentices.

6. According to informants Banri and Tsubasa, many cosplayers decide to stop cosplaying once they reach age thirty.

7. Fukuyama (1999) described "the body of informal values and standards shared by members of a group" in terms of social capital that enables collaboration between group members. Putnam (2000) also argued that, in a social organization that is based on social capital facilitating collaboration, interactions between group members result in the creation of a "generalized reciprocity" standard.

8. Whether the governor likes or dislikes otaku is not the point here. Banri's statement is significant because it is evidence of how cosplayers are embedded in the cultural practice of avoiding stigmatization.

9. According to Ueno (1999), places such as schools and workplaces that may appear top-down at first glance actually depend on students and apprentices for maintaining and reproducing the communities.

10. In colloquial parlance, noncontributing members of communities are called "leechers."

References

Arimoto, Norifumi, and Daisuke Okabe. 2008. *Designed reality: Hankei 300m no bunka shinrigaku.* Tokyo: Hokuju shupan.

Bucholtz, Mary. 1999. Why be normal? Language and identity practices in a community of nerd girls. *Language in Society* 28 (2): 203–224.

Butler, Judith. 1990. *Excitable speech: A politics of the performative.* New York: Routledge.

Cole, Michael. 1996. *Cultural psychology: A once and future discipline.* Cambridge, MA: Belknap Press of Harvard University Press.

Comic Market Junbikai. 2006. *Comic market 70.* Tokyo: Yugengaisha Comiket.

Dreier, Ole. 1999. Participation, intercontextuality, and personal trajectories. In *Challenges to theoretical psychology*, ed. Wolfgang Maiers, Betty Bayer, Barbara D. Esgalhado, René Jorna, and Ernst Schraube, 269–277. York, Canada: Captus Press.

Eckert, Penelope. 1990. Adolescent social categories, information and science learning. In *Toward a scientific practice of science education*, ed. Marjorie Gardner, James G. Greeno, Frederick Reif, and Alan H. Schoenfeld, 203–217. Hillsdale, NJ: Lawrence Erlbaum.

Fukuyama, F. 1999. *The great disruption: Human nature and the reconstruction of social order.* New York: The Free Press.

Hamano, Satoshi. 2008. *Architecture no seitaikei.* Tokyo: NTT Press.

Hebdige, Dick. 1979. *Subculture: The meaning of style.* London: Methuen.

Jenkins, Henry. 1992. *Textual poachers: Television fans and participatory culture: Studies in culture and communication.* New York: Routledge.

———. 2006. *Convergence culture.* New York: NYU Press.

Johnson, W. David, Roger T. Johnson, and Edythe Johnson Holubec. 1993. *Circles of learning: Cooperation in the classroom.* Edina, MN: Interaction Book Co.

Koizumi, Kyoko. 2003. Isei wo yosoou shojo tachi: Visual rock band no cosplay fan. In *Visual kei no jidai: Rock, kesho, gender*, ed. Takako Inoue, Takuo Morikawa, Naoko Murota, and Kyoko Koizumi, 208–245. Tokyo: Seikyusha.

Lave, Jean, and Etienne Wenger. 1991. *Situated learning: Legitimate peripheral participation.* Cambridge: Cambridge University Press.

Meito, Takako. 2007. Onna doshi ga miseru yume: Fan wa "Takarazuka" wo dou mite iruka. In *Sorezore no fan kenkyu: I am a fan*, 53–70. Tokyo: Fujinsha.

Okabe, Daisuke. 2008. Fujoshi no identity game: Identity no kashi/fukashi wo megutte. *Cognitive Science* 15 (4): 671–681.

Penley, Constance. 1997. *Nasa/Trek: Popular science and sex in America*. London: Verso Books.

Putnam, Robert D. 2000. *Bowling alone: The collapse and revival of American community*. New York: Simon & Schuster.

Rogoff, Barbara. 2003. *The cultural nature of human development*. New York: Oxford University Press.

Saeki, Yutaka. 1983. *"Wakaru" to iu koto no imi*. Tokyo: Iwanami Shoten.

Shinomiya, Aki. 1998. Watashi wo comike ni tsuretette: Kyodai comic doujinshi market no subete. In *Besatsu takarajima*, 358. Tokyo: Takarajimasha.

Ueno, Naoki. 1999. *Shigoto no naka deno gakushu*. Tokyo: Tokyo Daigaku Shupankai.

Ushiyama, Miho. 2005. Shojo no subculture ni miru gender parody no jisen: Cosplay shojo no jirei kara. *Anthropological Study* 6: 146–162.

Vygotsky, S. Lev. 1987. *The collected works of L. S. Vygotsky*. Ed. Robert W. Rieber and Aaron S. Carton. Trans. Norris Minick. New York: Springer.

Wenger, Etienne. 1998. *Communities of practice: Learning, meaning and identity*. Cambridge: Cambridge University Press.

Wertsch, James. 1998. *Mind as action*. New York: Oxford University Press.

Wieder, D. Lawrence. 1974. Telling the code. In *Ethnomethodology*, ed. Roy Turner, 144–172. Harmondsworth, UK: Penguin Education.

Willis, Paul E. 1977. *Learning to labor: How working class kids get working class jobs*. New York: Columbia University Press.

11

The Fighting Gamer Otaku Community: What Are They "Fighting" About?

YOSHIMASA KIJIMA

FIGHTING GAME OTAKU

Game arcades are ubiquitous in urban space. If one had no interest in them, perhaps they would escape notice, but shopping districts, shopping arcades, and shopping malls all tend to have game centers where many couples and families go for entertainment. In the depths of an arcade, or on one of the higher floors, you can always find the fighting gamers going head-to-head.

Gamers can face off one-on-one in a variety of electronic games that fall into three main categories: fighting games, rhythm action games (also known as music games), and trading card games. Most of these games are also available for home entertainment consoles. In this chapter, I focus on fighting games situated in game arcades and the surrounding game otaku community, drawing from a historical review of related game genres and fieldwork among fighting gamers. First, however, I address the question of whether fighting gamers are otaku and, if so, in what ways they fit the category. I begin by describing the typical gamer otaku.

Moe and *Yarikomi*

It is widely recognized that the gaming industry, along with the anime industry, plays a central role in the Japanese content industry. Driven by the ongoing technical innovation in gaming consoles, the gaming industry has grown to become Japan's premier form of visual entertainment. Gamer and anime otaku inhabit a shared sphere of contemporary Japanese popular culture.

Both anime and games share visual styles and genres and often even the same characters. Fans of both often become emotionally attached to characters, a phenomenon called *chara-moe* (see Chapter 2). In particular, dating simulation games such as *galge* (gal games) and *otome* (maiden) games are explicitly designed to cultivate moe in players.[1] In this respect, anime and gamer otaku are nearly indistinguishable.

The subject of moe does not come up as often, however, in the gaming world as it does in anime. One reason may be the difference between the two media. While anime is primarily for viewing, games are meant to be viewed and manipulated at the same time. Gamers become emotionally invested in the characters as they interact with them. It is here that anime otaku and gamer otaku diverge. If moe exemplifies the joy of viewing, *yarikomi*, or power gaming, exemplifies the joy of manipulation. Yarikomi is exhaustive and intensive gaming that goes beyond casual play or the goal of simply finishing a game. Instead, game otaku go after the ultimate achievements possible in a particular game. For example, this could involve gaining the maximum stats for a game character or clearing a level in the minimum amount of time.

Although yarikomi is a prerequisite, it is not a sufficient qualification for acquiring gamer otaku status. Many games in the market have been explicitly designed to encourage yarikomi, and some games—most notably role-playing games—are designed so anyone can beat the game as long as he or she invests enough time in it. In other words, the majority of games are designed to allow more casual gamers to indulge in yarikomi, so it has become a pervasive feature of game culture rather than something that defines elite gaming (Kijima 2007b, 191–195).

What specific kinds of yarikomi, then, are associated with otaku? Most simply put, the otaku favor self-punishing forms of game play. Otaku tend to handicap themselves with self-imposed rules and restrictions and seek out difficult games that require sophisticated skills and strategies for completion.

Performers and Makers

Just as it has become difficult to say that yarikomi is exclusively a gamer otaku activity, it is also difficult to say that moe is exclusively the province of anime otaku. Both moe and yarikomi have rapidly become mainstream since about 2005 and have come to symbolize the consumer culture of today's Japanese youth (Kijima 2008, 147–148). This rise of "pan-otaku"—or "commonplace" otaku—has led some scholars to posit that "*otaku* are dead" (Okada 2008, 138). An additional qualification will help delineate the otaku categories.

If the embrace of moe is the first baseline characteristic of anime otaku, the second key characteristic would be that anime otaku broadcast their passions to the anime otaku community. As discussed elsewhere in this book, anime otaku do this in two main ways. At one end of the spectrum are cosplayers, who perform for spectators by becoming the characters they admire; at the other end of the spectrum are *doujin* (fan manga and software) authors who create stories about their favorite characters (see Chapters 9 and 10).[2]

The performer-maker continuum can be applied to gamer otaku to generate the following rough categories: "superplayers," who attract viewers with their superior gaming skills, and the "modders," who analyze game code and modify it. Here again is a parallel between game and anime otaku, but the categories are not isomorphic. Superplayers enjoy manipulating characters, whereas modders enjoy manipulating game systems. Both types of game otaku are similar in their in-depth knowledge and connoisseurship with regard to game mechanics, traits that bring them close to being computer geeks.

Otaku and Fighting Games

We now have the groundwork to describe the characteristics specific to fighting game otaku. In Figure 11.1, the means of consumption (viewer versus manipulator) lie along the horizontal axis, and the means of displaying their passion (performer versus maker) lie along the vertical axis. The different categories, or ideal types, of visual-entertainment otaku discussed above have been placed along these two axes. Fighting game otaku fall into the superplayer category and differ from cosplayers in that they perform for their audience by manipulating, not becoming,

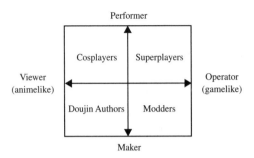

Figure 11.1. Typology of visual culture otaku. Credit: Yoshimasa Kijima.

the characters. Since they play the commercial product, they do not share the fascination for creating artifacts that doujin authors and modders have. Instead, their passion is focused on conducting exhaustive research on game mechanisms and masochistically pursuing difficult game play. In sum, fighting game otaku are characterized by their self-punishing and exhaustive game play, obsession with game mechanics, and how they display their passions by performing to an audience.

In addition to the rather obvious point that fighting gamers like games focusing on aggressive combat, such traits indicate that fighting gamers fall squarely in the camp of more masculine otaku culture. However, they do not fit the male otaku stereotype of the introverted hermit with no social skills. Fighting game otaku organize their social lives around game arcades and play regularly with total strangers. In this sense, they are extroverts who provide some insight into the complexity and diversity of otaku identities.

THE RISE OF THE FIGHTING GAME GENRE

I have described the characteristics of fighting gamers as a unique category of otaku, but I have yet to establish why it is that they have chosen arcade gaming over other platforms and sites of gaming (Kijima 2007a, 114–117). A broad overview of the rise of fighting games will help illuminate this point. In this section, I describe the historical transition from shooter games, which were initially the star attraction in game arcades, to fighting games.[3] This transition in turn epitomizes the shift in popular game play away from discovery to social interactions, a shift that was central to the growing appeal of fighting games.

From Outer Space to City Streets

Any historical account of video games includes a chapter on shooter games (e.g., Akagi 2005). Shooting down invading enemy ships or aliens in the vast reaches of outer space using fighters and cannons was a common motif even in the era when electronic gaming was limited to university computer labs. Beginning with *Spacewar!* (1962), the first shooter game, *Computer Space* (1971), the first arcade game, and *Space Invaders* (1979), the first game to enjoy nationwide popularity, shooter games were the bright stars of video games until the 1970s.

After the 1970s, however, the space motif began to fade in popularity. Advancements in graphic display technology, especially side scrolling, made it possible for designers to depict more familiar, everyday virtual worlds. The popularity of side-scroll shooting games in the early 1980s, followed by belt-scroll action games in the late 1980s, is a testament to this fact.[4]

In side-scroll shooting games, the player-controlled shooter moves at a fixed speed while the background scrolls from the left to right or from the bottom to top of the screen. Games in this genre mix everyday elements with otherworldly settings. For example, in *Xevious* (1982), a fantastical space opera setting with the high-speed aircraft Solvalou and the enormous fortress Andor Genesis is combined with familiar landscapes of mountains and forests.[5] The game constituted a curious fusion of a vast fictional world, complete with its own hieroglyphs and a history spanning 10,000 years, and more mundane aerial views that included real-life elements taken from the Nazca Lines in Peru.

The mixing of real-world and fantasy elements is even more apparent in two contrasting shooting games developed in 1985 by Konami, *Gradius* and *Twinbee*. The former boasted stunningly beautiful graphics and a soundtrack that still garners high praise, both of which supported the game's space opera world. The in-game appearance of flying Easter Island *moai* statues spitting rings of fire in space also shocked the players (see Figure 11.2).

In contrast, *Twinbee* featured rotund characters and pastel backgrounds in a pop parody of the sci-fi genre. The game even had kitchen items such as green peppers and knives emerge from the clouds, winning the hearts of many gamers.

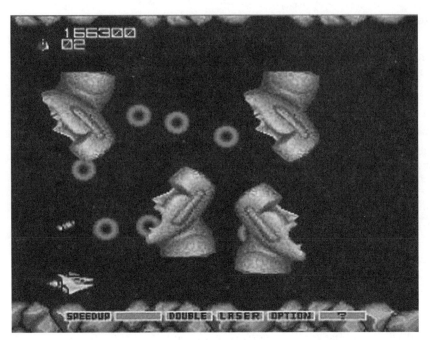

Figure 11.2. Moai statues that emit rings of fire from their mouths. Credit: *Gradius.* © KONAMI.

In belt-scrolling action games, conversely, otherworldly elements are introduced into everyday settings. With *Nekketsu Koha Kunio-kun* (Passionate Hardliner Kunio) (1986) as the progenitor, the genre reached its first peak with *Final Fight* (1989). The hallmark of this genre is that the street fighting takes place in a fictional city, a world with a five-kilometer radius. Gamers play characters such as a street thug with a heart of gold and a mayor who was formerly a pro wrestler, defeating wave after wave of evildoers. The protagonist deals with a variety of close-combat situations, such as being subjected to a nelson hold or grabbing an enemy by his collar and kneeing him. The player can also pick up and brandish an iron pipe as well as deal out special fighting moves. Once all the on-screen enemies have been defeated, the screen scrolls and new enemies appear. The scrolling action gives a sense of being on a conveyor belt, which is where this genre gets its name.

The backdrop for the fighting gradually changes as the game progresses. After fighting on the platform at a train station, players fight inside moving trains and then get off the train in the next city to fight in discos, bars, and factories. From the neon signs lighting up the city

Figure 11.3. Kunio fighting gang girls in front of a cabaret. Credit: *Nekketsu Koha Kunio-kun.* © Technos Japan.

at night to the spray-can graffiti on the bathroom walls, the background art is very detailed for each setting and tends to depict somewhat dated settings (see Figure 11.3). Players thus feel as though they are exploring a familiar city as they make their way step by step toward a "bastion of evil," such as a *yakuza* (gangster) headquarters.

From Sightseeing to Performance

With the commercial arcade games of the 1980s, players tended to feel as though they were travelers. As Bourbon Kobayashi (2005) has pointed out, playing games was like sightseeing at the time. What was important to the players was not the results, such as completing a level or achieving high scores, but rather the process of traversing and exploring the game world. Above all, as long as the players enjoyed the journey, long play times were not a problem. "I was never very good at shooters. Even if there weren't so many bullets flying around, you still died a lot. I wasn't good at them, but I still tried my best to play them. I never tried as hard with the other things I wasn't good at. I only stuck with the shooters because I wanted to see what happened next. . . . The fact that [mid-1980s arcade games such as] *Sky Kid* and *City Connection* had the Statue of Liberty and that *Bomb Jack* had the Sphinx made them a kind of sightseeing. Gaming was about enjoying the journey, not the ending. Most games didn't have an ending for the most part" (Kobayashi 2005, 27).

On the other hand, the scale of the journey undertaken in games became increasingly prosaic in successive generations. The focus shifted from flying the skies to walking the cities, from shooting bullets to dealing punches. At the end of this transition was the emergence of hand-to-hand combat fighting games that discarded the notion of the journey altogether.[6]

The fighting game genre became fully established after the commercial success of *Street Fighter II*, which was released in 1991. In fighting games, the arena was limited to a square area spanning no more than a few screens. Although the games included depictions of famous landmarks and historic sites around the world (for example, the Great Wall and the Eiffel Tower), they were treated more as props and backdrops than as a way to provide an immersive experience for the players. Instead, characters took center stage. Drawn at a larger scale, characters were minutely detailed down to the contours of their muscles, folds in their clothing, and the movement of their hair in the wind (see Figure 11.4). In addition, players could deal out a myriad of attacks using a combination of buttons and the joystick, thus allowing players to enjoy total control over their characters' actions—the joy of manipulation.

In addition, playing fighting games in game arcades directly mimics the act of street fighting in that players pick fights with other real-life opponents, though the fighting happens on-screen rather than on the street. Players do not compete indirectly by comparing scores but fight an opponent right in front of them by attacking their opponent's life points. Players choose their character from more than ten options and doggedly take on one opponent after another.

Figure 11.4. Ryuu and Chun-Li squaring off in Chinatown.
Credit: *Street Fighter II*.
© CAPCOM U.S.A., INC. 1992. All rights reserved.

As the source of pleasure of gaming shifted from the journey to the interpersonal give-and-take of the moment, the relationship between players and their audience also shifted. When games were still focused on sightseeing, the goal was to reach the next screen, rendering the relationship between the players and their audience roughly analogous to how a conductor relates to passengers. The player leads the audience through the journey. This changed with fighting games. The fight itself became the spectacle, and the player was transformed into a performer for a gallery audience.

Gaming Communities

Arcade fighting games thus became a platform for expanding social networks directly through game play, laying the groundwork for a new type of gaming community. Previously, social interactions mediated by gaming were indirect in that participants connected not by playing games together but by talking about games. Of course, gamers still socialize today by exchanging strategies, comparing scores, and sharing character illustrations. However, such communities should be considered game-information communities and not game-play communities. When the community centers on individual consumption and the social exchange of information, it is difficult to distinguish game-information communities from other communities centered on visual entertainment such as anime, novels, movies, and manga.

Games were originally designed to support direct social interaction. For example, *Tennis for Two* (1958), which is generally recognized as the first computer game available in the consumer market, and *Pong* (1972), which was the most popular commercial game until *Space Invaders*, both involved playing against an opponent. *Mario Bros.* (1980), another arcade game that later ported to a home console, had an immensely popular two-player mode in which players could try to kill each other's character. In other words, since the early days of electronic gaming culture, direct player-to-player interactions have been far more central than human-computer interaction.

These early interactions were not widespread enough to constitute a community, however. Gaming competitions were conducted in small groups of acquaintances or friends. When home consoles became widespread after the mid-1980s, sports games became a vehicle to strengthen relationships among friends. Players would often gather at somebody's home and compete with one another, forming local player friendships rather than communities per se.

Today, players can interact easily with strangers through games. The current trend is epitomized by various online multiplayer games, and most recently with the megahit action game *Monster Hunter Portable 2nd G*7. Released in 2008, the game sold nearly two million copies within the first week. The game's slogan is "Let's go hunting!" It encourages players to interact casually with one another through the PSP's WLAN feature.[7] Players can recruit fellow hunters at various locations in the city, such as at fast-food restaurants and cafés with wireless networks. The casual nature of this process has worked against the social cohesion and longevity that we typically associate with communities. These groups can be more rightfully called encounters, involving robust but temporary one-time interactions (Goffman 1961, 15–81).

Arcade fighting games, in contrast, became nodes of interaction before the spread of communication technologies and nurtured a cohesive gaming community that has survived to this day. Because the arcade fighting game has spawned a well-established game culture, it is a rich source of information for analyzing the characteristics of the gamer otaku.

THE ROAD TO BECOMING A FIGHTING GAMER

In this section, I will discuss the cultural characteristics of the fighting gamer community (called the fighting game world by its members) from the gamers' perspective. I conducted fieldwork at three game centers in the greater Osaka area between August and November in 2008. The fieldwork consisted of on-site observations of fighting gamers and on-site interviews spanning approximately forty minutes with twelve gamers whom I observed playing for at least ninety minutes. All interview participants were male and ranged in age from fifteen to forty-one. When quoted or referenced in this section, the interview data's source will be identified with the participant's age and a short descriptor provided by the participant in advance. Interviews were based on a semistructured interview protocol. Interview data were coded using Miles and Huberman's "two confirmations and no contradiction" decision rule: coding was reserved for ideas that were confirmed by at least two participants (1994, 131). A fighting game expert was recruited to verify analyses to increase the credibility of the interpretations.

A Dog-Eat-Dog World

"Is this seat open?" asks a gamer (Curly Hair) to a solitary gamer (Glasses), and then sits down without waiting for an answer and fishes out a one-hundred-yen coin from his wallet. With a slight smile on his lips, Glasses also doesn't bother to respond and merely cracks his knuckles. The two brusque gamers thus plunge into an intense face-off while being watched by three men, each of them standing about three meters away from the players. One of them appears to be Glasses's friend, periodically nagging Glasses with comments such as "No way!" but Glasses remains impassive, conveying the message "Don't bother me" with the position of his back. . . .

Twenty-seven minutes later, after repeated rounds of fighting, words have yet to be exchanged between Curly Hair and Glasses. We can hear occasional outbursts, however, especially from Curly Hair, who seems to be the noisy type, yelling, "Seriously?!" "Arrgh!" "Dammit!" and

"Gimme a break!" By contrast, Glasses says nothing and stays focused on the controls, although he utters an occasional "tsk-tsk" from time to time. Once, after winning a close match, his shoulders shudder. . . .

Twelve minutes later, Curly Hair suddenly stands up, acknowledges his opponent with a slight bow and karate-chop gesture, and tries to leave. That is when Glasses finally reacts, letting out a tiny "oh" and respectfully extending his right hand to Curly Hair. Five seconds later, Glasses shyly returns to his seat as if to resume his solitary gaming, but one of the observers who had been fidgeting for a while now walks forward and sits down in the opponent's chair.

This exchange is excerpted from my field notes documenting my observations at game arcades. The outlined exchange illuminates the fact that the community is not defined by physical boundaries but by cognitive ones. The community is an interpretive community of sorts, established only when members who have a similar appreciation of games recognize each other as peers (Fish [1980] 1992).[8]

The most fundamental criterion for evaluating a potential member is skill level. No other genre of games has consequences of defeat as severe as those in fighting games, in which the survival of the fittest is distilled to its purest form. The fighting game world is a black-and-white world with a very clear line drawn between the winners and the losers. No round can be completed unless one of the players is defeated in a knockout or a count out; there is no gray zone. Furthermore, defeat carries a financial consequence. Each game consists of three rounds, and while it is possible to play indefinitely as long as one keeps winning, losing means the player has instantly been parted from his or her money. The winner does not make a profit, but the loser feels robbed by the winner because the winner's attacks have led to this outcome. Further, the pain of defeat is visually underscored by having to watch one's character grovel in humiliation on-screen. In this sense, fighting games recreate the ignominy of defeat in a very realistic way.

Victory is sweet and defeat is bitter. Fighting games are games of competition, or agon (Caillois [1958] 1961). Little is left to chance; the games are designed so that only the players' abilities determine their ranking. Fighting game otaku are picky about their opponents because of this; casual gamers and gamers who are not fully committed to the genre are not suitable opponents. Players want someone who is as devoted to fighting games as they are. Only by defeating such worthy opponents can players fully enjoy the competition and savor the sweet wine of well-won victory.

Fighting gamers scan for various cues to determine whether their opponents are serious players. The opponents' handling of the controls, their sitting angle, their characters' timing and distance from the other character—fighting gamers analyze these behavioral minutiae to gauge their opponents' ability level, be it novice, intermediate, or expert. This ability to gauge an opponent's level against one's own is the ticket for entry into the fighting gamer community.

A Life of Training and Research

We can discern how fighting gamers develop this analytical skill by observing their daily practice. As gamers get involved in fighting games, competition at game arcades becomes integrated into their everyday lives. The question on the table is not whether a gamer will play:

> It's not a question of whether you will play, but just how much you will play. (thirty-five-year-old banker)

Players often distinguish between serious and informal gaming. In the former, gamers engage their opponent in a competitive face-off; in the latter, gamers do not particularly care about the outcome. The latter is therefore sometimes called hobby gaming. Informal gaming is far less recreational and playful than it may appear at first glance, however, because fighting gamers use informal gaming for the purpose of training and research.

Training is a process of gaining mastery over the game controls. Fighting games require split-second manipulation of the joystick and buttons to produce complex moves. Accomplished gamers practice the same move hundreds of times until the motion becomes ingrained as muscle memory and they execute the move without any conscious thought. Research involves devising new strategies and mapping out the flow of events in hypothetical fights. Careful research enables players to anticipate their opponents' moves in actual fights. Since they do not know who their opponents will be in advance, players anticipate a diverse range of attack patterns and devise countermeasures. When predictable patterns are derived through trial and error, they are called theories. These theories then become fodder for further research, and research continues indefinitely.

These thought experiments are conducted in relative secrecy, and the efforts are hidden from view.[9] Given that all fighting gamers engage in this kind of research, however, in this sense these efforts are part of the public culture of gaming. During matches, players keep an eye out for evidence of such training or research in their opponents' play to inform their analysis of their opponents' skill level.

> Researcher: Are skill levels immediately obvious?
>
> T:[10] Sure. When it comes down to it, fighting games are mind games. You try to read each other's minds. Just being able to do the moves only takes you halfway; you have to be able to predict your opponents' moves before you can call yourself a fighting gamer. That's why I can tell that a player's an apprentice from the way he can deal out combo attacks or that a player's an expert from the way he calculates his next move and tries all sorts of tricks. (twenty-six-year-old beer company employee)

The Uniqueness of Fighting Gamers

Fighting gamers clearly invest so much effort into their game play out of a desire to win, but they are also seeking to enthrall their audiences. They are always aware that their moves are subject to scrutiny by their opponents but also by a circulating audience of variable size. As such, fighting gamers reserve some of their attention for the spectators, and they derive much of their pleasure from showing off their game play. Their game play is an assertion of their individual style.

Fighting games have an aspect of mimicry, or mimesis (Caillois [1958] 1961). Just because one is a strong player in fighting games does not make one good at actual fighting or martial arts. However, fighting games are different from mimesis games in that players are not pretending to be the fantasy characters. The mimicry in fighting games is much closer to mimicking the players' "true" selves, with the individuality of the characters and of the players being inseparably linked with each other.

> Researcher: Did you just say you feel as though it's actually you fighting in the game?

> Y: Yes. I'm one with the character—a twitch of my fingers decides whether the character lives or dies. It's like the stand in *JoJo*.[11] When people prefer using a certain character, they refer to themselves as user of a particular character. (twenty-four-year-old cook)

One of the key characteristics of fighting games is that players can exhibit their individuality. The sheer variety of characters and their skills and moves allow players to select one or more *my-chara* (chosen character) and develop their own style of play.[12] My-chara are the characters a player chooses for ongoing play, and play style is a particular gamer's attack style. Fighting gamers therefore select a particular character and hone their fighting styles for use in face-offs.[13] Identifying oneself as a user of a certain character is a display of individuality.

On its own, simply choosing a particular character is not evidence that the characters are reflecting the players' true selves. Consider, however, that during a game, the players are also among the spectators observing the characters in action on-screen. Thus, the players are watching characters that they are manipulating on-screen. This gaming experience is similar to that of an actor acting in front of a mirror; it is impossible to separate the player's individuality from the character's individuality. Drawing from Goffman (1974), Yasukawa (1993) suggests that video games enable players to strongly sense "multiple laminations of experience" that go largely unnoticed in everyday life. In the case of arcade fighting games, a player cannot help but acknowledge leading a dual existence as a performer and as an observer of the self (Omura 1985, 7).

Dojo Storming

The unique cultural characteristics of the fighting gamer community are evident in how members manifest their individuality and acknowledge the individuality of their peers. For fighting gamers, one opportunity to showcase their individualism is the formal face-off in game tournaments. A wide variety of different types of game tournaments take place almost daily, sponsored by game shops and companies and pitting individual players and teams against each other. The size of the community is most visible in national tournaments that are held in large public halls and attract gamers in the tens of thousands in a festival-like setting.[14]

The fervor of these national tournaments indicates how fighting games are a pathway into a certain masculine culture. As players progress through store-run, regional, and national tournaments, the stakes rise, and players are motivated to compete in an effort to achieve the pinnacle of gaming status as the best fighting gamer in the nation. This goal is deeply rooted in a vision of a dog-eat-dog competitive world depicted in *shonen* (boys') manga. This worldview represents a collusion between the industry and the desire of gamers themselves.[15]

In tournaments, the individuality of the gamers also manifests in areas other than game mechanics and character selection. Players adopt ring names and affiliate themselves with specific teams that are linked to specific areas. Figure 11.5 is an example of a tournament bracket. The team World-Class Kotteri Sancho consisted of ZAP (vanguard), Brun Brun Maru (center field), and Daimon Rau (team captain); the team Kanto No. 3 & the Funny Mo-GYUs consisted of Man the Saturn Shark (vanguard), Kasai Rau (center field), and Bun Bun Maru (captain). Two things are of note: (1) team names are always listed with the "home" game center their players frequent, and (2) ring names are often constructed by adding the player's home-ground region to his preferred character's name (for example, Daimon Rau and Kasai Rau). Thus these locations play a large role in fighting gamers' identity construction.

The naming scheme also sheds light on how players connect with each other and develop a sense of camaraderie. As players rise through

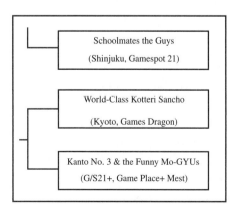

Figure 11.5. Excerpt from a tournament bracket.
Credit: *Monthly Arcadia*, 2003.

Schoolmates the Guys

(Shinjuku, Gamespot 21)

World-Class Kotteri Sancho

(Kyoto, Games Dragon)

Kanto No. 3 & the Funny Mo-GYUs

(G/S21+, Game Place+ Mest)

the ranks, they tend to expand their fields of activity in search of stronger opponents, foraying from familiar local haunts to regional game centers and on to nationally recognized arcades. In the process, they make friends out of enemies; fellow gamers in the same sphere of activity are peers working toward a common goal of becoming a nationally recognized gamer. For them, their local arcade is like a dojo—a training gym—that is part of their home turf. *Dojo yaburi* (dojo challenges) are a tradition that is part of the martial arts scene in Japan, in which members of training gyms will storm a rival gym and challenge its members to a fight. Similarly, fighting gamers also have a practice of dojo yaburi, with players teaming up to challenge other players with a reputation at a rival arcade.[16] Among them, the most popular opponents are the star players, players who repeatedly finish with high rankings in tournaments. They are local celebrities, and whatever game center they hang out in attracts challengers from nearby locales and from all over the nation. Star players welcome such challengers, posting provocative messages (for example, "If you think you've got the skills, come on over!") and schedules (for example, "I'm at so-and-so game center from this hour to that hour, see you there!") on their personal blogs and game center bulletin boards. They are always itching for a chance to fight a strong opponent.

The fighting game world thus has a kind of street fighting culture similar to the turf wars waged by yakuza and student gang leaders depicted in *seinen* (young adult) manga. Fighting gamers expand their influence by first conquering their home base (a nearby game arcade), then challenging a new base (a faraway game arcade), and so on. These aggressive competitive practices also mark the fighting gamer community as a highly masculine culture.

RESTRUCTURING THE GAMING WORLD

The line between the fighting game community and communities of martial arts and competitive sports is blurring.[17] Although fighting gamers do not exert themselves physically, the passion with which they play and the close-knit relationships they build with other gamers through their shared experiences are similar. They have the guts and grit of athletes and act in accordance with the three famous principles outlined in the boys' manga magazine *Shonen Jump*'s motto: effort, friendship, and victory. And yet it is still a game, and they are behaving like otaku. To further clarify the difference between fighting games and competitive sports, I will discuss the otaku aspects of the fighting gamer community.

Defection from Fighting Games

Sega's 2005 release of the fighting game *Fist of the North Star* heralded a series of changes in the fighting game world. The game was notable in that its popularity hinged on its appeal to other genres of game play that were not strictly part of the fighting genre. Many years after its release, it continues to attract a devoted following, and its popularity is actively maintained by its fans through their active evangelism.

At first, fighting gamers labeled it a "crap game." The characters' strengths were unevenly distributed, so a player could win by simply picking one of the stronger characters. Ironically, however, the poorly made game was recast as a "miracle game" after players uncovered a bug that could be exploited to execute certain moves. These "bug moves" could be used to make even weak characters effective in battle.

The game's nonsensical premise was also a source of appeal. The game was based on a popular shonen manga series by the same name from the 1980s. Players could use characters that practiced a special kind of kung fu to execute unrealistic moves, such as causing stone tablets to rain on the opponent or firing volleys of one's aura. Mastering bug moves allowed players to take this absurdity to the next level. For example, one bug move allowed players to execute a combination attack that lasted indefinitely. Fans of the game began competing to see who could keep up the attacks the longest and with the most skill. Reframing the game as a kind of new-era sports action game, players talked about "dribbling" the other players like a ball around the battlefield.

Spreading the Word

Discovery without dissemination is meaningless, so gamers try to spread the word. Sharing information and recommendations is central to how gamers encounter one another. Evangelism on the Internet has a particularly significant influence. *Fist of the North Star* aficionados reach out to new players by compiling notes on the moves they have uncovered (called "recipes"), sharing them on blogs and Internet forums, and posting screen casts of their game play on video-sharing sites. The Tokyo Ranking Fighters (TRF) game arcade in Nakano, Tokyo, is at the epicenter of these kinds of outreach activities.[18] TRF attracts a variety of star players, some of whom have achieved local celebrity status with live commentators who enliven an ongoing match, analysts who dissect matches and explain the outcomes, and reporters who edit the recording of the match and disseminate the video. The players are collectively called the "TRF Crowd" on online bulletin boards, and their accomplishments are widely celebrated.

TRF is considered the mecca of *Fist of the North Star* and attracts pilgrims from all over the nation, sometimes even from overseas. TRF's setup is slightly different from that of other game arcades. It ranks players in categories based on names in the original series—Mohican (novice), Warrior (apprentice), and Successor (expert). It also takes steps to help newcomers have fun and improve their skills, such as setting aside a few machines as Mohican units (a player scoring consecutive wins on a Mohican unit is allowed to graduate to a higher rank), having Mohican-only tournaments, and setting a lower fee for Mohican units (for example, three games for fifty yen). The game therefore unites online and offline evangelism efforts by consumers (players) and managers (game arcade staff). The result has been a grassroots growth in fans who built a huge following for what was originally considered a "crap game." In fact, fans of the game pushed for it to occupy a special category that allowed bug moves in Togeki, one of Japan's largest fighting game tournaments.[19]

Creating a Hypothetical World

I have described the ways in which committed fighting gamers exhibit otaku qualities. These include perceiving value in objects that most do not attribute social value to, broadcasting their attachment to the object in question, and, as a result, influencing the existing industry in some way. They also exhibit traits specific to gaming otaku in ways that can be understood by first unpacking some of the characteristics of games.

According to Shun Inoue (1977), all games share the same over-arching qualities of competitive play that follows a set of rules. Games are extremely diverse. For example, games may require physical skill (sports), strategy (chess and checkers), and chance (roulette and dice) (Roberts, Arth, and Bush 1959). Even so, they still share this quality of rule-based competitive play. All games also mobilize rules to create an alternate world. "Competitive play presupposes the existence of rules. Without rules, there can be no games. However, the rules do not exist merely to advance the game and decide the game's outcome—they create a world. Rules determine the structural framework of the game world and provide an internal order. This hypothetical world is distinct from everyday reality and is structured differently from reality. All of this is integrated with a structuring framework that gives meaning to the world" (Inoue 1977, 4). Drawing from competitions and conflicts in the real world, the game world abstracts, reconstructs, and distills them (Inoue 1977). The game world is far more defined, simplistic, and consistent relative to the complexity and contradictions of reality. In other words, the game world is a self-sustaining micro-cosm (Riezler 1941). It is constructed by borrowing specific meanings from reality that serve the microcosm's unique context, or by creating new kinds of meanings.

The distinction can be observed in the differences between physical fights and combative sports. In a street fight, knocking down an opponent does not necessarily lead to triumph. When news reports describe street fights as starting because perpetrators "just felt like it," the coverage is always extremely negative. Social mores dictate that real-world fighting should not be undertaken lightly. In contrast, the world of combat sports is constructed from a different set of rules. Within the ring, athletes are liberated from restraints normally placed upon them in the real world. They can beat each other up as equals because it is a world where they can fight each other to their hearts' content. However, they cannot fight exactly as they please as in the case of a physical fight. They are disqualified by the referee and lose the fight if they attack any vital organ. Instead, they must strive to score points while beating each other up in a nonlethal manner.

Game Otaku Rules

Combative sports involve a reconstruction of the real world. The reconstruction in the fighting games world is more twisted. While the fighting games world is fundamentally a replica of the combative sports world, it is based on a different structural framework. Despite the complexity involved in controlling the joystick and buttons, fighting games are much simpler to manipulate than the human body. The outcome of a match is also decided by a computer. The fighting game world is reconstructed from the combative sports world by taking meaning from it and making additional changes, adapting the frame to suit the purposes of the fighting games world. Typically, the changes involve both drastic abbreviations and exaggerations. The abbreviations ensure that the world includes only "fun" elements. The sequence of events from the time the match begins to the time the outcome is decided is depicted repeatedly, and all other events are excised as extraneous scenes. The exaggerations allow for participants to go all out, even more so than in real-world fights—players are freed from physical pain and enjoy combat that would be impossible in reality. They can emit rays from their eyes and possess other superhuman powers, and the damage incurred by their opponents, normally invisible to the human eye, is made visible.

This does not mean, however, that combat sports are real and fighting games are pure fiction. I have argued that fighting gamers experience their game play as real. The difference lies mostly in the modus operandi. Instead of using his entire body in the fight, a gamer fights by controlling buttons and analog sticks. Punches and kicks are executed by rapidly inputting the required command. Fighting games are not fictional versions of combative sports but are combative sports executed by one's fingertips. Normally, fighting gamers enjoy competing within the game world's constructed framework. However, *Fist of the North Star* enthusiasts have offered some alternatives. They chose to betray the "common sense" principles in the game world and established their own rules, executing bug moves, reshaping the properties of the characters, and creating their own value systems. In this way, they took the reconstruction process a step further by reconstructing the fighting games world (see Figure 11.6).

Figure 11.6. The process of game rule and world reconstruction.
Credit: Yoshimasa Kijima.

Other game otaku also reconstruct their game worlds in different ways, though they do not generally take the reconstruction to the extremes that the fans of *Fist of the North Star* have. For example, gamers regularly impose handicaps on themselves to create restrictions on the game world, and modders subvert game systems with cheats. Because the game world is based on code, it is relatively easy to engage in the satisfying activity of world modification.

Despite their seeming disparities, fighting gamer otaku share many characteristics with anime otaku. Although *Fist of the North Star* enthusiasts do not create actual games, they enjoy creating a derivative game world just as doujin authors enjoy creating derivative narratives. They also enjoy showing off their prowess to their peers just as cosplayers enjoy showing off their flamboyant costumes. This ability to extend the play experience is the reason why many members of the fighting gamer community continue playing the same game for years. The fighting game community thus represents a version of otaku culture that has many shared characteristics with anime otaku, but with a unique form of competitive performance at its core.

ACKNOWLEDGMENTS

I am deeply grateful to Yoshihiko Yamauchi for providing sources and checking my work.

Notes

1. Dating simulation games are games in which players date in-game characters and experience virtual romance. Games in which the protagonist is a male character attempting to date female characters are called *galge*, and games in which the genders are reversed are called *otome* games.

2. Of course, the two methods lie on a continuum, so they are difficult to separate. For example, hard-core cosplayers will take the initiative to create costumes

that they find satisfactory, and doujin authors are creating stories to appeal to fellow fans. With this caveat in mind, I have created these rough categories based on differences in emphasis.

3. The transition can be observed in the reader polls to determine the best arcade games for the Gamest Awards, conducted by *Monthly Gamest*, a now-defunct arcade game magazine (see Figure 11.7). The magazine had a niche audience, so the poll results do not represent the general gamer population but rather the tastes of more hard-core gamers.

4. These are also known as "beat 'em up" genre games.

5. The main developer behind *Xevious*, Masanobu Endo, is known for being the first man in Japan to call himself a game designer. His innovative ideas and comments granted him status as one of the standard-bearers for a new generation of free thinkers called *shinjinrui* (the new breed) and enabled him to wield an enormous influence. He is known to have been a close acquaintance of other such standard-bearers along the likes of Shigesato Itoi, a copywriter, and Haruomi Hosono, the lead musician of the techno-pop band YMO.

6. Of course, an element of sightseeing was not completely absent in subsequent games. It appeared in console games for more casual game play at home, most notably role-playing games such as the 1986 game *Dragon Warrior* (later renamed *Dragon Quest* in North America) and its successors, such as *Dragon Quest III*, which became a national phenomenon after its release in 1988.

Year (Award)	*Recipient* (Distributor)
1987 (1st)	*Darius* (TAITO)
1988 (2nd)	*Gradius II* (KONAMI)
1989 (3rd)	*Tetris* (SEGA)
1990 (4th)	*Final Fight* (CAPCOM)
1991 (5th)	*Street Fighter II* (CAPCOM)
1992 (6th)	*Street Fighter II Dash* (CAPCOM)
1993 (7th)	*Samurai Spirits* (SNK)
1994 (8th)	*The King of Fighters '94* (SNK)
1995 (9th)	*Virtua Fighter II* (SEGA)
1996 (10th)	*Street Fighter Alpha 2* (CAPCOM)
1997 (11th)	*Vampire Savior* (CAPCOM)
1998 (12th)	*Psychic Force 2012* (TAITO)

Figure 11.7. Gamest Awards recipients. Credit: Yoshimasa Kijima.

7. The PlayStation Portable Wireless Local Area Network enables players to make ad hoc connections with other portable game devices in the vicinity and to play together.

8. Broadly speaking, fighting games (and their community) can be grouped into 2-D and 3-D subcategories. The difference between these two subcategories is analogous to the difference between fantasy and realistic representation. Games in the 2-D category target gamers who want to take advantage of the virtual medium to enjoy fantastic battles involving superpowers (for example, the Kamehameha attack used by Goku in *Dragon Ball Z*). Games in the 3-D category target gamers who enjoy high-fidelity realistic street fights. Games in the former subcategory are typified by the *Street Fighter* series, the latter by the *Virtua Fighter* series. The issue of realism applies to the characters' movement or motion; clearly a battle between a sumo wrestler and a Tai Kwon Do expert is not fundamentally reality based.

9. Some players have persuaded game-center employees to reserve a machine for them for protracted training sessions, while others have bought their own machines to conduct research at home.

10. Initials in transcript are the first letter of the informant's name.

11. The player is referring to the supernatural powers, called "stands," showcased in the manga series *JoJo's Bizarre Adventure*. In *JoJo*, characters wield phantasmal projections of their imaginations that fight each other in vicious battles. Although each character has only one stand, in fighting games each player can technically wield multiple characters and be adept with several.

12. The term *my-chara* is used in a wide range of gaming genres. The term's meaning is slightly different in nonfighting games, however, tending to refer to player-made custom avatars.

13. Games requiring players to use IC cards have been introduced recently, strengthening the attachment players feel toward their chosen character's individuality. The IC cards record players' wins and losses, leading the players to believe that "even though the character may be the same, the character I play and the character someone else plays are different" (twenty-seven-year-old barber). Some games allow players with IC cards to change their characters' outfits.

14. Only expert players who survived the elimination rounds at the store and regional levels can compete in national tournaments. Organizers put on a good show by interviewing contenders before their matches about their determination and expectations and by providing live commentary during the matches. The use of spotlights and smoke machines is also common, and the entire spectacle is projected onto a giant screen in the hall.

15. Not all fighting gamers are trying to gain notoriety in tournaments. Some insist on staying anonymous throughout the tournament, and some never seek matches outside of their home ground. Gamers play in accordance with their own gaming philosophy.

16. In gaming, dojo challenges existed even in the early years of game arcades, before the rise of fighting games. The practice became well established, however, after the popularization of fighting games. In addition to the obvious fact that fighting games are based on face-to-face combat, there are two other reasons: (1) the emergence of the Internet permitted gamers to form more close-knit ties of communication, and (2) the proliferation of tournaments meant a related proliferation of certified "star players." In addition, the catchphrase of the fighting game trailblazer *Street Fighter II*, "I'm going to meet someone stronger than me," fueled a culture of dojo challenges, encouraging players to go on expeditions to seek worthy opponents.

17. This sentiment is frequently expressed by fighting gamers, who describe how their gaming investments and friendships go beyond what many expect of game culture. One gamer I interviewed gives voice to this stance:

Researcher: Beyond gaming?

U: Yeah. I think it's no different from music and sports—you can graduate or not be in any special clubs and still practice and be really into it. It connects you with people and lets you communicate with each other beyond just having pure fun. I wouldn't call it my life, but because it lets me meet people in this way, I can seriously say it's my most important hobby. (twenty-one-year-old technical college student)

18. If Akihabara is the eastern mecca of otaku culture in Tokyo, Nakano is the western mecca (see Chapter 6). TRF is in Nakano Broadway (also known as the otaku building), a shopping complex in the heart of Nakano.

19. The following admission information provides evidence of Togeki's popularity: "Admission tickets may be purchased in advance or the day of. Reserved seating can be purchased in the S and A seating classes; tickets will cover one day with reserved seating plus two additional days without reserved seating. Three-day reserved seating tickets are also available, but S class tickets are sold out" (Gekkan Arcadia Henshuubu 2008, 6). As this excerpt demonstrates, a match between star players is prime entertainment. S-class tickets (advance tickets cost 2,300 yen) sell out instantly, and various merchandise such as commemorative T-shirts are sold on-site. Events are reported on in various media, including magazines, TV, and the Internet, and memorable matches have been compiled into dozens of commercial DVDs.

References

Akagi, Masumi. 2005. *Sore wa "pong" kara hajimatta arcade TV game no naritachi*. Tokyo: Amusement Tsushinsha.

Caillois, Roger. 1961 [1958]. *Man, play and games*. Trans. Meyer Barash. New York: Free Press of Glencoe.

Fish, Stanley. [1980] 1992. *Is there a text in this class? The authority of interpretive communities.* Cambridge, MA: Harvard University Press.

Gekkan Arcadia Henshuubu. 2008. *Tougeki damashii.* Tokyo: Enterbrain.

Goffman, Erving. 1961. *Encounters: Two studies in the sociology of interaction—Fun in games and role distance.* Indianapolis: Bobbs-Merrill.

———. 1974. *Frame analysis: An essay on the organization of experience.* New York: Harper & Row.

Inoue, Shun. 1977. Game no sekai. In *Asobi no shakaigaku,* 3–32. Tokyo: Sekaishisousha.

Kijima, Yoshimasa. 2007a. Video game no genzai—Game ga motarasu asobi no kouzai. In *Digital media training—Johoka jidai no shakaigakuteki shikouhou,* ed. Tomita Hidenori, Minamida Katsuya, and Tsuji Izumi, 113–134. Tokyo: Yuhikaku.

———. 2007b. Video game no tanjou—Asobikata no saihakken. In *Digital media training—Johoka jidai no shakaigakuteki shikouhou,* ed. Hidenori Tomita, Minamida Katsuya, and Tsuji Izumi, 181–201. Tokyo: Yuhikaku.

———. 2008. Naze character ni "moeru" no ka?—Postmodern no bunka shakaigaku. In *Bunka shakaigaku no shiza—Nomerikomu media bunka ni aru nichijou no bunka,* ed. Minamida Katsuya and Tsuji Izumi, 147–168. Tokyo: Minerva Shobou.

Kobayashi, Bourbon. 2005. *Jyu • Game • Moanan • Puryu.* Tokyo: Ota Shuppan.

Miles, Matthew B., and Michael A. Huberman. 1994. *Qualitative data analysis: An expanded sourcebook.* Thousand Oaks, CA: Sage.

Okada, Toshio. 2008. *Otaku wa sudeni shinderu.* Tokyo: Shinchousha.

Omura, Eisho. 1985. Goffman ni okeru double-life no theme—Engi girei ron no igi. In *Gendai shakaigaku 19 tokusu Erving Goffman,* ed. Shakaigaku Kenkyukai, 5–29. Kyoto: Akademia shuppankai.

Riezler, Kurt. 1941. Play and seriousness. *Journal of Philosophy* 38 (19): 505–517.

Roberts, John M., Malcolm J. Arth, and Robert R. Bush. 1959. Games in culture. *American Anthropologist* 61 (4): 597–605.

Yasukawa, Hajime. 1993. Video game keiken no kouzou—Interaction to iu genzaikouzou. In *Genzai no esupuri 312 johoka to taishuka—Video game to karaoke,* ed. Tyuyoshi Sato, 25–43. Tokyo: Shibundou.

12

"As Long as It's Not *Linkin Park Z*": Popularity, Distinction, and Status in the AMV Subculture

· ·

MIZUKO ITO

Fan conventions (cons) in the United States include a colorful mix of programming that showcases the original Japanese anime at the heart of the fandom, as well as a wide variety of fan-made creative productions, such as fan art, cosplay, and anime music videos (AMVs). One of the most popular events in any major North American con is the AMV competition, featuring videos in which fans edit anime to a soundtrack of the editor's choosing. Generally this soundtrack is popular Euro-American music, but it could also be the soundtrack to a movie trailer or dialogue from a TV show, movie, or fan-created script. Fans wait in long lines to get into the AMV screenings of the larger conventions, and they receive ballots to vote on the viewers' choice awards. AMV editors showcase their most recent videos, organized by genre such as action, drama, parody, or technical. The videos vary from dramatic character profiles to celebrations of fight and action sequences to videos that are an amusing commentary on the anime fandom itself. The videos that are screened at large conventions represent the cream of the crop of the AMV world; these are works that have made it past a variety of initial screening mechanisms and are deemed eligible to be showcased in front of hundreds or even thousands of fans, possibly taking home a winning title. The editorial virtuosity of these winning videos rivals and often exceeds that of professional music video production.

During the past decade, AMVs have become a well-established feature of the overseas fandom for anime. An award at a major convention represents the pinnacle of achievement in the creative communities surrounding AMVs, giving the winning editors reputation and visibility in the AMV community and in the anime fandom as a whole. Editors with work recognized in this way often go on to become established names within a relatively small but growing cohort of editors who are central to the AMV scene. The work of these "elite" editors provides inspiration for the growing cohort of new AMV makers to improve their craft and eventually aspire to the competitions. Con competitions are one among a variety of mechanisms that the AMV community has adopted to support feedback, exchange, and reputation building, creating an ecology that is inviting to new aspiring editors and rewarding for more experienced ones. This noncommercial and amateur scene illustrates how high-quality creative work can be supported by a social and cultural logic quite different from commercial distribution and more formal, professionalized production.

AMV production, circulation, and viewing provide an illustrative case study of key trends in contemporary digital, networked, and transnational culture. First, AMVs are concrete representations of transnational cultural flow, in which fans mash up the visual referents from Japanese media with local audio and musical sources. Second, AMVs illustrate how digital and online culture democratizes access to creative production through accessible digital-production tools, online distribution, and a peer-based learning ecology. Finally, the social networks and hierarchies of the AMV community are uniquely keyed to a niche digital media subculture. Centered on lowbrow popular culture, AMV communities are accessible, open to new participants, and animated by an ethic of sharing and volunteerism. At the same time, video editor and curatorial communities also engage in a wide variety of practices to mark distinctions and status in the community, and they develop insider forms of knowledge and referents that are inaccessible to outsiders and newcomers. While these two dimensions may at first blush seem at odds with one another, I argue that they are in fact integrally related. It is the accessible and open nature of amateur digital media production that demands processes of distinction in order for the subculture to survive as a distinctive cultural niche. Conversely, the elite creative core of the community is sustained by the broader viewership and ongoing influx of new creators into its midst.

This chapter describes how AMV creators, supporters, and viewers engage in processes of social inclusion as well as processes for marking status and reputation that delineate the center and peripheries of the creative community. Amateur, fan, and hobby communities have historically been more open and inclusive than their professional counterparts, with fewer formal and institutionalized barriers to entry. As these communities have moved into the digital age, they have become much more visible to general publics, resulting in a rapid influx of new aspiring creators. The AMV scene is an example of an amateur creative community that has successfully weathered this transition by developing new kinds of social norms and mechanisms to deal with the greater openness and accessibility that online media afford. Where technical and economic barriers to entry were more salient in the early years, these have increasingly been supplanted by social and normative barriers that define the center and periphery of participation in the scene. This chapter starts by outlining the conceptual framework and methodology behind this study and then moves to historical background on the AMV scene before turning to descriptions of three dimensions of the AMV scene drawn from ethnographic fieldwork.[1] I describe the properties of open access and sharing that support the amateur ethos, processes of connoisseurship and distinction making, and how status and reputation are established and negotiated among the elite editors who comprise the core of the scene.

FAN PRODUCTION IN A DIGITAL AGE

In their review of fan studies, Jonathan Gray, Cornel Sandvoss, and C. Lee Harrington (2007) describe three waves of fan studies. In the 1980s, the first wave of fan studies took the stance of "fandom is beautiful," arguing for the merits of a subculture that was often stereotyped and reviled by the mainstream. As fan studies have matured, scholars have begun to look more closely at the ways in which fan communities were embedded in existing social hierarchies and structures rather than being fully outside and resistant to dominant culture. Gray, Sandvoss, and Harrington see Sarah Thornton's (1996) work on subcultural capital as a key text in defining this second wave of work that focuses on "fan culture and social hierarchy." A third, current wave of fan studies focuses on "fandom and modernity" and how fan culture is embedded in modern life more broadly. They write: "It is precisely *because* fan consumption has grown into a taken-for-granted aspect of modern communication and consumption that it warrants critical analysis and investigation more than ever" (9). In a similar vein, Henry Jenkins (2007) argues that fannish consumption has become thoroughly normalized in the digital age. Many of the buzzwords of contemporary networked culture have applied to fans for decades— prosumers, connectors, inspirational consumers, multipliers, and lead users. Rather than having to argue for the importance and legitimacy of fan activity, he sees public opinion as increasingly acknowledging that "fandom is the future," and fannish activities have become part of the everyday life of mainstream consumers.

As fannish subjectivity and production have become more mainstream and more visible, video remix has come to occupy a unique position in the fan culture landscape. Compared to fan fiction or fan art, which have been historically open and accessible forms of amateur production, until recently video was largely inaccessible to amateurs. In *Remix*, Lawrence Lessig (2008) argues that we are still in the early stages of developing shared conventions for how to reference and remix video. "While writing with text is the stuff that everyone is taught to do, filmmaking and record making were, for most of the twentieth century, stuff that professionals did" (Lessig 2008, 54). Particularly when considering the legal and policy landscape for video remix, shared conventions are still very much under negotiation. Yet in the span of one decade, we have seen remixes of movies and television catapulted from a marginal practice confined to small communities of fan creators to a highly visible and popular media form. Today, remixes of Harry Potter movies, *Star Trek*, and amateur videos are widely shared on sites such as YouTube and have become part of our shared cultural vocabulary.

Even as popular video remixes get millions of views on YouTube, there continue to be resilient subcultural niche groups that traffic in more exclusive and inaccessible forms of fan videos. Fan production is still deeply implicated in discourses and infrastructures that differentiate it from "mainstream" sensibilities of cultural production and consumption. While recognizing the key insight of third-wave fan culture studies, I find that Thornton (1996) and second-wave work have on-going salience. Rather than considering club cultures purely in relation to discourses of resistance to mainstream and commercial music cultures, Thornton suggests that subcultures have unique forms of cultural capital, reputation, and distinction that are constructed through specific forms of media production, circulation, and uptake. Similarly, fandom functions as a subculture with unique reputational schemes, hierarchies, and subcultural capital. These are mechanisms by which cult media producers distinguish their cultural world from both the mainstream commercial sector and common, everyday media production and consumption (see Chapter 10).

To say that fan production, remixes, and mashups are growing in cultural prominence is not the same as saying that they are becoming mainstream or that they aspire toward commercial regimes of circulation. Noncommercial cultural production of popular media remixes occupies a space of amateur cultural production that is distinct from everyday personal media creation (such as home videos and everyday performance) on the one hand and commercial media production on the other. What makes AMV creation, circulation, and viewing distinct from both commercial and everyday media production is a unique set of genre conventions in the content, and a particular set of social and community norms, grounded in a noncommercial, amateur ethos. As Yochai Benkler (2006) has argued, economies of volunteerism, sharing, and noncommercial cultural production have been a long-standing feature of our social and cultural landscape. In tandem with new networked and digital media, these noncommercial regimes that have existed for decades in the shadows of professional production are becoming more visible, but they retain distinctive norms and cultural markers that distinguish them from commercial media regimes.

In fact, the digital age is one in which the very notions of "mainstream" or "popular" culture are becoming increasingly destabilized. While there are clearly cultural referents and media franchises that are broadly shared within particular national and even transnational contexts, the ways in which these media sources are taken up and reframed are highly diverse. Fans are united through their consumption of popular media franchises, but they produce their own distinctive niche media works by appropriating these found materials. In describing the relationship between commercial and fannish media cultures, Jenkins

(2006) argues that fan activity and commercial activity are becoming increasingly synergistic. It is not that amateur media production is replacing professional media, but rather that both are occupying a shared and convergent media ecology. Far from ushering in an era of cultural homogeneity, networked media have supported the proliferation of niche cultural production.

The goal of this chapter is to describe how niche and subcultural sensibilities are maintained in the context of an increasingly accessible and participatory digital media scene. As Thornton (1996) notes in the case of club cultures, the core taste makers of a subculture must constantly resist the perception that they have gone "mainstream" or that they have "sold out." Similarly, in the AMV scene, as certain anime series become more accessible through mainstream channels, or certain forms of remix become more common, the scene has continuously worked to raise the bar of what it means to be a true anime connoisseur and insider. Digital and networked media have posed particular challenges to the AMV scene in that earlier barriers to participation, largely technical and economic in nature, eroded very rapidly in a short time. As I document in the historical background section, the scene responded to this new attention by the mainstream and the influx of new creators by developing mechanisms for marking status and distinction. In this way, the AMV scene has evolved into one that retains a populist and inclusive character while also maintaining a subcultural identity defined in opposition to more accessible forms of anime consumption.

My description of the AMV scene provides a window into understanding some key dynamics of media and fan culture in the digital age. This study speaks to a growing body of work examining how amateur media culture challenges existing social and cultural structures, such as intellectual property regimes (Lessig 2004), commercial culture (Benkler 2006), processes of innovation (Hippel 2005; Lakhani and Panetta 2007), and organizational forms (Shirky 2008). Just as early fan studies framed their objects in relation to mainstream culture, however, digital culture studies have also tended to frame new networked culture as a domain of "free culture" and a challenge to dominant forms of commercial and proprietary culture rather than as constituting cultural forms with their own unique norms and structure. Detailed ethnographic work that examines the infrastructures, social structures, and cultural norms specific to amateur, noncommercial digital culture provides grounding for these discussions of broader trends in media and communications. This perspective also serves to qualify and specify some of the contemporary debates in fan studies. My analysis of the AMV scene describes how fan cultures are *simultaneously* becoming more accessible and more exclusive, and how these two dynamics are integrally dependent on one another.

A BRIEF HISTORY OF AMVs

Although AMVs are now an established part of the overseas anime fandom, they are a relatively recent addition to the pantheon of fan practices. Digital video-editing tools became accessible consumer technologies only in the late 1990s. Before then, editing required analog editing tools that demanded tremendous patience to use. Longtime participants in the AMV scene generally date the origins of AMV making to some early videos made by U.S. fans in the early 1980s. In Japan, anime fans had been making video remixes known as MADs since the late 1970s, and fans of U.S. television had been creating remix "vids" since around that time as well (Coppa 2008; Jenkins 1992). By all accounts, however, AMV making evolved on a trajectory that was quite separate from these other fan video scenes. Vlad G. Pohnert (2005) notes that in those days, "AMVs were a cult of a small group of people and AMV contests were shown in rooms the size of shoe boxes." By the late 1990s, AMVs were being shown at anime conventions that were starting to crop up around the country, though the creator community was still small. EK, who began creating AMVs in the late 1990s, recalls the scene around 1998 and 1999. "I think at one point, pretty much every AMV editor in the U.S. knew each other, or knew of each other." She describes a snail mail–based VHS trading network "that mostly overlapped with fansub trading at that point."

By the late 1990s, editors were beginning to transition to digital tools, and in 2000, animemusicvideos.org was founded. Before the establishment of this site, which AMV creators affectionately call "the org," AMV makers hosted their videos on independent sites. The org quickly became a central clearinghouse for editors to upload their videos and to communicate with one another and their audiences (LantisEscudo 2008; Pohnert 2005; Springall 2004). The embrace of digital culture had a profound effect on the AMV scene by broadening access to video editing and distribution. This move toward digital creation and distribution happened in tandem with a surge in anime's popularity overseas and the growth of digital fansubbing (Springall 2004). Today, what was once a practice restricted to highly committed adult fans is now being adopted by much younger and more casual creators. In our 2006 online questionnaire, the majority of video creators responded that they had started creating AMVs during their teenage years. Video remix has entered the ranks of other fan creative practices such as fan art, fan fiction, and costuming as accessible forms of creative production. At the same time, responses to our questionnaire suggest that there are still significant barriers to entry because of the technical nature of editing practice and the kind of subcultural capital needed to participate. At least among the active participants in the org who responded to our questionnaire, the male/female split was 62 percent/38 percent. Respondents were overwhelmingly white (81 percent) and came predominantly from college-educated households.[2] Editors have unusually high levels of technology access, with 91 percent reporting that they had their own computers by the age of thirteen. Although the viewership of AMVs is likely much more diverse, the core editing community shares demographic characteristics with other geek technology subcultures in being predominantly white, male, and highly educated.

Today's AMV scene is distributed across a variety of online sites and conventions. English-language fandoms and conventions in North America and the United Kingdom continue to be the center of gravity for the AMV scene, but it has spread to other countries in Europe and to other regions such as Latin America. Online, the org continues to be a central congregation site for AMV editors, but AMV viewers are turning to more accessible video-streaming sites such as YouTube or Vimeo to watch AMVs. This has been a source of controversy within the AMV scene, as editors worry about their videos being made more accessible to publics that are not part of the anime fandom. The number of videos uploaded to the org grew steadily from 2000, with a dramatic jump between 2003 and 2004. Since 2005, which is the year that YouTube opened its doors, the number of uploads per year has steadily dropped, pointing to the gradual decentralization of the AMV scene.[3] This transition to a networked and open distribution ecology, the greater visibility of AMVs among anime fans and the general public, and the growing pervasiveness of video remix as an everyday media production process are the backdrop to today's AMV scene. I turn now to a more detailed treatment of the social structure of the contemporary AMV scene, beginning with a description of an amateur ethic of open and participatory media culture, and then going on to outline processes of distinction through appeals to more sophisticated forms of media connoisseurship. The final descriptive section examines how an "elite" core of editors is maintained and recognized.

EVANGELISM AND VOLUNTEERISM

In North America until fairly recently, anime was largely unavailable through mainstream commercial distribution. As described in Chapter 4, on the history of otaku culture in the United States, much of the early spread of anime overseas can be attributed to fan distribution of VHS tapes and translated scripts, and fans often explicitly saw themselves as evangelists for anime overseas (see Chapter 7). Even today, when there is a robust localization industry that translates and distributes anime to overseas fans, most fans rely on peer-to-peer fan networks to gain access to at least some of their anime (see Chapter 8). Unlike fandoms around domestic television, anime fans see their ability to access and acquire the media content as itself a unique marker of commitment and subcultural capital.

AMV creators position themselves as evangelists and translators for an inaccessible form of cult media, acquiring subcultural capital through their insider knowledge of anime and trying to stay as close and true as possible to the original Japanese source. At the same time, they display this insider knowledge by creating works that translate cult media to local referents and make it more accessible to a broader cut of the fandom. In discussions with AMV makers, they often describe their videos as "advertisements" for particular anime series. For example, in a description of one of his AMVs, *Sail On*, on animemusicvideos.org, Inertia advocates for *One Piece*, a series that he thinks has not gotten enough recognition overseas: "One Piece is an epic series, long running and always fresh, but it hasn't got the best recognition this side of the pond, barely anyone here had heard of it a year or two ago. . . . So here I'm trying to expose a little of that ;) Do note this is from the original One Piece, not the hacked up American dub version with water pistols, cork guns and no blood or plot."

Sail On was picked up by one of the fansub groups for *One Piece* and promoted on its site as part of its three-year anniversary and celebration of the *One Piece* series and the group's ongoing work. Although remix videos can vary from highly critical and political works to more fannish ones, AMVs most commonly are created in an appreciative and celebratory mode. Editors will often point to this characteristic of AMVs as a reason that the original creators should allow AMVs to flourish. Carolina, an AMV editor, argues: "The most likely result of a fan video and fan fiction is to gain greater exposure for the original product—free advertising!—and that exposure is also almost always positive, since people tend to love the original sources they use for fan productions." This stance was echoed by all the creators to whom I spoke.

Fans recognize that they are "borrowing" and "sharing" in an amateur and noncommercial mode that they believe is synergistic with the commercial industry, but that is also defined in opposition to its norms and values. Many AMV creators mentioned the fact that they value AMVs and the surrounding communities because they embody this kind of amateur, participatory ethic, and any financial motive on the fan side of the equation is explicitly frowned upon. Darius, an AMV maker and con organizer, describes how AMVs are a mechanism for people to start to get involved in a creative practice and a welcoming peer-based creative community: "It is one way that people can educate themselves creatively and technically. . . . It's basically people just having fun with each other and they aren't trying to make a profit. People don't try to sell AMVs. Nobody does that. It's basically just giving, and oh, that's a cool show. . . . It is all a community-type effort, village minded, whatever." I spoke to some AMV creators who were studying or working in adjacent fields such as media education, game design, or anime localization, but all creators saw the AMV scene as a space of noncommercial and community-based creativity, and not a direct pathway to professionalization.

A communal spirit of volunteerism was most evident among fans supporting the infrastructures of the AMV scene—the org and various AMV competitions and screenings at cons. In my interviews with the organizers of AMV competitions at cons, I was stunned by the amount of time, effort, and financial resources that the organizers poured into the events. Organizers spend all of their free time leading up to an event and almost all their time at the event in coordination activities, and they receive at most a free hotel room and some meals for their labors. For example, ScottAnime describes how during his peak years of con organizing he would be the lead organizer of the con or AMV competition organizer at eight or nine shows a year. Quu, who is credited for developing the first computer-based systems for running AMV competitions, describes how he donated thousands of dollars' worth of video and computer equipment, and his own programming expertise, to develop a system optimized for AMV competitions and screenings, setting a new standard for the scene.

The org is also sustained entirely on volunteer effort and member contributions. The site includes many modules programmed by the site administrators and is highly customized to cater specifically to the AMV scene. It offers functionality for members to upload and download high-quality video, to rank and comment on videos, write in blogs and forums, and aggregate information about competitions. In addition, the site hosts a wealth of member-generated content that caters to both newcomers and old hands. While the forums often include insider discussions and opinions about AMVs and anime, the site also features lengthy guides, targeted to the aspiring editor, on how to make and evaluate AMVs. In our interviews with editors, many described how they relied on these guides in making their first forays into AMV making. Editors also described how they would turn to the forums on the org for questions about AMVs and how they could count on somebody with expertise to respond. These kinds of resources, where experienced editors freely share their expertise in an open environment, have been key to the expansion of the base of AMV makers.

In contrast to their relation to professionally created videos, fans see AMVs as an accessible media practice that they can aspire to. The fannish appreciation of anime and AMVs is integrally tied to the impulse to create. One aspiring editor, Starfire2258, describes how viewing his first AMV competition "inspired me immediately to 1) Find out how to get more of these awesome creations . . . 2) Watch some of the cool anime series that these AMVs showed me and 3) Figure out if I could create one myself." Fan viewers of AMVs will often identify with the video creator rather than in the more distanced relation of a media consumer. For example, Gepetto says: "Today I don't think much of it, but back then I was amazed at the idea that such a pretty little videoclip was made by a fan just like me. . . . I put it on loop and watched it several times in a row. . . . I left the computer on all night and downloaded a few AMVs. I liked them all, and began thinking 'what kind of video would I really want to see?' Since I had no idea where else to look for AMVs, I decided, 'Why don't I make some myself?' "

All the editors we spoke to described how they started making AMVs as part of their participation in the anime fandom, and that they picked up video-editing skills in the process of working to make their own AMVs. That the AMV scene includes highly polished videos as well as videos by new and less accomplished editors is an important component of the overall ecology, providing a diversity of works that editors can emulate. Unlike professional practices, which weed out beginners and the less talented, amateur scenes thrive on a diverse range of quality and skill. Beginning editors may start by imitating popular kinds of genres and mashups. As editors get more involved in the scene, they will start modeling their work on that of more experienced editors, developing more individual styles, and aspire to broader visibility through competitions. For example, at the time of our interview, Earendil had created two AMVs and had still not entered any competitions, though he was considering it. He said he did not have personal relationships with other editors in the scene but had "a list of 'videos to aspire to.' "

Drawing from "how-to" guides on the Internet, posting questions on forums, and through trial and error, editors almost always learn how to create AMVs through a self-directed learning process. In the past decade, with the growing availability of AMVs, information about AMV creation, and accessible video-editing tools, the ability to create AMVs is within arm's reach of a much larger cut of the anime fandom. Jbone reflects on how digital technology has been "a blessing and a curse" to the AMV community. "It lets people who know what they are doing do it more easily, but it allows people who don't know what they are doing to do things much more easily as well." While many we interviewed valued the democratization of AMV creation, some of the more established editors described how this trend can come into conflict with the community's ability to support and recognize quality work. XStylus notes:

Around the time when AnimeMusicVideos.org came around, the bar-
rier for entry started to drop. DVD ripping eliminated the need for
complex video equipment, and computers were starting to include rudi-
mentary video editing programs. . . . Eventually they'd get their hands
on a bootleg copy of Premiere, and then they'd go on to make their first
AMV, usually with Linkin Park music and DragonBallZ footage. I feel
the community and craft suffered as a result of a deluge of carelessly
made AMVs. Quality got replaced by quantity. . . . Now that practically
anyone can make one, everyone does make one. It makes it supremely difficult for a new video of quality to stand out unless the creator already
has a reputation.

Here we see the tension between the open and populist ethos
of the community and the maintenance of subcultural capital. XStylus
gives voice to a common refrain among experienced editors—that
there is a glut of AMVs that combine two highly accessible media
sources popular among teenage boys: *Dragon Ball Z* and Linkin Park.
Lone Wolf, another experienced editor, says that he is fairly open to
viewing a wide range of AMVs "as long as it's not *Linkin Park Z*." The
Linkin Park Z video has become a stand-in for the degradation in quality that has accompanied an expansion of the base of AMV editors
to include a younger population and anime that is readily available
through mainstream cable sources. In the early years of AMV making, the scene was characterized by comparatively older editors (in
their twenties) and a flat, peer-based structure, with technical and
economic barriers to entry that kept casual creators away. Today, the
AMV scene is characterized by a finer set of internal distinctions that
enable the scene to welcome new participants and maintain subcultural capital that is out of reach of the casual fan.

CONNOISSEURSHIP AND SUBCULTURAL CAPITAL

AMVs not only expose viewers to new kinds of anime, but they
also interpret and reframe the source material in new and often unexpected ways. The pleasure of viewing an AMV is in connecting
with how other viewers have experienced a particular series or interpreted a particular character. Like fan fiction or fan art, AMVs appropriate and reframe found materials, engaging in a critical practice of
connoisseurship and interpretation by creating an incredibly diverse

range of media works. In many cases, fan-created transformative works give voice to marginalized subjectivities and viewpoints and offer alternative interpretations of popular texts. In the case of *Star Trek* fandom, for example, Francesca Coppa (2008) has argued that female fans have used fanvids to offer alternative representations of media texts to "heal wounds created by the marginalization, displacement, and fragmentation of female characters." AMVs are not dominated by the critical, feminist edge that is evident in much of the vidding community, but AMVs still represent the unique viewpoints and interpretations of overseas fans who are reframing and recontexualizing Japanese media to their local referents. While some AMVs are done to J-pop and other Japanese audio sources, the vast majority of AMVs are edited to Euro-American audio sources for cultural mashups that give voice to the experiences and interpretations of foreign fans of Japanese media.

As in the case of professional music videos, viewers and creators look for good editing, effects, timing, and high video quality. At the same time, because AMVs are amateur, noncommercial, derivative works, what people look for in AMVs differs fundamentally from the standards applied to their professional counterparts. As Coppa (2008) has argued in the case of vidding, AMVs are made primarily as a form of commentary on the anime source material, not as a way of illustrating popular music. These are works that grow out of anime fandoms, not music fandoms. Further, the goal of much of AMV creation is participation in ongoing fan exchange and sociability, not creating a media work that is going to stand on its own apart from this social and cultural context. Many creators, particularly beginning creators, see the process of AMV creation as an end in itself and may share their videos with only a few close friends. Even AMVs that are submitted to animemusicvideos.org or to a convention screening are designed to circulate among a community of peers who share similar subcultural interests, rather than being media works meant for broad and undefined audiences. Older fans of anime often speak nostalgically of the early years of the U.S.-based anime fandom in the 1980s and early 1990s, when content was scarce and the fandom was still small.

Even though anime and AMVs became more accessible in the past decade, AMVs continue to perform an important role in introducing anime fans to series that they might not have otherwise been exposed to. The advertising role that AMVs play in the community is tied to a tension in how AMVs are valued and evaluated that tracks along the tension between popularity and subcultural status. AMVs created using already popular source material will be catering to an existing fan base, but those using more obscure material can stake a stronger claim to the AMV's role in evangelizing to new audiences. Experienced editors will generally place a premium on source material that is less accessible or more sophisticated than the material that has been picked up by U.S. cable networks. Darius, an old-timer in the AMV scene, specializes in AMVs made from classic anime from the 1980s and early 1990s. He laments the fact that most of the AMVs that get shown at today's conventions are made from the current popular shows. "There's so much more. . . . I don't want to just limit it to what is most popular at the time. I want to really kind of send some of that up . . . and expose it with different people so they can go track it down themselves if they want."

Experienced editors will explicitly avoid themes that have been overdone and often chastise new editors for picking source material that is too common. For example, MercyKillings says he was motivated to start editing because of the low quality of many of the AMVs he saw on the Internet. "I was watching AMVs and I noticed that the quality was just crap, and it was really annoying because they were all the same thing. They were all *Naruto* based, or they were all *Dragon Ball Z*, and everybody used Linkin Park." One editor, interviewed as part of Annie Manion's (2005) master's thesis on anime fans, described how he started making AMVs with a *Dragon Ball Z* video and was promptly smacked down by another editor for using such common footage.

> I tried it once and I took . . . a *Dragon Ball Z* video—and I edited that to a piece of music and I put it on there and there was one guy who came on there right away and was like, wow, this is great editing, I love it, but you used *Dragon Ball Z*. Why the hell would you do that? Nobody likes that. . . . And they were accusing me of not being very creative because the anime has been so overdone. . . . These are people who get so worked up and they'll look at, like I said, the most obscure animes. They'll know about the most obscure topics. They won't say anything in English about anime. Then you also have like anime conventions where people just I mean go all out with their love for it.

He gives voice to the tension in the community between sharing a common, collective imagination and enthusiasm with other fans, "where people just I mean go all out with their love for it," and those in the discerning "elite," who traffic in the exclusive subcultural capital of obscure anime, Japanese language, and insider knowledge. Even editors who are well established in the community have to take their hits for using common source material. Inertia notes that people are critical of his videos because they draw from popular series. His AMV that combined *Naruto* footage with the audio track from a *Matrix* movie trailer was widely viewed and won several prominent awards. At the same time, "the *Narutrix* being so popular for such a popular series, it tends to get a lot of backlash from the higher authors. It took a lot of criticism for being a crowd pleaser. That was its main critique." Similarly, during the AMV awards for Anime Expo 2007 (a major anime con), one of the featured entries made use of *Naruto* footage, and the organizer "praised [the editor] for his video, stating that normally they can't stand to watch Narutard videos but they could not take their eyes off this video" (Suwatanapongched field note).[4]

This tendency for AMV editors and curators to mark their practice as exclusive and discerning has not been lost on those who take part in other dimensions of the fandom. Kohjiroh, who has dabbled in AMV making but does not socialize with AMV makers, thinks "a good portion of them seems like assholes." He notes that there is a "hierarchy within the anime con community" that segments different ways of participating in the fandom. "Cosplayers get treated like celebs, AMV creators get treated like professors, and the average con goer is like a commoner." While this professorial status can be viewed as elitist by those outside of the core, it is a source of status and subcultural capital that becomes a magnet for viewers and aspiring editors. AbsoluteDestiny, a well-known editor, says that "I think it's the point in which any community becomes a real community is when a selection of that community gets accused of being elitist."

RECOGNITION AND STATUS

As Thornton (1996) describes in the case of club cultures, maintaining subcultural capital and status requires ongoing processes of distinction making. Participants in a subculture must work to distinguish their practices from the mainstream and also to establish hierarchies and distinctions within the subcultural scene. Although the kinds of subcultural capital that anime fans traffic in is quite different from the club cultures that Thornton describes, the processes of distinction are similar. Within the anime fandom, the AMV editor community is positioned as elite taste makers and commentators. Further, within the different communities of AMV editors are various formal and informal mechanisms for creating status, reputation, and distinction. These mechanisms have been proliferating as AMVs have become a more popular and accessible media form. Lacking the formal gatekeeping functions that define the boundaries of professional practices, amateur creative communities must rely on more distributed mechanisms for developing status and reputation.

The more formal mechanisms for evaluating and ranking AMVs include various feedback and ranking mechanisms on online sites, as well as formal competitions online and at conventions. After animemusicvideos.org was established in 2000, it quickly became a central site for members of the AMV community to congregate, share, and comment on each other's videos. As the site has evolved, the site administrators have added a range of different mechanisms to allow people to rate and give feedback on videos and to compete for recognition and visibility. For example, when a viewer downloads a video from the site he or she is automatically asked to provide a five-star ranking of the video. Viewers can also provide more detailed opinions on the videos, add them to their favorites lists, or make comments. All of these metrics are aggregated into different "top video" lists that are easily viewable on the site. Further, the org hosts an annual viewers' choice competition, and it provides indexes and listings of all the major AMV competitions both online and at conventions, archiving the winners lists. These kinds of ranking systems have become more crucial as the base of the AMV community has broadened. As Jbone notes, "The lowest common denominator has always existed, but it feels like over time people have become less shy about sending the lowest common denominator for public viewing." More established creators say that they largely rely on their existing networks of editors or competitions to filter the AMVs that they view.

How AMVs are ranked and evaluated is also embedded within the structure and hierarchy of the AMV community, which employs a variety of more informal and peer-based practices for developing reputation. AbsoluteDestiny describes how moving from entry-level participation to a more central role in the AMV scene means both developing social connections and producing quality work. "You move from first trying to make something and showing it to a few friends. And then if you start getting to know some people online you might upload it to the org. Or you could enter a competition. When you decide to go to a big convention and meet other AMV creators, then that's another level again. It's at the big AMV conventions, when we get together to talk about each other's videos, that you start to understand that the videos are actually conversations among AMV creators. You wouldn't necessarily know that just from downloading the videos. The videos are a result of conversations that editors are having through a lot of private channels like at conventions or on IM."

He describes how he won notoriety for his signature *Shameless Rock Video* by first participating actively online, becoming known by other editors, and then eventually releasing a video that made a splash and went on to win competition awards. He says the social connection with other editors gives people the initial impetus to take a look at a video. "Having some sort of name recognition even if it's not for your videos but for your general participation in the community, will aid your presence. . . . When there are so many videos out there now, it's incredibly difficult to get noticed." Other editors describe how they may not be part of the con scene or the core elite crowd but develop reputations through online participation and contributions.

Editors in the inner circle share social connections and an ongoing give-and-take. They look to their peers for feedback and critique in a way that is not necessarily visible in the public AMV forums on the org or in other AMV discussions such as the Yahoo group or the IRC (Internet relay chat) channel. For example, dokidoki describes how the feedback he gets from other editors on his beta videos is invaluable, and this communication generally happens via instant messaging or e-mail. For those who are established members of the inner circle of editors, the community operates at a scale that is akin to that in the early years of the AMV scene in the late 1990s. Editors know each other personally and are in frequent contact, giving each other feedback, commentary, and help in improving their craft. Many of these established editors are also involved in the organizing of AMV competitions and events and in judging. In discussions with both new editors and those who are more central to the scene, people would generally name the same established creators as the well-known names in the scene. Although the claims to fame vary to some extent, the key factors are whether their videos have won awards in conventions, their longevity in the AMV scene, and whether they are socially active in the convention circuit or in online forums. Alan Clontz, who was one of the coordinators of a large collaborative editing project, *AMV Hell*, describes how "the community aspect is probably one of my favorite aspects though. Not so much having other people watch my videos but just talking and socializing with other creators." He sees his community specifically as being the other creators and not the broader audience for his AMVs. As editors move into more elite status in the scene, they tend toward affiliation with the core social community of editors rather than with the broader fandom.

Although editors rely on a mixture of inspiration, creativity, and hard work to create their videos, most will also acknowledge the importance of social support within the creative community. What constitutes an original and creative work is something that can be understood only within the social back-and-forth of commentary about videos. While a new editor with less experience in the scene may think that his or her *Linkin Park Z* video is innovative, more established editors will see the video as a rehash of a well-established formula that requires little technical or interpretive skill. Many highly acclaimed videos will rely on bringing together a set of uncommon referents into a unique interpretation. E-Ko's *Tainted Donuts*, for example, is a video that is celebrated for being one of the first to tell a story by seamlessly melding characters and scenes from two different anime series. Other videos are acclaimed because of their innovation in developing a new technique or a new genre. For example, Kevin Caldwell's *Engel* raised the bar for lip-synch and timing, and Scorpion Unlimited's *Whisper of the Beast* set a new standard for the use of digital effects in AMVs. Some of the most highly acclaimed videos rely heavily on insider knowledge about the AMV community itself and are "meta" commentaries on the community or the creative process of editing. Dokidoki's *Right Now* is still a favorite among many fans because it comments on many shared referents in the fandom. More specific to the AMV scene, EK's *Failed Experiments* is a parody of her own experiences as an

AMV editor, and it is considered one of the classics. Similarly, XStylus's *A Total Waste of 6 min 35 sec* pokes fun at many of the common mistakes that AMV editors make, and it received a tremendous ovation when screened at Anime Expo 2002.

As the AMV scene has matured, the distinctions and distance between elite editors, newbie editors, and the viewers of AMVs have grown. The quality and technical sophistication of the best videos have also grown in tandem with this growth in social distinctions. While interactions between the core group of editors still retain the feel of a close peer-based community and an ethic of sharing and reciprocity, those on the periphery can often experience social distance. Many of the more successful editors produce works of professional quality and have an aura of celebrity at the conventions, with committed fandoms of their own, something that often sits uneasily with the more populist ethos that animates many amateur and hobby cultures. For example, Jbone describes how one of his fellow editors has a fannish following among younger fans. "I can say that I don't have screaming schoolgirls running after me, which I think is a good thing. I've known people who've had that." He goes on to describe an awkward interaction he had with a "creepy fanboy" at one of the conventions he attended. "I mean, it happens sometimes where you meet somebody for the first time and you're a little starstruck because, wow, this person did this really awesome thing. And then after five minutes, it's like, oh, yeah they're cool, you know? It's when the five minutes are up and people are still like 'Wow, you're awesome. Wow, you're awesome. Wow, you're awesome,' it just doesn't work."

Despite the fact that renowned editors have a status that is elevated above that of the casual creator and viewer of AMVs, a communal and populist ethic still pervades the scene. Fannishness is a stance more appropriately reserved for a fan's relationship with commercial media and professional creators, not for other fans, no matter how much status they may have in the scene. While there is clearly an elite group of editors with status, overall the scene remains welcome and open to newcomers, and there is a certain expectation of parity and sharing among even elite fans. The way in which the AMV scene promotes this open and noncommercial ethic, while also supporting achievement, status, distinction, and recognition of high-quality work, is an important property of an amateur creative community that has successfully weathered a transition to a digital and networked age.

CONCLUSIONS

Today's AMV scene incorporates both diversity and cohesion by integrating the populist and open affordances of networked media with mechanisms for developing the status and reputation that define the core leadership of the scene. My intention in describing the various forms of distinction, hierarchy, reputation, and status making in the AMV scene is not to portray the community as elitist or exclusionary. Quite the contrary, my argument is that to maintain a democratic and open ethos toward participation and media making, amateur creative communities must rely on distributed and peer-based processes for distinguishing new and experienced participants and recognizing high-quality and innovative work. The AMV scene is an example of a creative community that has been highly successful in recruiting a very broad base of young creators into video-editing practices, keeping barriers to entry low and the pleasure of creation high. At the same time, the community has developed ways of highlighting and celebrating those who have the commitment and skills to develop exceptional work. Although participants in the scene experience tension between the more "common" and "elite" forms of participation in the AMV scene, I have argued that in fact they are integrally related and synergistic. The health of the AMV scene as a thriving amateur, noncommercial, and networked creative practice is predicated on the diversity and hierarchies that have evolved through the years.

The AMV scene is supported by differentiated forms of participation, which allow people to participate as newcomers and with varying levels of social commitment, with only a small cut of participants going on to join the elite inner circle. This dynamic is evident in other online platforms and scenes that support robust participation in effective forms of distributed innovation; the barriers to entry must be low enough to support entrants outside of the usual suspects, and the scene must reward diverse motivations for participating (Lakhani 2008; Lakhani and Panetta 2007). Newcomers participate because of opportunities to learn from more experienced editors, experienced editors get recognition for high-quality work, and all participants can benefit from the social interaction and the pleasure of creation. By achieving this balance, the AMV scene collectively produces high-quality creative work as well as a wide range of technical innovations in video editing.

As more and more creative and hobby communities become digitally networked, the productive tension between open and populist tendencies and processes of subcultural distinction will be a persistent feature of the cultural landscape. Noncommercial, amateur, and peer-based production scenes thrive on models of open participation and access, but processes for differentiating participation, recognizing leadership, and developing status and reputation are also central to the scene. Processes for maintaining an elite core, competitions, and other systems of recognition provide important incentives that drive the quest for quality and innovation among the more committed creators. Unlike professional practices, driven by financial incentives and formal institutional structures, communities such as those we see at anime conventions and at the org are driven by different kinds of motivations and rewards. We see organizers, site administrators, and editors putting in truly extraordinary amounts of effort and their own financial resources to support AMVs as a passionate hobby. The value people get out of participation is a complex alchemy of community participation, recognition, and the pleasures of creation and connoisseurship.

ACKNOWLEDGMENTS

First and foremost, thanks goes to all the AMV editors and anime fans who took the time to speak with me and my research team. I would particularly like to thank Jonathan Cullinane (Inertia), whose videos and curation at our first video fest were what hooked me irretrievably on the AMV scene, and phade, who was kind enough to help get the word out about our questionnaire. Though I have barely scratched the surface of the AMV community, I would not have gotten anywhere without the patient guidance, good humor, and encyclopedic knowledge of Tim Park (dokidoki). This work was supported by a grant from the John D. and Catherine T. MacArthur Foundation and by the Annenberg Center for Communication at the University of Southern California. My research assistants included Rachel Cody, Renee Saito, Annie Manion, Brendan Callum, and Judy Suwatanapongched. Becky Herr-Stephenson kindly stepped in to clean up the data from our AMV creator questionnaire, and Jennifer Urban was a valued collaborator in this research.

Notes

1. This chapter draws from ethnographic fieldwork with the AMV scene in 2006 and 2007, which included interviews, online observations, and observations at conventions in Los Angeles, San Jose, and Atlanta. This chapter relies primarily on interviews with twenty-three AMV editors. I was the lead researcher of a team that included several graduate and undergraduate students, including Rachel Cody, Annie Manion, Renee Saito, Brendan Callum, and Judy Suwatanapongched. Jennifer Urban, a collaborator on this work, also participated in the fieldwork. When the observation or interview was conducted by somebody other than me, this is noted in the text. This work is part of a broader study of the overseas anime fandom, and in addition to the interviews with the editors, we interviewed forty-two other fans involved in different dimensions of the fandom, varying from casual con-goers to fan fiction writers, con organizers, fansubbers, cosplayers, and fan artists. These interviews with the broader fandom contextualize the more focused case study work on AMV makers. Finally, we also fielded an online questionnaire for AMV editors in the fall of 2006, asking about background information as well as some details on how they create their AMVs and participate in conventions and the online scene. The questionnaire was featured on animemusicvideos.org and garnered 277 valid responses.

2. For mother's level of education, 43 percent reported it to be some college or college degree, and 22 percent reported some graduate school or graduate degree. For father's level of education, 37 percent reported it to be some college or college degree, and 26 percent reported some graduate school or graduate degree.

3. These numbers are from personal communication with Tim Park, one of the site administrators at the org, and are derived from the numbers of videos in the "premiered" category entered into the org for each year from 2000 to 2008.

4. From the online *Urban Dictionary:* "Narutard is a derogatory term applied to otaku fans of the anime title Naruto. It is a word play on the combination of naruto and retard. This term surfaced during early 2004 at the beginning of the anime's popularity in America and characterizes the behavior of Naruto fans as being so blindly devoted to the series (with an almost religious cult-like fervor) that they act incredibly stupid and can be confused with retarded (er, mentally challenged) persons."

References

Benkler, Yochai. 2006. *The wealth of networks: How social production transforms markets and freedom.* New Haven, CT: Yale University Press.

Coppa, Francesca. 2008. Women, *Star Trek,* and the early development of fannish vidding. *Transformative Works and Cultures* 1, http://journal.transformativeworks.org/index.php/twc/article/view/44/64 (retrieved August 14, 2010).

Gray, Jonathan, Cornel Sandvoss, and C. Lee Harrington. 2007. Introduction: Why study fans? In *Fandom: Identities and communities in a mediated world*, 1–18. New York: New York University Press.

Hippel, E. V. 2005. *Democratizing innovation.* Cambridge, MA: MIT Press.

Jenkins, Henry. 1992. *Textual poachers: Television fans and participatory culture.* New York: Routledge.

———. 2006. *Convergence culture: Where old and new media collide.* New York: New York University Press.

———. 2007. The future of fandom. In *Fandom: Identities and communities in a mediated world*, ed. Jonathan Gray, Cornell Sandvoss, and C. Lee Harrington, 357–364. New York: New York University Press.

Lakhani, Karim R. 2008. *InnoCentive.com.* Harvard Business School Case 608-016. Cambridge, MA: Harvard Business.

Lakhani, Karim R., and Jill A. Panetta. 2007. The principles of distributed innovation. *Innovations: Technology, Governance, Globalization* 2 (3): 97–112.

LantisEscudo. 2008. "The history of the org." animemusicvideos.org, www .animemusicvideos.org/forum/viewtopic.php?f=2&t=91946&start=8 (retrieved August 14, 2010).

Lessig, Lawrence. 2004. *Free culture: How big media uses technology and the law to lock down culture and control creativity.* New York: Penguin Press.

———. 2008. *Remix: Making art and commerce thrive in the hybrid economy.* New York: Penguin Press.

Manion, Annie. 2005. *Discovering Japan: Anime and learning Japanese culture.* Master's thesis, University of Southern California, Los Angeles, CA. www.chanpon.org/ archive/manionthesis.pdf (retrieved June 9, 2010).

Pohnert, Vlad G. 2005. "History of AMV." animemusicvideos.org, www .animemusicvideos.org/forum/viewtopic.php?f=2&t=44607&start=14 (retrieved August 14, 2010).

Shirky, Clay. 2008. *Here comes everybody: The power of organizing without organizations.* New York: Penguin Press.

Springall, Dana. 2004. *Popular music meets Japanese cartoons: A history of the evolution of anime music videos.* Undergraduate thesis, Samford University, Birmingham, AL. www.doki.ca/tmp/AMVThesis.doc (retrieved August 14, 2010).

Thornton, Sarah. 1996. *Club cultures: Music media and subcultural capital.* Middletown, CT: Wesleyan Press.

Urban Dictionary. "Narutard." http://narutard.urbanup.com/1281292 (retrieved July 7, 2009).

Contributors

HIROKI AZUMA is a Japanese philosopher, cultural critic, and novel writer. He has published several books on contemporary Japanese culture and is widely regarded as one of the most influential cultural theorists of the Japanese otaku generation. His present research focuses on two distinct issues: the transformation of the literary imagination as a result of postmodernization/otaku-ization; and how the emergence of a ubiquitous information society can be made to support new forms of human liberty and freedom. Azuma is a professor at Waseda University.

LAWRENCE ENG is a social scientist specializing in otaku studies. He received his PhD in Science and Technology Studies from Rensselaer Polytechnic Institute in 2006. His doctoral research examined the ways in which anime otaku and related subcultures engage and appropriate science and technology. As of 2011, he is the online community manager for ServiceNow in San Diego, CA.

KIMI ISHIDA is a specialist in media education. Her focus is ethnographic studies of literacy practices of adolescent girls in relation to popular culture. She also conducts research on Japanese anime and manga fan culture as a youth subculture. She works at Tokiwa University.

MIZUKO ITO is a cultural anthropologist of technology use, focusing on children and youth's changing relationships to media and communications. She has been conducting ongoing research on kids' technoculture in Japan and the United States, and she is coeditor of *Personal, Portable, Pedestrian: Mobile Phones in Japanese Life*, coauthor of *Hanging Out, Messing Around, and Geeking Out: Youth Living and Learning with New Media*, and author of *Engineering Play: A Cultural History of Children's Software*. She is a professor in residence and MacArthur Foundation Chair in Digital Media and Learning at the University of California, Irvine. www.itofisher.com/mito.

YOSHIMASA KIJIMA is a sociologist specializing in cultural learning theory. His focus is interactional studies of video game play. He also conducts research on Japanese popular music culture. He works as a lecturer at St. Andrew's University in Japan.

AKIHIRO KITADA is a sociologist specializing in sociological theory and media history. His research analyzes contemporary Japanese media from a historical perspective. He is a well-known commentator on contemporary media culture in Japan. Kitada works as a research associate professor at the University of Tokyo.

KAICHIRO MORIKAWA is an architectural studies scholar specializing in theory of design. He is an associate professor at Meiji University. He studies the relationship between social structure and hobbies by examining how hobbies relate to communities and urban space.

DAISUKE OKABE is a cognitive psychologist specializing in situated learning theory. His focus is interactional studies of learning and education in relation to new media technologies. He also conducts research on Japanese anime and manga fan culture. He is a coeditor of *Personal, Portable, Pedestrian: Mobile Phones in Japanese Life* and a lecturer at Tokyo City University.

HIROAKI TAMAGAWA is a specialist in media consumption and media history. He focuses on Japanese popular entertainment media. As part of the Graduate School of Social and Cultural Studies at Kyushu University in Japan, he belonged to the study group for the Comic Market 30th Anniversary Survey, a joint project between the organizing committee of the Comic Market and academic scholars to conduct comprehensive research on Comic Market participants. He works as a researcher at Media Development Research Institute in Japan, a consulting company for media and advertising industries.

IZUMI TSUJI is a sociologist specializing in the sociology of culture. He has conducted extensive research on Japanese fan culture, including a study of fans of young idol musicians and train otaku. He is coauthor of *Sore Zore no Fan Kenkyuu–I am a fan*, a book on Japanese fan culture. He works as an associate professor at Chuo University in Japan.

Index